C000129916

the **heart** sutra

OSHO

Extemporaneous talks given by Osho at
the OSHO International Meditation Resort, Pune, India

the **heart** sutra

Becoming a Buddha through Meditation

TALKS ON SUTRAS OF GAUTAMA THE BUDDHA

OSHO

Copyright © 1977, 2011 OSHO International Foundation
www.osho.com/copyrights

Osho image Copyright © OSHO International Foundation

All rights reserved. No part of this book may be reproduced or transmitted
in any form or by any means, electronic or mechanical, including
photocopying, recording, or by any information storage and retrieval
system, without prior written permission from the publisher.

OSHO is a registered trademark of OSHO International Foundation
www.osho.com/trademarks

This book is a series of original talks by Osho, given to a live audience. All
of Osho's talks have been published in full as books, and are also available
as original audio recordings. Audio recordings and the complete text archive
can be found via the online OSHO Library at www.osho.com/library

The material in this book is a transcript of a series of original OSHO
Talks, *The Heart Sutra*, given to a live audience. All of Osho's talks have
been published in full as books, and are also available as original audio
recordings. Audio recordings and the complete text archive can be found via
the online OSHO Library at www.osho.com/library

We gratefully acknowledge the use of excerpts from *Buddhist Wisdom
Books*. Translated and explained by Edward Conze. ©1958: George Allen &
Unwin Ltd. Published: George Allen & Unwin Ltd., Ruskin House, Museum
Street, London.

OSHO MEDIA INTERNATIONAL
New York • Zurich • Mumbai
an imprint of
OSHO INTERNATIONAL
www.osho.com/oshointernational

Distributed by Publishers Group Worldwide
www.pgw.com

Library of Congress Catalog-In-Publication Data is available

Printed in India by Manipal Technologies Limited, Karnataka

ISBN 978-1-938755-90-3
Also available as eBook 978-0-88050-288-7

contents

I have told you the story: in Buddha's time there was a blind man who was a great logician. There is no difficulty; eyes are not needed to be a logician. And because he was a great logician, nobody could prove to him that light exists. He argued, and argued so clearly, "You are either just befooling yourself, or you want me to be humiliated as a blind man. But I say there is no light."

And his reasoning was very clear, crystal clear. He said, "I am ready for every experiment. I want to touch it – bring me to where there is light. I want to taste it. I am ready to smell it, I am ready to hear the sound of it."

Naturally the people were at a loss. What to do with this man? He is blind but he is a great debater. As far as arguments are concerned he is always a winner, because nobody can manage to make the sound of light; nothing like that exists, the taste of light, or the touch of light.

Once Gautam Buddha was just on the way towards the capital city of Vaishali, and he passed the village where the blind man lived. People thought, "This is a good opportunity. Perhaps this is the last opportunity – if this man can even defeat Buddha through his argumentation, then we are finished! Perhaps light does not exist. Perhaps we are dreaming about light."

That's what he used to say to people, "You are dreaming. Just cool down, be alert: there is no light, all is darkness."

They brought the man to Buddha. They thought that Buddha would argue with him, but instead of arguing, Buddha said, "You have brought him to a wrong person. He does not need more argumentation, because no argumentation can prove light. He needs a physician, a surgeon."

Buddha had his own personal physician, the best physician of those days, given to him by the king of Vaishali. The physician followed him continuously for forty-two years, till his last breath, just like a shadow taking care of him; he was fragile.

He said to his physician, "Take this case in your hands. I will be leaving tomorrow morning, but remain behind until you are finished with this case."

The physician looked into the man's eyes and he said, "It will not be long. I will soon catch up with you. His eyes are only covered with a thin layer which can be removed. Within a few weeks, he will be able to see light."

And after six weeks the physician came with the man to another village where Buddha had gone. The man came dancing. He fell unto the feet of Gautam Buddha and he said, "Just forgive me. I could not believe something which was not my experience; I am not a man of faith. But now that I can see light, a tremendous trust has arisen in me. In your compassion you did not argue about it but you simply diagnosed the case and handed me over to the physician."

Faith is for the blind; trust is for one who has tasted something of the ultimate. The faithful are the followers. I don't want anybody to believe or to have faith. I want you to trust in yourself; that if Gautam Buddha can become an Everest of consciousness, he has proved the point that every human consciousness has the same potential. Trust in it, trust in yourself.

This distinction has to be remembered. Belief is always in somebody else's ideology, and faith is in somebody else's personality.

Trust is in your own potentiality.

Osho
The Buddha: The Emptiness of the Heart

CHAPTER 1

the buddha within

Homage to the perfection of wisdom, the lovely, the holy!

Avalokita, the holy lord and bodhisattva, was moving in the deep course of the wisdom which has gone beyond. He looked down from on high, he beheld but five heaps, and he saw that in their own being they were empty.

I salute the buddha within you. You may not be aware of it, you may not have ever dreamed about it – that you are a buddha, that nobody can be anything else, that buddhahood is the very essential core of your being, that it is not something to happen in the future, that it has happened already. It is the very source you come from; it is the source and the goal too. It is from buddhahood that we move, and it is to buddhahood that we move. This one word, *buddhahood*, contains all – the full circle of life, from the alpha to the omega.

But you are fast asleep, you don't know who you are. Not that you have to become a buddha, but only that you have to recognize it, that you have to return to your own source, that you have to look within yourself. A confrontation with yourself will reveal your buddhahood. The day one comes to see one-self, the whole existence becomes enlightened. It is not that a person becomes enlightened – how can a person become enlightened? The very idea of being a person is part of the unenlightened mind. It is not that *I* have become enlightened; the "I" has to be dropped before one can become enlightened, so how can *I* become enlightened? That is absurdity. The day I became enlightened the whole existence became enlightened. Since that moment I have not seen anything other than buddhas – in many forms, with many names, with a thousand and one problems, but buddhas still.

So I salute the buddha within you.

I am immensely glad that so many buddhas have gathered here. The very fact of your coming here to me is the beginning of the recognition. The respect in your heart for me, the love in your heart for me, is respect and love for your own buddha-hood. The trust in me is not trust in something extrinsic to you, the trust in me is self-trust. By trusting me you will learn to trust yourself. By coming close to me you will come close to yourself. Only a recognition has to be attained. The diamond is there – you have forgotten about it, or you have never remembered it from the very beginning.

There is a very famous saying of Emerson: "Man is a God in ruins." I agree and I disagree. The insight has some truth in it – man is not as he should be. The insight is there but a little upside down. Man is not God in ruins, man is God in the making; man is a budding buddha. The bud is there, it can bloom any moment: just a little effort, just a little help is needed. And the help is not going to cause it – it is already there! Your effort is only going to reveal it to you, help to unfold what is there, hidden. It is a discovery, but the truth is already there. The truth is eternal.

Listen to these sutras because these are the most important sutras in the great Buddhist literature. Hence they are called the *Heart Sutra*; it is the very heart of the Buddhist message.

But I would like to begin from the very beginning. From this point only does Buddhism become relevant: let it be there in your heart that you are a buddha. I know it may look presumptuous, it may look very hypothetical; you cannot trust it totally. That is natural, I understand it. Let it be there, but as a seed. Around that fact many things will start happening, and only around that fact will you be able to understand these sutras. They are immensely powerful – very small, very condensed, seedlike. But with this soil, with this vision in the mind, that you are a buddha, that you are a budding buddha, that you are potentially capable of becoming one, that nothing is lacking, all is ready, things just have to be put in the right order, that a little more awareness is needed, a little more consciousness is needed... The treasure is there; you have to bring a small lamp inside your house. Once the darkness disappears you will no longer be a beggar, you will be a buddha; you will be a sovereign, an emperor. This whole kingdom is yours and it is just for the asking; you have just to claim it.

But you cannot claim it if you believe that you are a beggar. You cannot claim it, you cannot even dream about claiming if you think that you are a beggar. This idea that you are a beggar, that you are ignorant, that you are a sinner, has been preached from so many pulpits down the ages that it has become a deep hypnosis in you. This hypnosis has to be broken. To break it I start with: I salute the buddha within you.

To me, you are buddhas. All your efforts to become enlightened are ridiculous if you don't accept this basic fact. This has to become a tacit understanding, that you *are* it! This is the right beginning, otherwise you go astray. This is the right beginning. Start with this vision, and don't be worried that this may create some kind of ego: "I am a buddha." Don't be worried, because the whole process of the *Heart Sutra* will make it clear to you that the ego is the only thing that doesn't exist – the *only* thing that doesn't exist! Everything else is real.

There have been teachers who say the world is illusory and the soul is existential – the "I" is true and all else is illusory, *maya*. Buddha says just the reverse: he sees only the "I" is untrue and everything else is real. And I agree with Buddha more than with the other standpoint. Buddha's insight is very penetrating, the most penetrating. Nobody has ever penetrated into those realms, depths and heights of reality.

But start with the idea, with this climate around you, with this vision. Let it be declared to every cell of your body and every thought of your mind; let it be declared to every nook and corner of your existence: "I am a buddha!" And don't be worried about the "I," we will take care of it.

"I" and buddhahood cannot exist together. Once the buddhahood becomes revealed the "I" disappears, just like darkness disappears when you bring a light in.

Before entering into the sutras, it will be helpful to understand a little framework, a little structure.

The ancient Buddhist scriptures talk about seven temples. Just as Sufis talk about seven valleys, and Hindus talk about seven chakras, Buddhists talk about seven temples.

The first temple is the physical, the second temple is psychosomatic, the third temple is psychological, the fourth temple is psycho-spiritual, the fifth temple is spiritual, the sixth temple is spirituo-transcendental, and the seventh temple and the ultimate – the temple of temples – is the transcendental.

The sutras belong to the seventh. These are declarations of someone who has entered the seventh temple, the transcendental, the absolute. That is the meaning of the Sanskrit word, *pragyaparamita* – the wisdom of the beyond, from the beyond, in the beyond; the wisdom that comes only when you have transcended all kinds of identifications – lower or higher, this worldly or that worldly; when you have transcended all kinds of identifications, when you are not identified at all, when there is only a pure flame of awareness left with no smoke around it. That's why Buddhists worship this small book, this very, very small book; and they have called it the *Heart Sutra* – the very heart of religion, the very core.

The first temple, the physical, can correspond to the Hindu map with the *muladhar* chakra; the second, the psychosomatic, with *svadisthan* chakra; the third, the psychological, with *manipura;* the fourth, the psycho-spiritual, with *anahatta;* the fifth, the spiritual, with *vishudha;* the sixth, the spirituo-transcendental, with *agya;* and the seventh, the transcendental, with *sahasrar*. *Sahasrar* means one-thousand-petaled lotus. That is the symbol of the ultimate flowering: nothing has remained hidden, all has become unhidden, manifest. The thousand-petaled lotus has opened, the whole sky is filled with its fragrance, its beauty, its benediction.

In the modern world a great work has started in search of the innermost core of the human being. It will be good to understand how far modern efforts lead us.

Pavlov, B. F. Skinner and the other behaviorists, go on circling around the physical, the *muladhar*. They think man is only the body. They get so involved in the first temple, they get so involved with the physical that they forget everything else. These people are trying to explain man only through the physical, the material. This attitude becomes a hindrance because they are not open. When from the very beginning you deny that there is anything other than the body, then you deny the exploration itself. This becomes a prejudice. A Communist, a Marxist, a behaviorist, an atheist – people who believe that man is only the body – their very belief closes doors to higher realities. They become blind. And the physical is there, the physical is the most apparent; it needs no proof. The physical body is there, you need not prove it. Because it need not be proved, it becomes the only reality. That is nonsense. Then man loses all dignity. If there is nothing to grow in or to grow towards, there cannot be any dignity in life. Then man becomes a thing. Then you are not an opening, then nothing more is going to happen to you – you are a body: you will eat, and you will defecate, and you will eat and you will make love and produce children, and this will go on and on, and one day you will die. A mechanical repetition of the mundane, the trivia – how can there be any significance, any meaning, any poetry? How can there be any dance?

Skinner has written a book, *Beyond Freedom and Dignity*. It should be called *Below Freedom and Dignity*, not *Beyond*. It is below, it is the lowest standpoint about man, the ugliest. There is nothing wrong with the body, remember. I am not against the body, it is a beautiful temple. The ugliness enters when you think it is all.

Man can be conceived of as a ladder with seven rungs, and you get identified with the first rung. Then you are not going anywhere. And the ladder is there, and the ladder bridges this world and the other; the ladder bridges matter with godliness. The first rung is perfectly good if it is used in relationship to the whole ladder. If it functions as a first step it is immensely beautiful: one should be thankful to the body. But if you start worshipping the first rung and you forget the remaining six, you forget that the whole ladder exists and you become closed, confined to the first rung, then it is no longer a rung at all – because a rung is a rung only when it is part of a ladder. If it is no longer a rung then you are stuck with it. Hence, people who are materialistic are always stuck, they always feel something is missing, they don't feel they are going anywhere. They move in rounds, in circles, and they come again and again to the same point. They become tired and bored. They start contemplating how to commit suicide. And their whole effort in life is to find some sensations, so something new can happen. But what "new" can happen? All the things that we go on being occupied with are nothing but toys to play with.

Think of these words of Frank Sheed: "The soul of man is crying for purpose or meaning. And the scientist says, 'Here is a telephone.' Or, 'Look! Television!' – exactly as one tries to distract a baby crying for its mother by offering it sugar sticks and making funny faces at it. The leaping stream of invention has served extraordinarily well to keep man occupied, to keep him from remembering that which is troubling him."

All that the modern world has provided you with is nothing but sugar sticks, toys to play with – and you were crying for the mother, you were crying for love, and you were crying for consciousness, and you were crying for some significance in life. And they say, "Look! The telephone. Look! The television. Look! We have brought so many beautiful things for you." And you play around a little bit; again you get fed up, again you are bored, and again they go on searching for new toys for you to play with.

This state of affairs is ridiculous. It is so absurd that it seems almost inconceivable how we go on living in it. We have got caught at the first rung.

Remember that you are in the body, but you are not the body; let that be a continuous awareness in you. You live in the body, and the body is a beautiful abode. Remember, I am not for a single moment hinting that you become anti-body, that you start denying the body as the so-called spiritualists have done down the ages. The materialists go on thinking that the body is all that is, and there are people who move to the opposite extreme, and they start saying that the body is illusory, the body is not: "Destroy the body so the illusion is destroyed, and you can become really real."

This other extreme is a reaction. The materialist creates his own reaction in the spiritualist, but they are partners in the same business; they are not very different people. The body is beautiful, the body is real, the body has to be lived, the body has to be loved. The body is a great gift of existence. Not for a single moment be against it, and not for a single moment think that you are only it. You are far bigger. Use the body as a jumping board.

The second is: psychosomatic, *svadisthan*. Freudian psychoanalysis functions there. It goes a little higher than Skinner and Pavlov. Freud enters into the mysteries of the psychological a little bit more. He's not just a behaviorist, but he never goes beyond dreams. He goes on analyzing dreams.

The dream exists as an illusion in you. It is indicative, it is symbolic, it has a message from the unconscious to be revealed to the conscious. But there is no point in just getting caught in it. Use the dream, but don't become the dream. You are not the dream.

And there is no need to make so much fuss about it, as Freudians do. Their whole effort seems to be moving in the dimension of the dream world. Take note of it, take a very, very clear standpoint about it, understand its message; and there is really no need to go to anybody else for your dream analysis. If you cannot analyze your dream nobody else can, because your dream is your dream. And your dream is so personal that nobody else can dream the way you dream. Nobody has ever dreamed the way you dream, nobody will ever dream the way you dream; nobody can explain it to you. His interpretation will be *his* interpretation. Only you can look into it. And in fact there is no need to analyze a dream: look at the dream in its totality, with clarity, with alertness, and you will see the message. It is so loud! There is no need to go for psychoanalysis for three, four, five, seven years.

A person who is dreaming every night, and in the day is going to the psychoanalyst to be analyzed, becomes by and by surrounded by dreamy-stuff. Just as the first becomes too much obsessed with the *muladhara*, the physical, the second becomes too much obsessed with the sexual – because the second, the realm of psychosomatic reality, is sex. The second starts interpreting everything in terms of sex. Whatsoever you do, go to the Freudian and he will reduce it to sex. Nothing higher exists for him. He lives in the mud, he does not believe in the lotus. Bring a lotus flower to him, he will look at it and reduce it to the mud. He will say, "This is nothing, this is just dirty mud. Has it not come out of dirty mud? If it has come out of dirty mud then it has to be dirty mud." Reduce everything to its cause, and that is the real.

Then every poem is reduced to sex, everything beautiful is reduced to sex and perversion and repression. Michelangelo is a great artist? Then his art has to be reduced to some sexuality. And Freudians go to absurd lengths. They say all the great works of art by Michelangelo or Goethe or Byron which bring great joy to millions of people, are nothing but repressed sex – maybe Goethe was going to masturbate and was stopped.

Millions of people are stopped from masturbation, but they don't become Goethes. It is absurd. But Freud is the master of the world of the toilet. He lives there, that is his temple. Art becomes pathology, poetry becomes pathology, everything becomes perversion. If Freudian analysis succeeds then there will be no Kalidas, no Shakespeare, no Michelangelo, no Mozart, no Wagner, because everybody will be normal. These are abnormal people, these people are psychologically ill, according to Freud. The greatest are reduced to the lowest. Buddha is ill, according to Freud, because whatsoever he is talking about is nothing but repressed sex.

This approach reduces human greatness to ugliness. Beware of it. Buddha is not ill; in fact, Freud is ill. The silence of Buddha, the joy of Buddha, the celebration of Buddha is not ill, it is the full flowering of wellbeing.

But to Freud the normal person is one who has never sung a song, who has never danced, who has never celebrated, never prayed, never meditated, never done anything creative, is just normal: goes to the office, comes home, eats, drinks, sleeps, and dies; leaves not a trace behind of his creativity, leaves not a single signature anywhere. This normal man seems to be very mediocre, dull and dead. There is a suspicion about Freud that because he himself could not create – he was an uncreative person – he was condemning creativity itself as pathology. There is every possibility that he was a mediocre person. It is his mediocreness which feels offended by all the great people of the world.

The mediocre mind is trying to reduce all greatness. The mediocre mind cannot accept that there can be any greater being than him. That hurts. This whole psychoanalysis and its interpretation of human life is revenge by the mediocre. Beware of it. It is better than the first, yes, a little ahead of the first, but one has to go, and go on going, beyond and beyond.

The third is psychological. Adler lives in the world of the psychological, the will to power; at least something – very egoistic, but at least something; a little more open than Freud. But the problem is, just like Freud reduces everything to sex, Adler reduces everything to the inferiority complex. People try to become great because they feel inferior. A person trying to become enlightened is a person who is feeling inferior, and a person trying to become enlightened is a person who is on a power trip. This is utterly wrong, because we have seen people – a Buddha, a Christ, a Krishna – who are so utterly surrendered that their trip cannot be called a power-trip. And when Buddha blooms he has no ideas of superiority, not at all. He bows down to the whole of existence. He has not that idea of holier-than-thou, not at all. Everything is holy, even the dust is divine. No, he is not thinking himself superior, and he was not striving to become superior. He was not feeling inferior at all. He was born a king; there was no question of inferiority. He was at the top from the very beginning, there was no question of inferiority. He was the richest man in his country, the most powerful man in his country: there was no more power to be attained, no more riches to be attained. He was one of the most beautiful men ever born on this earth, he had one of the most beautiful women as his beloved. All was available to him.

But Adler would go on searching for some inferiority because he could not believe that a man could have any goal other than the ego. It is better – better than Freud, a little higher. Ego is a little higher than sex; not much higher, but a little higher.

The fourth is psycho-spiritual, *anahatta*, the heart center. Jung, Assagioli and others penetrate that realm. They go higher than Pavlov, Freud and Adler, they open more possibilities. They accept the world of the irrational, the unconscious: they don't confine themselves to reason. They are more reasonable people – they accept "irreason" too. The irrational is not denied but accepted. This is where modern psychology stops – at the fourth rung. And the fourth rung is just in the middle of the whole ladder: three rungs on this side and three rungs on that side.

Modern psychology is not yet a complete science. It is hanging in the middle. It is very shaky, not certain about anything. It is more hypothetical than experiential. It is still struggling to be.

The fifth is spiritual: Islam, Hinduism, Christianity – the mass-organized religions remain stuck with the fifth. They don't go beyond the spiritual. All the organized religions, the churches, remain there.

The sixth is the spirituo-transcendental – Yoga and other methods. All over the world, down the ages, many methods have been developed which are less like a church organization, which are not dogmatic but are more experiential. You have to do something with your body and mind; you have to create a certain harmony within yourself so that you can ride on that harmony, you can ride on that cloud of harmony and go far away from your ordinary reality. Yoga can comprehend all that; that is the sixth.

And the seventh is transcendental: Tantra, Tao, Zen. Buddha's attitude is of the seventh – *pragyaparamita*. It means wisdom that is transcendental, wisdom that comes to you only when all the bodies have been crossed and you have become just a pure awareness, just a witness, pure subjectivity.

Unless man reaches to the transcendental, man will have to be provided with toys, sugar sticks. He will have to be provided with false meanings.

Just the other day I came across an American car advertisement. On top of a beautiful car it says: "Something to believe in." Man has never fallen so low. Something to believe in! You believe in a car? Yes, people believe – people believe in their houses, people believe in their cars, people believe in their bank balances. If you look around you will be surprised – God has disappeared, but belief has not disappeared. God is no longer there: now there is a Cadillac or a Lincoln! God has disappeared but man has created new gods – Stalin, Mao. God has disappeared and man has created new gods – movie stars.

This is for the first time in the history of human consciousness that man has fallen so low. And even if sometimes you remember God, it is just an empty word. Maybe when you are in pain, maybe when you are frustrated, then you use God – as if God is aspirin. That's what the so-called religions have made you believe: they say, "Take God three times a day and you won't feel any pain!" So whenever you are in pain you remember God. God is not an aspirin, God is not a painkiller.

A few people remember God habitually, a few others remember God professionally. A priest remembers professionally. He has nothing to do with God, he is paid for it. He has become proficient. A few people remember habitually, a few professionally, but nobody seems to remember God in deep love. A few people invoke his name when they are miserable; nobody remembers him when they are in joy, celebrating. And that is the right moment to remember – because only when you are joyous, immensely joyous, are you close to God. When you are in misery you are far away, when you are in misery you are closed. When you are happy you are open, flowing; you can hold God's hand.

So either you remember habitually, because you have been taught from very childhood – it has become a kind of habit, like smoking. If you smoke you don't enjoy it much; if you don't smoke you feel you are missing something. If you remember God every morning, every evening, nothing is attained, because the remembrance is not of the heart – just verbal, mental, mechanical. But if you don't remember you start feeling something is missing. It has become a ritual. Beware of making God a ritual, and beware of becoming professional about it.

I have heard a very famous story:

The story is about a great yogi, very famous, who was promised by a king that if he could go into deep *samadhi* and remain under the earth for one year, the king would give him the best horse in the kingdom as a reward. The king knew that the yogi had a soft heart for horses, he was a great lover of horses.

The yogi agreed; he was buried alive for a year. But in the course of the year the kingdom was overthrown and nobody remembered to dig up the yogi.

About ten years later someone remembered: "What happened to the yogi?" The king sent a few people to find out. The yogi was dug up; he was still in his deep trance. A previously agreed to mantra was whispered in his ear and he was roused, and the first thing he said was, "Where is my horse?"

Ten years of remaining in silence underneath the earth, but the mind has not changed at all – "Where is my horse?" Was this man really in trance, in *samadhi?* Was he thinking about God? He must have been thinking about the horse. But he was professionally proficient, skillful. He must have learned the technique of how to stop the breathing and how to go into a kind of death – but it was technical.

Remaining ten years in such deep silence, and the mind has not changed a little bit! It is exactly the same as if these ten years had not passed by. If you technically remember God, if you professionally remember God, habitually, mechanically remember God, then nothing is going to happen. All is possible, but all possibilities go through the heart. Hence the name of this scripture: the *Heart Sutra*.

Unless you do something with great love, with great involvement, with great commitment, with sincerity, with authenticity, with your total being, nothing is going to happen.

For some people religion is like an artificial limb: it has neither warmth nor life. And although it helps them to stumble along it never becomes part of them; it must be strapped on each day.

Remember, this has happened to millions of people on the earth, this can happen to you too. Don't create an artificial limb, let real limbs grow in you. Only then will your life have a warmth, only then will your life have joy – not a false smile on the lips, not a pseudo kind of happiness that you pretend to, not a mask, but in reality. Ordinarily you go on wearing things: somebody wears a beautiful smile, somebody wears a very compassionate face, somebody wears a very, very loving personality – but these are like clothes that you put on yourself. Deep down you remain the same.

These sutras can become a revolution.

The first thing, the beginning, is always the question, "Who am I?" And one has to go on asking. When first you ask, "Who am I?" the *muladhar* will answer, "You are a body! What nonsense! There is no need to ask, you know it already." Then the second will say, "You are sexuality." Then the third will say, "You are a power-trip, an ego" – and so on and so forth.

Remember, you have to stop only when there is no answer coming, not before it. If some answer is coming: "You are this, you are this," then know well that some center is providing you with an answer. When all the six centers have

been crossed and all their answers canceled, you go on asking, "Who am I?" and no answer comes from anywhere, it is
utter silence. Your question resounds in yourself: "Who am I?"
and there is silence, no answer arises from anywhere, from
any corner. You are absolutely present, absolutely silent,
and there is not even a vibration. "Who am I?" – and only
silence. Then a miracle happens: you cannot even formulate
the question. Answers have become absurd; then finally the
question also becomes absurd. First answers disappear, then
the question also disappears – because they can live only
together. They are like two sides of a coin – if one side has
gone, the other cannot be retained. First answers disappear,
then the question disappears. And with the disappearance of
question and answer, you come to realize: that is transcendental. You know, yet you cannot say; you know, yet you
cannot be articulate about it. You know from your very being
who you are, but it cannot be verbalized. It is life-knowledge;
it is not scriptural, it is not borrowed, it is not from others. It
has arisen in you.

And with this arising, you are a buddha. And then you
start laughing because you come to know that you have been
a buddha from the very beginning; you had just never looked
so deep. You were running around and around outside your
being, you had never come home.

The philosopher, Arthur Schopenhauer, was walking down
a lonely street. Buried in thought, he accidentally bumped
into another pedestrian. Angered by the jolt and the apparent
unconcern of the philosopher, the pedestrian shouted, "Well!
Who do you think you are?"

Still lost in thought the philosopher said, "Who am I? How
I wish I knew."

Nobody knows. Knowing this – that I don't know who I am
– the journey starts.

The first sutra:

Homage to the perfection of wisdom, the lovely, the holy!

This is an invocation. All Indian scriptures start with an invocation for a certain reason. This is not so in other countries and in other languages; this is not so in Greece. The Indian understanding is this: that we are hollow bamboos, only the infinite flows through us. The infinite has to be invoked; we become just instruments to it. We invoke it, we call it forth to flow through us. That's why nobody knows who wrote this *Heart Sutra*. It has not been signed because the person who wrote it didn't believe that he was the author of it. He was just instrumental. He was just like a steno; the dictation was from beyond. It was dictated to him, he has faithfully written it, but he is not the author of it – at the most, just the writer.

Homage to the perfection of wisdom, the lovely, the holy! This is the invocation, a few words, but every word is very, very pregnant with meaning.

Homage to the perfection of wisdom... "Perfection of wisdom" is the translation for *pragyaparamita*. *Pragya* means wisdom. Remember, it does not mean knowledge. Knowledge is that which comes through the mind, knowledge is that which comes from the outside. Knowledge is *never* original. It can't be original, by its very nature; it is borrowed. Wisdom is your original vision: it does not come from the outside, it grows in you. It is not like an artificial plastic flower that you go to the market and purchase. It is a real rose that grows on the tree, through the tree. It is the song of the tree. It comes from its innermost core; from its depth it arises. One day it is unexpressed, another day it is expressed; one day it was unmanifest, another day it has become manifest.

Pragya means wisdom, but in the English language even wisdom has a different connotation. In English, *knowledge* means without experience: you go to the university, you gather knowledge. *Wisdom* means you go to life and you gather experience. So a young man can be knowledgeable but never wise, because wisdom needs time. A young man can have degrees: he can be a PhD or a DLitt – that is not difficult – but only an old man can be wise. *Wisdom* means knowledge gathered through one's own experience, but it is still from the outside.

Pragya is neither knowledge nor wisdom as ordinarily

understood. It is a flowering within – not through experience, not through others, not through life and life's encounters, no, but just by going within in utter silence, and allowing that which is hidden there to explode. You are carrying wisdom as a seed within you; it just needs a right soil so that it can sprout. Wisdom is always original. It is always yours, and only yours.

But remember again, when I say "yours" I don't mean that there is any ego involved in it. It is yours in the sense that it comes out of your self-nature, but it has no claim to the ego – because again ego is part of the mind, not of your inner silence. *Paramita* means of the beyond, from the beyond, beyond time and space; when you move to a state where time disappears, when you move to an inner place where space disappears, when you don't know where you are and when, when both references have disappeared. Time is outside you, so is space outside you. There is a crossing point within you where time disappears.

Somebody asked Jesus, "Tell us something about the kingdom of God. What will be special there?" Jesus is reported to have said, "There will be time no longer." There is eternity, a timeless moment. That is the beyond – a spaceless space and a timeless moment. You are no longer confined, so you cannot say where you are.

Now look at me: I cannot say I am here, because I am there too. And I cannot say I am in India, because I am in China too. And I cannot say that I am on this planet, because I am not. When the ego disappears you are simply one with the whole. You are everywhere *and* nowhere. You don't exist as a separate entity, you are dissolved.

Look! In the morning, on a beautiful leaf, there is a dew-drop shining in the morning sun, utterly beautiful. And then it starts slipping, and it slips into the ocean. It was there on the leaf: there was time and space, it had a definition, a personality of its own. Now once it has dropped into the ocean you cannot find it anywhere – not because it has become nonexistential, no. Now it is everywhere; that's why you cannot find it anywhere. You cannot locate it because the whole ocean has become its location. Now it doesn't exist separately.

When you don't exist in separation from the whole, there arises *pragyaparamita*, the wisdom that is perfect, the wisdom that is from the beyond.

Homage to the perfection of wisdom, the lovely, the holy! A beautiful provocation. It says: my homage is to that wisdom that comes when you move into the beyond. And it is lovely, and it is holy – holy because you have become one with the whole; lovely because that ego that created all kinds of ugliness in your life is no more.

Satyam, shivam, sunderam: it is true, it is good, it is beautiful. These are the three qualities.

Homage to the perfection of wisdom... Truth... That's what truth is: the perfection of wisdom, the lovely, the beautiful, the holy, the good.

Why is it called holy? – because buddhas are born out of it. It is the womb of the buddhas. You become a buddha the moment you partake of this perfection of wisdom. You become a buddha when the dewdrop disappears into the ocean, loses separation, is no longer struggling against the whole, is surrendered, is with the whole, no longer against it. Hence my insistence to be with nature, never be against it. Never try to overcome it, never try to conquer it, never try to defeat it. If you try to defeat it you are doomed to failure, because the part cannot defeat the whole – and that's what everybody is trying to do. Hence there is so much frustration, because everybody seems to be a failure. Everybody is trying to conquer the whole, trying to push the river. Naturally you become tired one day, exhausted – you have a very limited source of energy; the river is vast. One day it takes you, but you give in, in frustration.

If you can give in joyfully it becomes surrender. Then it is no longer defeat, it is a victory. You win only with existence, never against existence. And remember, existence is not trying to defeat you. Your defeat is self-generated. You are defeated because you fight. If you want to be defeated, fight; if you want to win, surrender. This is the paradox: that those who are ready to give in become the winners. The losers are the only winners in this game. Try to win and your defeat is absolutely certain – it is only a question of time, of when, but it is certain it is going to happen.

It is holy because you are one with the whole. You throb with it, you dance with it, you sing with it. You are like a leaf in the wind: the leaf simply dances with the wind, it has no will of its own. This will-lessness is what I call sannyas, what the sutra calls holy.

The Sanskrit word for holy is *bhagavati*. That is even more important to be understood than the word *holy*, because the word *holy* may carry some Christian connotation to it. *Bhagavati* is feminine for *bhagavan*. First, the sutra does not use the word *bhagavan*, it uses *bhagavati*, the feminine – because the source of all is feminine, not masculine. It is yin, not yang, it is a mother, not a father.

The Christian concept of God as father is not so beautiful. It is nothing but male ego. The male ego cannot think that God can be a "she"; the male ego wants God to be a "he." And you see the whole Christian trinity: all three persons are men, woman is not included there – God the father, and Christ the son, and the Holy Ghost. It is an all-male club. And remember well that the feminine is far more fundamental in life than the man, because only the woman has a womb, only the woman can give birth to life, to new life. It comes through the feminine.

Why does it come through the feminine? It is not just accidental. It comes through the feminine because only the feminine can allow it to come – because the feminine is receptive. The masculine is aggressive; the feminine can receive, absorb, can become a passage.

The sutra says *bhagavati*, not *bhagavan*. It is of immense importance. That perfect wisdom out of which all the buddhas come is a feminine element, a mother. The womb has to be a mother. Once you think of God as father, you don't seem to understand what you are doing. Father is an unnatural institution. The father does not exist in nature. The father has existed only for a few thousand years; it is a human institution. The mother exists everywhere, the mother is natural.

The father came into the world because of private property. The father is part of economics, not of nature. And once private property disappears – if it ever disappears – the father will disappear. The mother will remain there always and always. We cannot conceive of a world without the mother, we can conceive of a world without the father very easily. And the very idea is aggressive. Have you not seen? Only Germans call their country "fatherland," every other country calls it "motherland." These are dangerous people! "Motherland" is okay. By calling your country "fatherland" you are starting something dangerous, you are putting something dangerous on foot. Sooner or later the aggression will come, the war will come. The seed is there.

All the religions that have thought of God as the father have been aggressive religions. Christianity is aggressive, so is Islam. And you know perfectly well that the Jewish God is a very angry and arrogant God. And the Jewish God declares: "If you are not for me, then you are against me, and I will destroy you. And I am a very jealous God; only worship me!" The people who have thought of God as mother have been nonviolent people.

Buddhists have never fought a war in the name of religion. They have never tried to convert a single human being by any force, by coercion of whatsoever sort. Mohammedans have tried to convert people with the sword, against their will, against their conscience, against their consciousness. Christians have tried to manipulate people to become Christians in all kinds of ways – sometimes through the sword, sometimes through bread, sometimes through other persuasions. Buddhism is the only religion that has not converted a single human being against his conscience. Only Buddhism is a nonviolent religion, because the concept of the ultimate reality is feminine.

Homage to the perfection of wisdom, the lovely, the holy!
Remember, truth is beautiful. Truth is beauty because truth is a benediction. Truth cannot be ugly, and the ugly cannot be true; the ugly is illusory.

When you see an ugly person don't be deceived by his

ugliness; search a little deeper and you will find a beautiful person hidden there. Don't be deceived by ugliness. Ugliness is in your interpretation. Life is beautiful, truth is beautiful, existence is beautiful – it knows no ugliness.

It is lovely, it is feminine and it is holy. But remember, what is meant by holy is not what is ordinarily meant – as if it is otherworldly, as if it is sacred against the mundane and the profane, no. All is holy. There is nothing which can be called mundane or profane. All is sacred because all is suffused with one.

There are buddhas and buddhas! – buddha-trees and buddha-dogs and buddha-birds and buddha-men and buddha-women – but all are buddhas. All are on the way. Man is not God in ruins, man is God in the making, on the way.

The second sutra:

> Avalokita, the holy lord and bodhisattva, was moving in the
> deep course of the wisdom which has gone beyond. He looked
> down from on high, he beheld but five heaps, and he saw that in
> their own being they were empty.

Avalokita is a name of Buddha. Literally it means one who looks from above – *avalokita* – one who looks from above, one who stands at the seventh center, *sahasrar*, the transcendental, and looks from there. Naturally, whatsoever you see is contaminated by your standpoint, is contaminated by the space you are in.

If a man who lives at the first rung – the physical body – looks at anything, he looks from that standpoint. A man who lives at the physical only looks to your body when he looks at you, he cannot look at more than that, he cannot see more than that. Your vision of things depends on from where you are looking.

A man who is sexually disturbed, sexually involved in fantasies, only looks from that standpoint. A man who is hungry looks from that standpoint. Watch in your own self. You look at things, and each time you look at things they appear different because you are different. In the morning the world looks a little more beautiful than in the evening. In the morning you are fresh, and in the morning you have come from a depth of great sleep, the deep sleep, the dreamless sleep. You have tasted something of the transcendental, although unconsciously. So in the morning everything looks beautiful. People are more compassionate, more loving; people are purer in the morning, people are more innocent in the morning. By the time evening arrives these same people will become more corrupted, more cunning, clever, manipulating, ugly, violent, deceiving. These are the same people, but in the morning they were very close to the transcendental. By the evening they have lived in the mundane, in the worldly, in the physical too much, and they have become focused there.

The man of perfection is one who can move through all these seven chakras easily – that is the man of freedom – who is not fixed at any point, who is like a dial: you can adjust it to any vision. That is what is called a *mukta*, one who is really free. He can move in all the dimensions and yet remain untouched by them. His purity is never lost, his purity remains of the transcendental.

Buddha can come and touch your body and heal your body. He can become a body, but that is his freedom. He can become a mind and he can talk to you and explain things to you, but he is never the mind. He comes and stands behind the mind, uses it, just as you drive your car – you never become the car. He uses all these rungs, he is the whole ladder. But his ultimate standpoint remains the transcendental. That is his nature.

Avalokita means one who looks from the beyond at the world.

Avalokita, the holy lord and bodhisattva, was moving in the deep course of the wisdom which has gone beyond. The sutra says this state of beyondness is not a static thing. It is a movement, it is a process, riverlike. It is not a noun, it is a verb. It goes on unfolding. That's why Hindus call it the one-thousand-petaled lotus: "one thousand" simply means infinite, it is symbolic of infinity. Petals upon petals, petals upon petals go on opening, to no end. The journey begins but never ends. It is eternal pilgrimage.

Avalokita, the holy lord and bodhisattva, was moving in the deep course of the wisdom which has gone beyond. He was flowing like a river into the world of the beyond. He is called the holy lord and bodhisattva. Again the Sanskrit word has to be remembered. The Sanskrit word is *iswara,* which is translated as "holy lord." *Iswara* means one who has become absolutely rich from his own riches, whose riches are of his own nature; nobody can take them away, nobody can steal them, they cannot be lost. All the riches that you have can be lost, can be stolen, *will* be lost – one day death will come and will take everything away. When somebody has come to that inner diamond that is one's own being, death cannot take it away. Death is irrelevant to it. It cannot be stolen, it cannot be lost. Then one has become *iswara*, then one has become a holy lord. Then one has become *bhagavan.*

The word *bhagavan* simply means "the blessed one." Then one has become the blessed one. Now his blessing is eternally his; it depends on nothing, it is independent. It is not caused by anything so it cannot be taken away. It is uncaused, it is one's intrinsic nature.

And he is called bodhisattva. Bodhisattva is a very beautiful concept in Buddhism. *Bodhisattva* means one who has become a buddha but is still holding himself in the world of time and space – to help others. *Bodhisattva* means "essentially a buddha," is just ready to drop and disappear, is ready to go into nirvana. Nothing remains to be solved, all his problems are solved. There is no need for him to be here, but he is still here. There is nothing else to be learned here, but he is still here. And he is keeping himself in body-form, in mind-form – he is keeping the whole ladder. He has gone beyond, but he is keeping the whole ladder – to help, out of compassion.

A story is told that Buddha reached the doors of the ultimate, nirvana. The doors were opened, the angels were dancing and singing to receive him – because it rarely happens that a human being becomes a buddha, in millions of years. Those doors open, and that day is naturally a great day of celebration. All the ancient buddhas had gathered, and there was great rejoicing, and flowers were showering, and music was played, and everything was decorated – it was a day of celebration.

But Buddha did not enter the door. And the ancient buddhas, all with folded hands, asked him, requested him to come in: "Why is he standing outside?" And Buddha is reported to have said, "Unless all others who are coming behind me enter, I am not going to enter. I will keep myself outside, because once I come in then I disappear. Then I will not be of any help to these people. I see millions of people stumbling and groping in the dark. I have myself been groping the same way for millions of lives. I would like to give them my hand. Please close the door. When everybody has come I myself will knock, then you can receive me."

A beautiful story. This is called the state of bodhisattva: one who is ready to disappear but still is holding – in body, in mind, in the world, in time and space – to help others.

Buddha says: "Meditation is enough to solve your problems, but something is missing in it – compassion." If compassion is also there, then you can help others solve their problems. He says: "Meditation is pure gold; it has a perfection of its own. But if there is compassion then the gold has a fragrance too – then a higher perfection, then a new kind of perfection, gold with fragrance. Gold is enough unto itself – very valuable – but with compassion, meditation has a fragrance."

Compassion keeps a buddha remaining a bodhisattva, just on the borderline. Yes, for a few days, a few years, one can hold, but not for long – because by and by things start disappearing on their own. When you are not attached with the body you become dislocated from there. You can come sometimes, with effort. You can use the body, with effort, but you are no longer settled there. When you are no longer in the mind you can use it sometimes, but it no longer functions as well as it used to function before. You are no longer flowing in it. When you are not using it, it is lying there: it is a mechanism, it starts gathering rust.

When a man has reached to the seventh, for a few days, for a few years, he can use the six rungs. He can go back and use them, but by and by they start breaking. By and by, they start dying. A bodhisattva can be here for only one life, at the most. Then he has to disappear, because the mechanism disappears.

But all those who have attained have tried, as far as they can, to use the body-mind to help those who are in body and mind, to help those who can understand only the language of the body and the mind, to help the disciples.

Avalokita, the holy lord and bodhisattva, was moving in the deep course of the wisdom which has gone beyond. He looked down from on high, he beheld but five heaps, and he saw that in their own being they were empty. When you look from that point... For example, I was just telling you that I salute the buddha in you. That is one vision from the beyond: that I see you as potential buddhas. And another vision is just that I see you as empty shells.

What you think you are is nothing but an empty shell. Somebody thinks he is a man; that is an empty idea. Consciousness is neither male nor female. Somebody thinks he has a very beautiful body, he is beautiful, strong, this and that – that is an empty idea, just ego deceiving you. Somebody thinks he knows much – that is just meaningless. His mechanism has accumulated memories and he is deceived by the memories. These are all empty things.

So when seeing from the transcendental, on the one side I see you as budding buddhas, on another side I see you just as empty shells.

Buddha has said that man consists of five elements, five *skandhas,* which are all empty. And because of the combination of the five, a by-product arises called the ego, the self. It is just like a clock functioning: it goes on ticking. You can listen and the tick is there; you can open the clock, you can separate all the parts to find where the tick is coming from. Where is the tick? You will not find it anywhere. The tick is a by-product. It is just a combination of a few things. A few things functioning together were creating a tick.

That's what your "I" is – five elements functioning together creating the tick called "I." But it is empty, it has nothing in it. If you go and search for anything substantial in it you will not find anything.

This is one of the Buddha's deepest intuitions, insights: that life is empty, that life as we know it is empty. And life is full too, but we don't know anything about it. From this emptiness you have to move towards a fullness, but that fullness is inconceivable right now – because that fullness from this state will look only empty. From *that* state your fullness looks empty – a king looks like a beggar; a man of knowledge, a knowledgeable man, looks stupid, ignorant.

A small story:

A certain holy man accepted a pupil and said to him, "It would be a good thing if you tried to write down all you understand about the religious life and what has brought you to it."

The pupil went away and began to write. A year later he came back to the master and said, "I have worked very hard on this, and though it is far from complete, these are the main reasons for my struggle."

The master read the work, which was many thousands of words, and then said to the young man, "It is admirably reasoned and clearly stated, but it is somewhat long. Try to shorten it a little." So the novice went away and after five years he came back with a mere hundred pages.

The master smiled, and after he had read it he said, "Now you are truly approaching the heart of the matter. Your thoughts have clarity and strength. But it is still a little long; try to condense it, my son."

The novice went away sadly, for he had labored hard to reach the essence. But after ten years he came back, and bowing low before the master offered him just five pages and said, "This is the kernel of my faith, the core of my life, and I ask your blessings for having brought me to it."

The master read it slowly and carefully: "It is truly

marvelous," he said, "in its simplicity and beauty, but it is not yet perfect. Try to reach a final clarification."

And when the master had reached the time appointed and was preparing for his end, his pupil returned to him again, and kneeling before him to receive his blessings handed him a single sheet of paper on which was written nothing.

Then the master placed his hands on the head of his friend and said, "Now... Now you have understood."

From that transcendental vision, what you have is empty. From your vision, your neurotic vision, what I have is empty.

Buddha looks empty – just pure emptiness – to you. Because of your ideas, because of your clingings, because of your possessiveness about things, Buddha looks empty. Buddha is full: you are empty. And his vision is absolute; your vision is very relative.

The sutra says:

> *Avalokita, the holy lord and bodhisattva, was moving in the deep course of the wisdom which has gone beyond. He looked down from on high, he beheld but five heaps, and he saw that in their own being they were empty.*

Emptiness is the key to Buddhism – *shunyata*. We will be going into it more and more as we enter into the deeper realms of the *Heart Sutra*.

Meditate over these sutras – meditate with love, with sympathy, not with logic and reasoning. If you go to these sutras with logic and reasoning you will kill their spirit. Don't dissect them. Try to understand them as they are, and don't bring your mind – your mind will be an interference.

If you can look at these sutras without your mind, great clarity is going to happen to you.

Enough for today.

CHAPTER 2

surrender is understanding

The first question:

Osho,
Sometimes while just sitting, the question comes up in the
mind: What is truth? But by the time I come here I realize
that I am not capable to ask. But may I ask what happens
in those moments when the question arises so strongly
that had you been nearby I would have asked it. Or if you
had not replied, I would have caught hold of your beard or
collar and asked, "What is truth, Osho?"

That is the most important question that can arise in any-body's mind, but there is no answer for it. The most important question, the ultimate question, cannot have any answer; that's why it is ultimate.

When Pontius Pilate asked Jesus, "What is truth?" Jesus remained silent. Not only that, the story says that when Pontius Pilate asked the question, "What is truth?" he did not wait to listen for the answer. He left the room and went away.

This is very strange. Pontius Pilate also thinks that there cannot be an answer for it, so he didn't wait for the answer. Jesus remained silent because he also knows it cannot be answered.

But these two understandings are not the same, because these two persons are diametrically opposite. Pontius Pilate thinks that it cannot be answered because there is no truth; how can you answer it? That is the logical mind, the Roman mind. Jesus remains silent not because there is no truth, but because the truth is so vast, it is not definable. The truth is so huge, enormous, it cannot be confined in a word, it cannot be reduced to language. It is there. One can *be* it, but one cannot say it.

For two different reasons they behaved almost in the same way: Pontius didn't wait to hear the answer, he already knew that there is no truth. Jesus remains silent because he knows truth, and knows that it cannot be said.

Chidvilas has asked this question. The question is absolutely significant. There is no question higher than that, because there is no religion higher than truth. It has to be understood; the question has to be analyzed. Analyzing the question, trying to understand the question itself, you may have an insight into what truth is. I will not answer it, I cannot answer it; nobody can answer it. But we can go deep into the question. Going deep into the question, the question will start disappearing. When the question has disappeared you will find the answer at the very core of your heart – you *are* truth, so how can you miss it? Maybe you have forgotten about it, maybe you have lost track of it, maybe you have forgotten how to enter into your own being, into your own truth.

Truth is not a hypothesis, truth is not a dogma. Truth is neither Hindu nor Christian nor Mohammedan. Truth is neither mine nor yours. Truth belongs to nobody, but everybody belongs to truth. Truth means that which is: that is exactly the meaning of the word. It comes from a Latin root, *verus*. *Verus* means: that which is. In English there are a few words which are derivations of the Latin root *verus*: *was*, *were* – they come from *verus*. In German, *war* – that comes from *verus*. *Verus* means that which is, uninterpreted. Once the interpretation comes in, then what you know is reality, not truth. That is the difference between truth and reality. Reality is truth interpreted. So the moment you answer the question, "What is truth?" it becomes reality; it is no longer truth. Interpretation has entered it, the mind has colored it. And realities are as many as there are minds; there are multi-realities. Truth is one because truth is known only when the mind is not there. It is mind that keeps you separate from me, separate from others, separate from existence. If you look through the mind, then the mind will give you a picture of truth. That will be only a picture, a photograph of that which is. And of course, the photograph depends on the camera, on the film used, on the chemicals, on how it has been developed, how it has been printed, who has done it. A thousand and one other things enter in; it becomes reality.

The word *reality* is also beautiful to understand. It comes from the root, *res*; it means thing or things. Truth is not a thing. Once interpreted, once the mind has grabbed it, defined it, demarked it, it becomes a thing.

When you fall in love with a woman there is some truth – if you have fallen absolutely unaware, if you have not "done" it in any way, if you have not acted, managed, if you have not even thought about it. Suddenly you see a woman, you look into her eyes, she looks into your eyes, and something clicks. You are not the doer of it, you are simply possessed by it, you simply fall into it. It has nothing to do with you. Your ego is not involved, at least not in the very, very beginning, when love is virgin. In that moment there is truth, but there is no interpretation. That's why love remains indefinable.

Soon the mind comes in, starts managing things, takes possession of you. You start thinking about the girl as your girlfriend, you start thinking of how to get married, you start thinking about the woman as your wife. Now these are things; the girlfriend, the wife – these are things. The truth is no longer there, it has receded. Now things are becoming more important. The definable is more secure, the indefinable is insecure. You have started killing, poisoning the truth. Sooner or later there will be a wife and a husband, two things. But the beauty is gone, the joy has disappeared, the honeymoon is over.

The honeymoon is over at that exact moment when truth becomes reality, when love becomes a relationship. The honeymoon is very short, unfortunately – I'm not talking about the honeymoon that you take. The honeymoon is very short. Maybe for a single moment it was there, but the purity of it, the crystal purity of it, the divinity of it, the beyondness of it – it is from eternity, it is not of time. It is not part of this mundane world, it is like a ray coming into a dark hole. It comes from the transcendental. It is absolutely appropriate to call love God, because love is truth. The closest that you come to truth in ordinary life is love.

Chidvilas asks: "What is truth?"

Asking has to disappear; only then do you know.

If you ask, "What is truth?" what are you asking? If I say *A* is truth, *B* is truth, *C* is truth, will that be the answer? If I say *A* is truth, then certainly *A* cannot be the truth: it is something else that I am using as synonymous with truth. If it is absolutely synonymous, then it will be a tautology. Then I can say, "Truth is truth," but that is silly, meaningless. Nothing is solved by it. If it is exactly the same, if *A* is truth, then it will mean truth is truth. If *A* is different, is not exactly truth, then I am falsifying. Then to say *A* is truth will be only approximate. And remember, there cannot be anything approximate. Either truth is or it is not. So I cannot say *A* is truth.

I cannot even say, "God is truth," because if God is truth then it is a tautology – "Truth is truth." Then I'm not saying anything. If God is different from truth, then I am saying something, but then I am saying something wrong. Then God is different, then how can he be truth? If I say it is approximate, linguistically it looks all right, but it is not right. "Approximately" means some lie is there, something false is there. Otherwise, why is it not a hundred percent truth? If it is ninety-nine percent truth, then something is there which is not true. And truth and untruth cannot exist together, just as darkness and light cannot exist together – because darkness is nothing but absence. Absence and presence cannot exist together, truth and untruth cannot exist together. Untruth is nothing but the absence of truth.

So no answer is possible, hence Jesus remained silent. But if you look at it with deep sympathy, if you look into the silence of Jesus, you will have an answer. Silence is the answer. Jesus is saying, "Be silent, as I am silent, and you will know" – not saying it in words. It is a gesture, it is very, very Zen-like. In that moment when Jesus remained silent, he comes very close to the Zen approach, to the Buddhist approach. He is a buddha in that moment. Buddha never answered these questions. He had eleven questions listed: wherever he would move his disciples would go around and declare to people, "Never ask these eleven questions of Buddha" – questions which are fundamental, questions which are really significant. You could ask anything else, and Buddha was always ready to answer. But don't ask the fundamental, because the fundamental can only be experienced. And truth is the most fundamental; the very substance of existence is what truth is.

Go into the question. The question is significant, it is arising in your heart: "What is truth?" – a desire to know that which is, is arising. Don't push it aside, go into it. Chidvilas, whenever it happens again, close your eyes, go into the question. Let the question become very, very focused – "What... is...truth?" Let there arise a great concentration. Forget everything, as if your whole life depends on this simple question, "What is truth?" Let it become a matter of life and death. And don't try to answer it, because you don't know the answer.

Answers may come – the mind always tries to supply answers – but see the fact that you don't know, that's why you are asking. So how can your mind supply you an answer? The mind knows not, so tell the mind, "Keep quiet." If you know, then there is no need for the question. You don't know, hence the question.

So don't be befooled by the mind's toys. It supplies toys: it says, "Look, it is written in the Bible. Look, it is written in the Upanishads. This is the answer. Look, this is written by Lao Tzu, this is the answer." The mind can throw all kinds of scriptures at you: the mind can quote, the mind can supply from the memory. You have heard many things, you have read many things; the mind carries all those memories. It can repeat in a mechanical way. But look into this phenomenon: the mind knows not, and all that mind repeats is borrowed. And the borrowed cannot help.

It happened at a railway crossing. The gates were closed, a train was to pass, and a man was sitting in his car, waiting for the train to pass, reading a book. A drunkard who was sitting just by the side of the gate came close, knocked on the air-conditioned car's window. The man opened the window and said, "What can I do for you? Do you need any help?"

And the bum said, "Yes, for two days I have not eaten anything at all. Can you give me two rupees? That will be enough for me, just two rupees."

The man laughed and said, "Never borrow and never lend money," and showed the book to the bum and said, "Shakespeare – Shakespeare says so. Look."

The bum pulled out of his pocket a very dirty paperback and said to the man, "You sonofabitch – D. H. Lawrence."

Beware of the mind. The mind goes on quoting, the mind knows all without knowing at all. The mind is a pretender. See into this phenomenon: this I call insight. It is not a question of thinking. If you think about it, it is again the mind. You have to see through and through. You have to look deeply into the very phenomenon, the functioning of the mind, how the mind functions. It borrows from here and there, it goes on borrowing and accumulating. It is a hoarder, a hoarder of knowledge. Mind becomes very knowledgeable, and then whenever you ask a question which is really important the mind gives a very unimportant answer to it – futile, superficial, rubbish.

A man bought a parrot from a pet shop. The shop-owner assured him the bird would learn to say hello within half an hour. Back home he spent an hour "helloing" to the parrot, but not a word from the bird.

As he was turning away in sheer despair, the bird said, "Number engaged."

A parrot is a parrot. He must have heard it in the pet shop. And this man was going on and on, "Hello, hello, hello," and the bird was listening, and waiting for him to stop. Then he could say, "Number engaged!"

You can go on asking the mind, "What is truth, what is truth, what is truth?" And the moment you stop, the mind will immediately say, "Number engaged" or something. The mind will give you an answer. Beware of the mind.

The mind is the Devil, there is no other Devil. And it is *your* mind. This insight has to be developed – of looking through and through. Cut the mind in two with a sharp blow of the sword. That sword is awareness. Cut the mind in two and go through it, go beyond it! And if you can go beyond the mind, through the mind, and a moment of no-mind arises in you, there is the answer – not a verbal answer, not a scripture quoted, not in quotation marks, but authentically yours, an experience. Truth is an existential experience.

The question is immensely significant, but you will have to be very respectful towards the question. Don't be in a hurry to find an answer, otherwise some rubbish will kill the question. Don't allow your mind to kill the question. And the way of the mind to kill the question is to supply answers, unlived, unexperienced.

You are truth! But it can happen only in utter silence, when not a single thought moves, when the mind has nothing to say, when not a single ripple is in your consciousness. When there is no ripple in your consciousness, your consciousness remains undistorted. When there is a ripple, there is a distortion.

Just go to a lake. Standing on the bank, look down at your reflection. If there are waves, ripples on the lake, and wind is blowing, your reflection is shaky. You cannot figure out what is what – where is your nose and where are your eyes – you can only guess. But the lake is silent and the wind is not blowing and there is not a single ripple on the surface; suddenly you are there. In absolute perfection, the reflection is there. The lake becomes a mirror.

Whenever there is a thought moving in your consciousness it distorts. And there are many thoughts, millions of thoughts, continuously rushing, and it is always rush-hour. Twenty-four hours a day it is rush-hour, and the traffic goes on and on, and each thought is associated with thousands of other thoughts. They are all holding hands and linked together and interlinked, and the whole crowd is rushing around you. How can you know what truth is? Get out of this crowd.

That's what meditation is, that's what meditation is all about: a consciousness without mind, a consciousness without thoughts, a consciousness without any wavering – an unwavering consciousness. Then it is there in all its beauty and benediction. Then truth is there – call it God, call it nirvana, or whatsoever you like to call it. It is there, and it is there as an *experience*. You are in it and it is in you.

Use this question. Make it more penetrating. Make it *so* penetrating; put everything at stake so that the mind cannot befool you with its superficial answers. Once the mind disappears, once the mind is no longer playing its old tricks, you will know what truth is. You will know it in silence. You will know it in thoughtless awareness.

The second question:

Osho,
My surrender is goal-oriented. I'm surrendering in order to
win freedom, so it is not real surrender at all. I'm watching
it, but the problem is: it is always "I" who is watching.
Therefore every realization out of that watching is a
reinforcement of the ego. I feel tricked by my ego.

You have not understood what surrender is. The first thing to remember about surrender is: you cannot do it, it is not a doing. You can prevent it from happening, but you cannot manage it to happen. Your power about surrender is only negative: you can prevent it, but you cannot bring it.

Surrender is not something that you can do. If you do it, it is not surrender, because the doer is there. Surrender is a great understanding that, "I am not." Surrender is an insight that the ego exists not, that, "I am not separate." Surrender is not an act but an understanding.

In the first place *you* are false, the separation is false. Not for a single moment can you exist separate from the universe. The tree cannot exist if uprooted from the earth. The tree cannot exist if the sun disappears tomorrow. The tree cannot exist if no water is coming to its roots. The tree cannot exist if it cannot breathe. The tree is rooted in all the five elements – what Buddhists call *skandhas,* the five groups we were talking about the other day. *Avalokita...* When Buddha came to the transcendental vision, when he passed through all the stages, when he passed through all the rungs of the ladder and came to the seventh – from there he looked down, looked back. What did he see? He saw only five heaps with nothing substantial in them, just emptiness, *shunyata.*

The tree cannot exist if these five elements are not constantly pouring energy into it. The tree is just a combination of these five elements. If the tree starts thinking, "I am," then there is going to be misery for the tree. The tree will create a hell for itself. But trees are not so foolish, they don't carry any mind. They are there, and if tomorrow they disappear, they simply disappear. They don't cling; there is nobody to cling. The tree is constantly surrendered to existence. *Surrendered* means it is never separate, it has not come to that stupid idea of the ego. And so are the birds, so are the mountains, so are the stars. It is only man who has turned his great opportunity of being conscious into being self-conscious. Man has consciousness. If consciousness grows, it can bring you the greatest bliss possible. But if something goes wrong and consciousness turns sour and becomes self-consciousness, then it creates hell, then it creates misery. Both alternatives are always open; it is for you to choose.

The first thing to be understood about ego is that it exists not. Nobody exists in separation. You are as much one with the universe as I am, as Buddha is, as Jesus is. I know it, you don't know it; the difference is only of recognition. The difference is not existential, not at all! So you have to look into this stupid idea of separation. Now if you start trying to surrender you are still carrying the idea of separation. Now you are thinking, "I will surrender, now I am going to surrender" – but you think you *are*.

Looking into the very idea of separation, one day you find that you are not separate, so how can you surrender? There is nobody to surrender! There has never been anybody to surrender. The surrenderer is not there, not at all – never found anywhere. If you go into yourself you will not find the surrenderer anywhere. In that moment is surrender. When the surrenderer is not found, in that moment is surrender. You cannot do it. If you *do* it, it is a false thing. Out of falsity only falsity arises. *You* are false, so whatsoever you do will be false, more false. And one falsity leads to another, and so on and so forth. And the fundamental falsity is the ego, the idea, "I am separate."

You say: "My surrender is goal-oriented." The ego is always goal-oriented. It is always greedy, it is always grabbing. It is always searching for more and more and more; it lives in the more. If you have money it wants to have more money; if you have a house it wants to have a bigger house; if you have a woman it wants to have a more beautiful woman, but it always wants more. The ego is constantly hungry. It lives in the future and in the past. In the past it lives as a hoarder – "I have this and this and this." It gets a great satisfaction: "I have got something" – power, prestige, money. It gives a kind of reality to it. It gives the notion: "When I have these things, I must be there." And it lives in the future with the idea of more. It lives as memory and as desire.

What is a goal? A desire: "I have to reach there, I have to be that, I have to attain." The ego does not live, *cannot* live in the present, because the present is real and the ego is false – they never meet. The past is false, it is no more. Once it was, but when it was present, ego was not there. Once it has disappeared, is no longer existential, ego starts grabbing it, accumulating it. It grabs and accumulates dead things. The ego is a graveyard: it collects corpses, dead bones.

Or, it lives in the future. The future is not yet – it is imagination, fantasy, dream. Ego can live with that too, very easily; falsities go together perfectly well, smoothly well. Bring anything existential and the ego disappears. Hence the insistence of being in the present, being herenow, just this moment. If you are intelligent there is no need to think about what I am saying; you can simply *see* into it this very moment! Where is the ego? There is silence, and there is no past, and there is no future, only this moment – and this dog barking... *This* moment, and you are not. Let this moment be, and you are not. And there is immense silence, there is profound silence, within and without. And then there is no need to surrender because you know you are not. Knowing that you are not is surrender.

It is not a question of surrendering to me, it is not a question of surrendering to existence. It is not a question of surrendering at all. Surrendering is an insight, an understanding that, "I am not." Seeing, "I am not, I am a nothingness, emptiness," surrender grows. The flower of surrender grows on the tree of emptiness. It cannot be goal-oriented.

The ego is goal-oriented. The ego is hankering for the future. It can hanker even for the other life, it can hanker for heaven, it can hanker for nirvana. It doesn't matter what it hankers for – hankering is what it is, desiring is what it is, projecting into the future is what it is.

See it! See into it! I'm not saying think about it. If you think about it you miss. Thinking again means past and future. Have a look into it – *avalokita!* – look into it. The English word *look* comes from the same root as *avalokita*. Look into it, and do it right now. Don't say to yourself, "Okay, I will go home and do it." The ego has entered, the goal has come, the future has entered. Whenever time enters you are falling into that falsity of separation.

Let it be here, this very moment. And then you suddenly see you are, and you are not going anywhere, and you are not coming from anywhere. You have always been here. *Here* is the only time, the only space. *Now* is the only existence. In that now, there is surrender.

"My surrender is goal-oriented," you say; "I'm surrendering in order to win freedom..." But you *are* free! You have never been unfree. You are free, but again there is the same problem: you want to be free, but you don't understand that you can be free only when you are free from yourself – there is no other freedom. When you think about freedom, you think as if you will be there and free. You will not be there; there will be freedom. Freedom means freedom *from* the self, not freedom *of* the self. The moment the prison disappears the prisoner also disappears, because the prisoner is the prison! The moment you come out of the prison, you also are not. There is pure sky, pure space. That pure space is called nirvana, *moksha,* liberation.

Try to understand rather than trying to achieve.

"I am surrendering in order to win freedom..." Then you are using surrender as a means, and surrender is the goal, is the end unto itself. When I say surrender is the goal, I'm not saying that surrender has to be achieved somewhere in the future. I'm saying that surrender is not a means, it is an end unto itself. It is not that surrender brings freedom, surrender *is* freedom! They are synonymous, they mean the same thing. You are looking at the same thing from two different angles.

"...so it is not real surrender at all." It is neither real nor unreal. It is not surrender at all. It is not even unreal.

"I am watching it, but the problem is it is always "I" who is watching. Therefore every realization out of that watching is a reinforcement of the ego. I feel tricked by my ego." Who is this "I" you are talking about who feels tricked by the ego? It is the ego itself. The ego is such that it can divide itself into fragments, into parts, and then the game starts. You are the chaser and you are the chased.

It is like a dog trying to catch hold of its own tail, and it goes on jumping. And you look and you see the absurdity of it – but you see the absurdity, the dog cannot see it. The more he finds it is difficult to catch hold of the tail, the more he becomes crazy, the more he jumps. And the faster and the bigger the jump, the more the tail jumps faster and bigger also. And the dog cannot conceive what is happening: he's such a great catcher of everything, and this ordinary tail, and he cannot catch hold of it?

This is what is happening to you. It is "I" who is trying to catch, and who is the catcher and the caught both. See the ridiculousness of it, and in that very seeing be free of it.

There is not a thing to be done – not a thing, I say, because you are already that which you want to become. You are buddhas, you have never been otherwise. Seeing is enough.

When you say, "I am watching..." it is again the "I." Watching, the "I" will be created again, because watching is again an act, there is effort involved. You are watching – then who is watching? Relax. In relaxation – when there is nothing to be watched and nobody as a watcher, when you are not divided into a duality – there arises a different quality of witnessing. It is not a watching, it is just passive awareness; passive, I say – remember. It has nothing aggressive in it. Watching is very aggressive: effort is needed, you have to be tense. But be non-tense, relaxed. Just be there. In that consciousness when you are simply there, sitting doing nothing, the spring comes and the grass grows by itself.

That is the whole Buddhist approach: that anything that you do will create and enhance the doer – watching also, thinking also, surrendering also. Anything that you do will create the trap. Nothing is needed to be done on your part. Just be, and let things happen. Don't try to manage, don't try to manipulate. Let the breeze pass, let the sunrays come, let life dance, and let death come and have its dance in you too.

This is my meaning of sannyas: it is not something that you do, but when you drop all doing and see the absurdity of doing. Who are you to do? You are just a wave in this ocean. One day you are, another day you will disappear; the ocean continues. Why should you be so worried? You come, you disappear. Meanwhile, for this small interval, you become worried and tense, and you take all the burdens on your shoulders, and you carry rocks on your heart – for no reason at all.

You are free this very moment!

I declare you enlightened in this very moment. But you don't trust me. You say, "That's right, Osho, but just tell us how to become enlightened." That becoming, that achieving, that desiring, goes on jumping on every object that you can find. Sometimes it is money, sometimes it is godliness. Sometimes it is power, sometimes it is meditation – but any object, and you start grabbing it. Non-grabbing is the way to live the real life, the true life, non-grasping, non-possessing.

Let things happen, let life be a happening, and there is joy, there is rejoicing – because then there is no frustration, ever, because you had never expected anything in the first place. Whatsoever comes is good, is welcome. There is no failure, no success. That game of failure and success has been dropped. The sun comes in the morning and wakes you, and the moon comes in the evening and sings a lullaby and you go to sleep. Hunger comes and you eat, and so on and so forth. That's what Zen masters mean when they say: "When hungry, eat, when sleepy, sleep, and there is nothing else to do."

I'm not teaching you inaction. I'm not saying don't go and work, I'm not saying don't earn your bread, I'm not saying renounce the world and depend on others and become exploiters; no, not at all. But don't be a doer. Yes, when you are hungry you have to eat, and when you have to eat you have to earn the bread – but there is nobody doing it. It is hunger itself that is working; there is nobody else doing it. It is thirst itself that is taking you towards the well or towards the river. It is thirst itself moving; there is nobody who is thirsty. Drop nouns and pronouns in your life and let verbs live.

Buddha says: "The truth is that when you see a dancer, there is no dancer but only a dance. When you see a river, there is no river but only rivering. When you see a tree, there is no tree but only treeing. When you see a smile, there is nobody who is smiling, there is only smile, smiling. When you see love, there is nobody who is a lover but only loving. Life is a process."

But we are accustomed to thinking in terms of static nouns. That creates trouble. And there is nothing static – all is flux and flowing. Flow with it, flow with this river, and never be a doer. Even when you are doing don't be a doer. There is doing but there is no doer. Once this insight settles in you there is nothing else.

Enlightenment is not something like a goal that has to be attained. It is the very ordinary life, this simple life that surrounds you. But when you are not struggling, this ordinary life becomes extraordinarily beautiful. Then trees are greener, then birds sing in richer tones, then everything that is happening around is precious. Then ordinary pebbles are diamonds.

Accept this simple, ordinary life. Just drop the doer. And when I say drop the doer, don't become a dropper! Seeing into the reality of it, it disappears.

The third question:

Osho,
Is there a difference between the shunyavada of Nagarjuna and avyakritopadesh, the unspoken and the undefinable teaching of Lord Buddha?

There is no difference at all. If a difference appears to be there, that is only because of the formulation. Nagarjuna is a great philosopher, one of the greatest of the world. Only a few people in the world, very few, have that quality of penetration that Nagarjuna has. So, his way of talking is very philosophical, logical, absolutely logical. Buddha is a mystic, not a philosopher. His way of saying things is more poetic than philosophical. The approach is different, but Nagarjuna is saying exactly the same thing as Buddha. Their formulation is certainly different, but what they are saying has to be understood.

You ask, "Is there any difference between *shunyavada*..." *Shunyavada* means the theory, the philosophy of nothingness. In English there is no word which can be equivalent, appropriately equivalent, to *shunya*. *Shunya* means emptiness; but not negative, a very positive emptiness. It means nothingness, but it does not mean simply nothingness; it means no-thing-ness. *Shunya* means void, void of everything. But the void itself is there, with utter presence, so it is not just void. It is like the sky which is empty, which is pure space, but which is. Everything comes in it and goes, and it remains.

Shunya is like the sky – pure presence. You cannot touch it although you live in it. You cannot see it although you can never be without it. You exist in it; just as the fish exists in the ocean, you exist in space, in *shunya*. *Shunyavada* means that everything arises out of no-thing.

Just a few minutes ago I was telling you the difference between truth and reality. *Reality* means the world of things, and *truth* means the world of no-thing, nothing – *shunya*. All things arise out of nothing and dissolve back into nothing.

In the Upanishads there is a story:

Svetaketu has come from his master's house, back to his parents. He has learned all. His father, Uddalaka, a great philosopher, looks at him and says, "Svetaketu, go outside and bring a fruit from yonder tree."

He goes out, brings a fruit. And the father says, "Break it. What do you see in it?" There are many seeds in it. And the father says, "Take one seed and break it. What do you see in it?"

And he says, "Nothing."

And the father says, "Everything arises out of this nothing. This big tree, so big that one thousand bullock carts can rest underneath it, has arisen out of just a seed. And you break the seed and you find nothing there. This is the mystery of life – everything arises out of nothing. And one day the tree disappears, and you don't know where; you cannot find it anywhere."

So does man: we arise out of nothing, and we are nothing, and we disappear into nothing. This is *shunyavada*.

And what is Buddha's *avyakritopadesh*, the unspoken and the undefinable teaching? It is the same. He never made it so philosophically clear as Nagarjuna has made it. That's why he has never spoken about it. That's why he says it is indefinable; it cannot be brought to the level of language. He has kept silent about it.

You know the Flower Sermon?

One day Buddha comes with a lotus flower in his hand and sits silently, saying nothing. And the ten thousand disciples are there, the ten thousand *bhikkhus* are there, and they are waiting for him to say something, and he goes on looking at the lotus flower. There is great silence, and then there is great restlessness too. People start becoming fidgety – "What is he doing? He has never done that before."
And then one disciple, Mahakashyapa, smiles.
Buddha calls Mahakashyapa, gives him the lotus flower, and says to the assembly, "What can be said I have said to you, and what cannot be said I have given to Mahakashyapa."

This is *avyakritopadesh*, this is the indefinable message. This is the origin of Zen Buddhism, the transmission. Something was transmitted by Buddha to Mahakashyapa, something which is nothing; on the visible plane nothing – no word, no scripture, no theory – but something has been transmitted. What?
The Zen monks have been meditating on this for two thousand five hundred years: "What? What was transmitted? What exactly was given?" In fact, nothing has been given from Buddha to Mahakashyapa; Mahakashyapa has certainly understood something. He understood the silence, he understood the penetrating silence. He understood that moment of clarity, that moment of utter thoughtlessness. He became one, in that moment, with Buddha. That's what surrender is. Not that he was doing it: Buddha was silent and he was silent, and the silences met, and the two silences dissolved into each other. And two silences cannot remain separate, remember, because a silence has no boundary, a silence is unbounded, a silence is simply open, open from all sides. In that great assembly of ten thousand monks there were two silences that day – Buddha and Mahakashyapa. The others remained outside. Mahakashyapa and Buddha met: that's why he smiled – because that was the greatest sermon that Buddha had ever preached. Not saying a single thing and he

had said all, all that could be said – and all that could not be said, that too.

Mahakashyapa understood and laughed. In that laughter Mahakashyapa disappeared totally, became a buddha. The flame from the lamp of Buddha jumped into Mahakashyapa. That is called the "transmission beyond scriptures" – the Flower Sermon. It is unique in the history of human consciousness. That is what is called *avyakritopadesh*: the unspoken word, the unuttered word.

Silence became so substantial, so solid; silence became so real, so existential; silence became tangible in that moment. Buddha was a nothing, Mahakashyapa also understood what it means to be a nothing, to be utterly empty.

There is no difference between Nagarjuna's *shunyavada* and Buddha's unuttered message. Nagarjuna is one of the greatest disciples of Buddha, and one of the most penetrating intellects ever. Only very few people – once in a while, a Socrates, a Shankara – can be compared with Nagarjuna. He was very, very intelligent. The uttermost that the intellect can do is to commit suicide; the greatest thing, the greatest crescendo that can come to the intellect is to go beyond itself – that's what Nagarjuna has done. He has passed through all the realms of intellect, and beyond.

The logical positivists say that nothing is merely an abstraction. In the various instances of negative assertions – for example: this is not sweet, I am not healthy, I was not there, he did not like me, etcetera, etcetera – negation has no substance of its own. This is what the logical positivists say. Buddha does not agree, Nagarjuna does not agree. Martin Heidegger, one of the most penetrating intellects of the modern age, does not agree.

Heidegger says there is an actual experience of nothing. It is not just something created by language; there is an actual experience of nothing. It is inseparably bound up with being. The experience that attests to this is that of dread. Kierkegaard, the Danish philosopher, also asks, "What effect does nothing produce?" and answers, "It begets dread."

Nothing is an actual experience. Either you can experience

it in deep meditation, or when death comes. Death and meditation are the two possibilities of experiencing it. Yes, sometimes you can experience it in love too. If you dissolve into somebody in deep love you can experience a kind of nothingness. That's why people are afraid of love – they go only so far, then panic arises, then they are frightened. That's why very few people have remained orgasmic – because orgasm gives you an experience of nothingness. You disappear, you melt into something and you don't know what it is. You go into the indefinable, *avyakrit.* You go beyond the social. You go into some unity where separation is no longer valid, where ego does not exist. And it is frightening, because it is deathlike.

So it is an experience, either in love, which people have learned to avoid – so many go on hankering for love, and go on destroying all possibilities for it because of the fear of nothingness – or, in deep meditation when thought stops. You simply see there is nothing inside, but that nothing has a presence; it is not simply absence of thought, it is presence of something unknown, mysterious, something very huge. Or, you can experience it in death, if you are alert. People ordinarily die in unconsciousness. Because of the fear of nothingness they become unconscious. If you die consciously... And you can die consciously only if you accept the phenomenon of death, and for that one has to learn, prepare for the whole life. One first has to love to be ready to die, and one has to meditate to be ready to die. Only a man who has loved and meditated will be able to die consciously. And once you die consciously then there is no need for you to come back, because you have learned the lesson of life. Then you disappear into the whole; that is nirvana.

The logical positivists look very logical, but they miss something – because reality is far more than logic. In ordinary experience we come only to what they say: this chair is here, this will be removed, then you will say there is no chair there. It simply indicates absence – the chair has been removed. These are ordinary instances of nothingness: there was once a house and then it has been dismantled, it is no longer there. It is only an absence.

But there are nothingnesses deep inside your being, at the very core. At the very core of life, death exists. Death is the center of the cyclone. In love you come close to that, in meditation you come close to that, in physical death also you come close to that. In deep sleep, when dreams disappear, you come close to it. It is very life-giving, it is life-enhancing. A man who cannot sleep deeply will become ill, because it is only in deep sleep, when he dies into his deepest depth, that he regains life, energy, vitality. In the morning he is again fresh and full of zest, gusto – vibrant, again vibrant.

Learn to die! That is the greatest art to be learned, the greatest skill there is.

Heidegger's standpoint comes very close to Buddha's, and his language is very modern, that's why I'm quoting him. He says: "Every being, so far as it is a being, is made out of nothing." There is a parallel Christian doctrine too – very neglected, because Christian theologicians cannot manage it, it is too much. The doctrine is *creatio ex nihilo*: the creation is out of nothing.

If you ask the modern physicist he will agree with Buddha: as you go deeper into matter, things start disappearing. A moment comes, when the atom is divided, that thing-hood completely disappears. Then there are electrons, but they are not things anymore, they are no-things. It is very difficult to understand. But physics, modern physics, has come very close to metaphysics – because it is coming closer and closer to reality every day. It is approaching through matter, but coming to nothing. You know matter no longer exists in modern physics. Matter is just an illusion: it only appears, it is not there. The solidity of it, the substantiality of it, is all illusion; nothing is substantial, all is flux and energy. Matter is nothing but energy. And when you go deeper into energy, energy is not a thing, it is a no-thing.

Death is the point at which knowledge fails, and we become open to being – that has been the Buddhist experience down the ages. Buddha used to send his disciples, when somebody had died, to see the body burning on the funeral pyre: "Meditate there, meditate on the nothingness of life." Death is the point at which knowledge fails, and when knowledge fails, mind fails. And when mind fails, there is a possibility of truth penetrating you.

But people don't know. When somebody dies you don't know what to do, you are very embarrassed. When somebody dies it is a great moment to meditate.

I always think that each city needs a Death Center. When somebody is dying and his death is very, very imminent he should be moved to the Death Center. It should be a small temple where people who can go deep in meditation should sit around him, should help him to die, and should participate in his being when he disappears into nothing. When somebody disappears into nothing great energy is released. The energy that was there, surrounding him, is released. If you are in a silent space around him, you will go on a great trip. No psychedelic can take you there. The man is naturally releasing great energy; if you can absorb that energy, you will also kind of die with him. And you will see the ultimate – the source and the goal, the beginning and the end.

"Man is the being by whom nothing comes into the world," says Jean-Paul Sartre. "Consciousness is not this or that object, it is not any object at all; but surely it is itself? No," says Sartre, "that is precisely what it is not. Consciousness is never identical with itself. Thus, when I reflect upon myself, the self that is reflected is other than the self that reflects. When I try to state what I am, I fail, because while I am speaking, what I am talking about slips away into the past and becomes what I was. I am my past and my future, and yet I am not. I have been the one, and I shall be the other. But in the present, there is nothingness."

If somebody asks you, "Who are you?" what are you going to say? Either you can answer out of the past, which is no more, or you can answer out of the future, which you are not yet. But who are you right in this moment? A nobody, a nothingness. This nothingness is the very core, the heart – the heart of your being.

Death is not the ax that cuts down the tree of life, it is the fruit that grows on it. Death is the very substance you are made of. Nothingness is your very being. Attain to this nothingness either through love or meditation, and go on having glimpses of it. This is what Nagarjuna means by *shunya*. This is what Buddha transferred that day when he delivered the Flower Sermon. This is what Mahakashyapa understood when he laughed. He saw nothingness, and the purity of it, the innocence of it, the primal innocence of it, the radiance of it, the immortality of it – because nothingness cannot die. Things die; nothingness is immortal, eternal.

If you are identified with anything, you will suffer death. But if you know that you are death, how can you suffer death? Then nothing can destroy you; nothingness is indestructible.

A Buddhist parable narrates that the king of hell asked a newly arrived spirit whether during life he had met the three heavenly messengers. And when he answered, "No, my Lord, I did not," he asked whether he had ever seen an old man bent with age, or a poor and friendless sick man, or a dead man?

Buddhists call these three "the messengers of God": old age, sickness, death – three messengers of God. Why? – because only through these experiences in life do you become aware of death. And if you become aware of death and you start learning how to go into it, how to welcome it, how to receive it, you are released from the bondage, from the wheel of life and death.

Heidegger says, and so does Søren Kierkegaard, that nothingness creates dread. That is only half of the story – it creates dread because these two people are just philosophers.

If you ask Buddha, Mahakashyapa, Nagarjuna, if you ask me, death looked at only partially creates dread; looked at absolutely, totally, it frees you from all dread, from all anguish, from all anxiety, it frees you from *samsara*. If you look partly then it creates fear that you are going to die, that you will become a nothing, that soon you will disappear. And naturally you feel nervous, shaken, uprooted. If you look at death totally, then you know you *are* death, you are made of it. So nothing is going to disappear, nothing is going to remain. Only nothingness is.

Buddhism is not a pessimistic religion as has been thought

by many people. Buddhism is the way to get rid of both opti-
mism and pessimism, to get rid of duality.

Start meditating on death. And whenever you feel death
close by, go into it through the door of love, through the door
of meditation, through the door of a man dying. And if some
day you are dying – and the day *is* going to come one day –
receive it in joy, benediction. If you can receive death in joy
and benediction, you will attain to the greatest peak, because
death is the crescendo of life. Hidden in it is the greatest
orgasm, because hidden in it is the greatest freedom.

Death is making love to existence, or existence making
love to you. Death is cosmic, total orgasm. So drop all ideas
that you carry about death – they are dangerous. They make
you antagonistic to the greatest experience that you need
to have. If you miss death you will be born again. Unless you
have learned how to die, you will go on being born again
and again and again. This is the wheel, *samsara*, the world.
Once you have known the greatest orgasm, then there is no
need; you disappear, and you remain in that orgasm forever.
You don't remain like you, you don't remain as an entity, you
don't remain defined, identified with anything. You remain as
the whole, not as the part.

This is Nagarjuna's *shunyavada*, and this is Buddha's
unspoken message, the unspoken word. They are both the
same.

The last question:

Osho,
I am afraid of taking sannyas, although I am immensely
attracted. I am afraid because of my husband. I don't think
he will be able to understand it.

You are not very respectful towards your husband. Do you
think he's stupid or something? Why should he not be able
to understand it? If he loves you, he will understand it. Love
is understanding. If he does not love you, then whether you
take sannyas or not, he's not going to understand you.

The second thing: if he does not understand your sannyas, it is his problem. You have to live your life. Never compromise, otherwise you will miss much. Never compromise! If you feel like becoming a sannyasin, become a sannyasin. Take the risk. If he loves you there is no problem, he will understand – because love gives freedom. If he does not love you then there will be difficulty because he will feel you are getting out of his possession, you are becoming independent, you are trying to be yourself. But to bow down to such expectations is suicidal. That is *his* problem. You have to live your life, he has to live his life. Nobody should try to impose things on the other.

But my feeling is that you must also be imposing things on him, that's why you are afraid. If you are not imposing anything on him, you can be independent. But it is a mutual arrangement: people are slaves to each other, and whenever you make a slave of somebody, remember, you are making somebody your master too. It is a mutual arrangement. You must be trying to manipulate your husband, you must be trying to force things upon him, you must be making him a cripple. Now you want to be independent, and deep down you are afraid that if you become independent, he will assert his independence too. Then he would like to go his own way, and that you cannot afford. That is the real fear.

But if you don't do something that you like, that you wanted to do, that you wanted to be, you will never be able to forgive him. And you will take revenge, and you will be angry, and you will be in a rage – because you will constantly think you wanted to become a sannyasin, and it is only because of this man that you did not. You will feel caged, imprisoned. Nobody likes being imprisoned. Then one hates the person who is the cause of your imprisonment, then one tries to take revenge in subtle ways. That will destroy your marriage.

Never create such a situation in which you cannot forgive the other. Only two independent persons can forgive each other. Slaves cannot forgive. And who knows, it may help him too, in some way.

I was reading an anecdote the other day:

Two explorers met in the wilds of the Amazon. The following exchange took place:

First explorer: "I came out here because the urge to wander is in my blood. Civilization sickens me. I like to see nature in its primitive form. I would like to plant my footprints where no human being has ever gone before. How about you? Why did you come out here?"

Second explorer: "My wife has become Osho's sannyasin, and she is doing Dynamic Meditation in the morning and Kundalini in the evening – that's why!"

But good! If your husband goes to the Amazon and becomes an explorer, this is giving him a good opportunity to do something.

Enough for today.

CHAPTER 3

negation of knowledge

Here, O Sariputra, form is emptiness and the very emptiness is form; emptiness does not differ from form, form does not differ from emptiness; whatever is form, that is emptiness, whatever is emptiness, that is form; the same is true of feelings, perceptions, impulses, and consciousness.

Here, O Sariputra, all dharmas are marked with emptiness; they are not produced or stopped, not defiled or immaculate, not deficient or complete.

Knowledge is the curse, the calamity, the cancer. It is through knowledge that man becomes divided from the whole. Knowledge creates the distance.

You come across a wildflower in the mountains, you don't know what it is; your mind has nothing to say about it, the mind is silent. You look at the flower, you see the flower, but no knowledge arises in you – there is wonder, there is mystery. The flower is there, you are there. Through wonder you are not separate, you are bridged.

If you know that it is a rose or a marigold, or something else, that very knowing disconnects you. The flower is there, you are here, but there is no bridge – you know! Knowledge creates distance. The more you know the bigger the distance; the less you know the less the distance. And if you are in a moment of not knowing, there is no distance, you are bridged.

You fall in love with a woman or a man – the day you fall in love there is no distance. There is only wonder, a thrill, an excitement, an ecstasy – but no knowledge. You don't know who this woman is. Without knowledge, there is nothing to divide you; hence the beauty of those first moments of love. You have lived with the woman for only twenty-four hours; knowledge has arisen. Now you have some ideas about the woman: you know who she is, there is an image. Twenty-four hours have created a past. Those twenty-four hours have left marks on the mind: you look at the same woman, there is no longer the same mystery. You are coming down the hill, that peak is lost.

To understand this is to understand much. To understand that knowledge divides, knowledge creates distance, is to understand the very secret of meditation. Meditation is a state of not knowing. Meditation is pure space, undisturbed by knowledge. Yes, the biblical story is true – that man has fallen through knowledge, by eating the fruit of the tree of knowledge. No other scripture of the world surpasses that. That parable is the last word; no other parable has reached to that height and insight.

It looks so illogical that man has fallen through knowledge. It looks illogical because logic is part of knowledge. Logic is all in support of knowledge. It looks illogical, because logic is the root cause of man's fall. A man who is absolutely logical, absolutely sane, always sane, never allows any illogic in his life is a madman. Sanity needs to be balanced by insanity; logic needs to be balanced by illogic. The opposites meet and balance. A man who is just rational is unreasonable – he will miss much. In fact he will go on missing all that is beautiful and all that is true. He will collect trivia, his life will be a mundane life. He will be the worldly man.

That biblical parable has immense insight. Why has man fallen through knowledge? – because knowledge creates distance, because knowledge creates "I" and "thou," because knowledge creates subject and object, the knower and the known, the observer and the observed. Knowledge is basically schizophrenic; it creates a split. And then there is no way to bridge it. That's why the more knowledgeable man has become, the less religious he is. The more educated a man, the less the possibility is for him to approach godliness.

Jesus is right when he says, "Only children will be able to enter into my kingdom." Only children... What is that quality that a child has and you have lost? The child has the quality of non-knowledge, innocence. He looks with wonder, his eyes are absolutely clear. He looks deep, but he has no prejudices, no judgments, no a priori ideas. He does not project, hence he comes to know that which is.

The other day we were talking about the distinction between reality and truth. The child knows the truth, you know only the reality. The reality is that which you have created around yourself – projecting, desiring, thinking. The reality is your interpretation of truth. Truth is simply that which is; reality is that which you have come to understand – it is your idea of the truth. Reality consists of things, all separate. Truth consists of only one cosmic energy. Truth consists of oneness, reality consists of "many-ness." Reality is a crowd, truth is integration.

Before we enter into the sutras, this has to become the foundation: that knowledge is a curse. J. Krishnamurti has said, "To negate is silence." To negate what? – to negate knowledge, to negate mind, to negate this constant occupation inside you; to create an unoccupied space. When you are unoccupied you are in tune with the whole. When you are occupied you have fallen out of tune. Hence, whenever it happens that you can attain a moment of silence, there is immense joy. In that moment life has significance, in that moment life has a grandeur beyond words. In that moment life is a dance. In that moment if even death comes it will be a dance and a celebration, because that moment knows nothing but joy. That moment is joyous, it is blissful.

Knowledge has to be negated – but not because I am saying so or because J. Krishnamurti says so or because Gautam Buddha has said so. If you negate because I am saying so, then you will negate your knowledge, and whatsoever I am saying will become your knowledge in its place; you will substitute it. The negation has not to come from the mind, otherwise the mind is very tricky. Then whatsoever I say becomes your knowledge, you start clinging to it. You throw away your old idols and you replace them with new ones. But it is the same game played with new words, new ideas, new thoughts.

Then how to negate knowledge? Not by other knowledge: just seeing the fact that knowledge creates distance, just seeing this fact intensely, totally, is enough. Not that you have to replace it with something else; that intensity is fire, that intensity will reduce your knowledge to ashes. That intensity is enough. That intensity is what is known as "insight." Insight will burn your knowledge, and it will not be replaced by other knowledge. Then there is emptiness, *shunyata*. Then there is nothingness, because then there is no content; there is undisturbed, undistorted truth.

You have to *see* what I am saying, you are not to learn what I am saying. Here, sitting with me every day, listening to me, don't start collecting knowledge. Here, listening to me, don't start hoarding. Listening to me should be an experiment in insight. You should listen with intensity, with totality, with as much awareness as is possible for you. In that very awareness you will see a point, and that very seeing is transformation. Not that you have to do something else afterwards; the seeing itself brings mutation. If some effort is needed, that simply shows you missed. If you come tomorrow and ask me, "I have understood that knowledge is the curse, that knowledge creates distance. Now, how do I drop it?" – then you missed. If the "how" arises, then you missed. The "how" cannot arise, because the "how" is asking for more knowledge. The "how" is asking for methods, techniques: "What should be done?" And insight is enough; it need not be helped by any efforts. Its fire is more than enough to burn all knowledge that you carry within you. Just see the point.

Listening to me, go with me. Listening to me, hold my hand and move into the spaces that I'm trying for you to move into. And see what I am saying, don't argue. Don't say yes, don't say no. Don't agree, don't disagree. Just be with me in this moment – and suddenly the insight is there. If you are listening attentively... And by attention I don't mean concentration; by attention I simply mean you are listening with awareness, not with a dull mind; you are listening with intelligence, with aliveness, with openness. You are here, now, with me. That's what I mean by attention: you are nowhere else. You are not comparing in the mind what I am saying with your old thoughts. You are not comparing at all, you are not judging. You are not there judging inside, within you, whether what I am saying is right or not, or how much is right.

Just the other day I was talking to a seeker. He has the quality of a seeker but is burdened by knowledge. While I was talking to him his eyes became full of tears. His heart was just going to open, and in that very moment the mind jumped in and destroyed the whole beauty of it. He was just moving towards the heart and opening, but immediately his mind came in. Those tears that were just on the verge of dropping, disappeared. His eyes became dry. What had happened? – I said something with which he could not agree. He was agreeing with me, up to a certain point. Then I said something which goes against his Jewish background, which goes against the Kabbala, and immediately the whole energy changed. He said, "Everything is right. Whatsoever you are saying is right, but this one thing: that God has no purpose, that existence exists purposelessly – with this I cannot agree, because the Kabbala says just the opposite: that life has purpose, that God is purposive, that he is leading us towards a certain destiny, that there *is* a destination."

He may not have even looked at it this way – that he missed in that moment because comparison came in. What does the Kabbala have to do with me? When you are with me, put away all your knowledge of the Kabbala, of Yoga, of Tantra, of this and that. When you are with me, be with me. If you are totally with me... And I am not saying that you are agreeing with me, remember. I am not saying that you are agreeing with me: there is no question of agreement or disagreement.

When you see a roseflower, do you agree with it or disagree with it? When you see the sunrise, do you agree or do you disagree? When you see the moon in the night, you simply see it! Either you see it or you don't see it, but there is no question of agreement or disagreement.

Be with me that way; that is the way of being with a master. Just be with me. I'm not trying to convince you about anything. I'm not trying to convert you to some theory, philosophy, dogma, to some church, no! I'm simply sharing what has happened to me, and in that very sharing, if you participate, it can happen to you too. It is infectious. Insight transforms.

When I am saying knowledge is a curse you can agree or disagree – and you have missed! Just listen to it, just see into it, go into the whole process of knowledge. You see how knowledge creates distance, how knowledge becomes a barrier, how knowledge stands in between, how knowledge goes on increasing and the distance goes on increasing, how innocence is lost through knowledge, how wonder is destroyed, crippled, murdered through knowledge, how life becomes a dull and boring affair through knowledge. Mystery is lost, and with the mystery godliness is lost.

Mystery disappears because you start having the idea that you know. When you know, how can there be mystery? Mystery is possible only when you don't know.

Remember, man has not known a thing! All that we have gathered is just rubbish. The ultimate remains beyond grasp. What we have gathered are only facts, truth remains untouched by our efforts. And that is the experience not only of Buddha, Krishna, Krishnamurti and Ramana; that is the experience even of Edison, Newton, Albert Einstein. That is the experience of poets, painters, dancers. All the great intelligences of the world – they may be mystics, they may be poets, they may be scientists – are in absolute agreement about one thing: that the more we know, the more we understand that life is an absolute mystery. Our knowledge does not destroy its mystery. It is only stupid people who think that because they know a little bit, now there is no more mystery in life. It is only the mediocre mind that becomes too attached to knowledge; the intelligent mind remains above knowledge. He uses it, certainly uses it – it is useful, it is utilitarian – but knows perfectly well that all that is true is hidden, remains hidden. We can go on knowing and knowing, but existence remains unexhausted.

Listen with insight, attention, totality, and in that very vision you will see something, and that seeing changes you. Don't ask how.

That is the meaning when Krishnamurti says, "To negate is silence." Insight negates. And when something is negated and nothing is posited instead, something has been destroyed and nothing has been put, replaced in its place, there is silence – because there is space. There is silence because the old has been thrown and the new has not been brought in. That silence Buddha calls *shunyata*. That silence is emptiness, nothingness. And only that nothingness can operate in the world of truth.

Thought cannot operate there. Thought works only in the world of things, because thought is also a thing – subtle, but it is also material. That's why thought can be recorded, that's why thought can be relayed, conveyed. I can throw a thought at you; you can hold it, you can have it. It can be taken and given, it is transferable, because it is a thing. It is a material phenomenon.

Emptiness cannot be given, emptiness cannot be thrown at you. You can participate in it, you can move into it, but nobody can give it to you. It is nontransferable. And only emptiness operates in the world of truth. Truth is known only when mind is not. To know truth mind has to cease, it has to go out of functioning. It has to be quiet, still, unmoving.

Thought cannot operate in truth, but truth can operate through thoughts. You cannot attain to truth by thinking, but when you have attained it you can use thinking in its service. That's what I am doing, that's what Buddha has done, that's what all the masters have done.

What I am saying is a thought, but behind this thought is emptiness. That emptiness has not been produced by thought, that emptiness is beyond thought. Thought cannot touch it, thought cannot even look at it.

Have you observed one phenomenon? – that you cannot think about emptiness, you cannot make emptiness a thought. You cannot think about it, it is unthinkable. If you can think about it, it will not be emptiness at all. Thought has to go for emptiness to come; they never meet. Once emptiness has come, it can use all kinds of devices to express itself.

Insight is a state of no-thought. Whenever you see something, you always see when there is no thought. Here also, listening to me, being with me, sometimes you see. But those moments are gaps, intervals. One thought has gone, another has not come, and there is a gap; and in that gap something strikes, something starts vibrating. It is like somebody playing on a drum: the drum is empty inside, that's why it can be played upon. That emptiness vibrates. That beautiful sound that comes out is produced out of emptiness. When you are, without a thought, then something is possible, immediately possible. Then you can see what I am saying. Then it will not be just a word heard, then it will become an intuition, an insight, a vision. You have looked into it, you have shared it with me.

Insight is a state of non-thinking, no-thought. It is a gap, an interval in the process of thought, and in that gap is the glimpse, the truth.

The English word *empty* comes from a root which means at leisure, unoccupied. It is a beautiful word if you go to the root. The root is very pregnant: it means at leisure, unoccupied. Whenever you are unoccupied, at leisure, you are empty. And remember, the proverb that says that the empty mind is the Devil's workshop is just nonsense. Just the opposite is the truth: the occupied mind is the Devil's workshop. The empty mind is God's workshop, not the Devil's. But you have to understand what I mean by "empty"– at leisure, relaxed, nontense, not moving, not desiring, not going anywhere, just being here, utterly here. An empty mind is a pure presence. And all is possible in that pure presence, because the whole existence comes out of that pure presence.

These trees grow out of that pure presence, these stars are born out of this pure presence; we are here – all the buddhas have come out of this pure presence. In that pure presence you are in God, you are God. Occupied, you fall; occupied, you have to be expelled from the Garden of Eden. Unoccupied you are back in the garden, unoccupied you are back at home.

When the mind is not occupied by reality, by things, by thoughts, then there is that which is. And that which is, is the truth. Only in emptiness is there a meeting, merging. Only in emptiness do you open to truth and truth enters in you. Only in emptiness do you become pregnant with truth.

These are the three states of the mind. The first is content and consciousness. You always have contents in the mind – a thought moving, a desire arising, anger, greed, ambition. You always have some content in the mind; the mind is never unoccupied. The traffic goes on, day-in, day-out. While awake it is there, while asleep it is there. While awake you call it thinking, while asleep you call it dreaming – it is the same process. Dreaming is a little more primitive, that's all – because it thinks in pictures. It does not use concepts, it uses pictures. It is more primitive; like small children think in pictures. So in small children's books you have to make big pictures, colorful, because they think through pictures. Through pictures they will learn words. By and by those pictures become smaller and smaller, and then they disappear.

The primitive man also thinks in pictures. The ancientmost languages are pictorial languages. Chinese is a pictorial language: it has no alphabet. It is the ancientmost language. In the night you again become primitive, you forget your sophistication of the day and you start thinking in pictures – but it is the same.

The psychoanalyst's insight is valuable – that he looks into your dreams. Then there is more truth, because you are more primitive; you are not trying to deceive anybody, you are more authentic. In the day you have a personality around you which hides you – layers upon layers of personality. It is very difficult to find the true man. You will have to dig deep, and it hurts, and the man will resist. But in the night, just as you put your clothes away, you put your personality away too. It is not needed because you will not be communicating with anybody, you will be alone in your bed. And you will not be in the world, you will be absolutely in your private realm. There is no need to hide and no need to pretend. That's why the psychoanalyst tries to go into your dreams, because they show much more clearly who you are. But it is the same game played in different languages; the game is not different. This is the ordinary state of the mind: mind and content, consciousness plus content.

The second state of the mind is consciousness without content; that's what meditation is. You are fully alert, and there is a gap, an interval. No thought is encountered, there is no thought before you. You are not asleep, you are awake – but there is no thought. This is meditation. The first state is called mind, the second state is called meditation.

And then there is a third state. When the content has disappeared, the object has disappeared, the subject cannot remain for long – because they exist together. They produced each other. When the subject is alone it can only hang around a little while more, just out of the momentum of the past. Without the content the consciousness cannot be there long; it will not be needed, because a consciousness is always a consciousness *about* something. When you say "conscious," it can be asked "About what?" You say, "I am conscious of..." That object is needed, it is a must for the subject to exist. Once the object has disappeared, soon the subject will also disappear. First go the contents, then consciousness disappears.

Then the third state is called *samadhi* – no content, no consciousness. But remember, this no-content, no-consciousness, is not a state of unconsciousness. It is a state of superconsciousness, of transcendental consciousness. Consciousness now is only conscious of itself. Consciousness has turned upon itself; the circle is complete. You have come home. This is the third state, *samadhi*; and this third state is what Buddha means by *shunyata*.

First drop the content – you become half-empty; then drop

consciousness – you become fully empty. And this full-emptiness is the most beautiful thing that can happen, the greatest benediction.

In this nothingness, in this emptiness, in this selflessness, in this *shunyata*, there is complete security and stability. You will be surprised to know about this complete security and stability when you are not. All fears disappear – because what is the basic fear? The basic fear is the fear of death. All other fears are just reflections of the basic fear. All other fears can be reduced to one fear: the fear of death, the fear: "One day I may have to disappear, one day I may have to die. I am, and the day is coming when I will not be" – that frightens, that is the fear.

To avoid that fear we start moving in such a way so that we can live as long as possible. And we try to secure our lives – we start compromising, we start becoming more and more secure, safe, because of the fear. We become paralyzed, because the more secure you are, the safer you are, the less alive you will be.

Life exists in challenges, life exists in crises, life needs insecurity. It grows in the soil of insecurity. Whenever you are insecure, you will find yourself more alive, more alert. That's why rich people become dull: a kind of stupidity and a kind of stupor surrounds them. They are so secure, there is no challenge. They are so secure, they need not be intelligent. They are so secure – for what do they need intelligence? Intelligence is needed when there is challenge, intelligence is provoked by challenge.

So because of the fear of death we strive for security, for a bank balance, for insurance, for marriage, for a settled life, for a home; we become part of a country, we join a political party, we join a religious church – we become Hindus, Christians, Mohammedans. These are all ways to find security. These are all ways to find some place to belong to – a country, a church. Because of this fear politicians and priests go on exploiting you. If you are not in any fear, no politician, no priest can exploit you. It is only out of fear that he can exploit because he can provide – at least he can promise – that this will make you secure: "This will be your security. I can guarantee it." The goods may never be delivered – that's another thing – but the promise... And the promise keeps people exploited, oppressed. The promise keeps people in bondage.

Once you have known the inner emptiness, there is no fear because death has already happened. In that emptiness it has happened. In that emptiness you have disappeared. How can you be afraid anymore? About what? About whom? And who can be afraid? In this emptiness all fear disappears because death has already happened. Now there is no longer any death possible. You feel a kind of deathlessness, timelessness. Eternity has arrived. Now you don't look for security; there is no need.

This is the state of a sannyasin. This is the state where a man need not be a part of a country, need not be a part of a church, or stupid things like that.

It is only when you have become nothing that you can be yourself.

It looks paradoxical. You need not compromise, because it is out of fear and greed that one compromises. And you can live in rebellion because there is nothing to lose. You can become a rebellion; there is nothing to fear. Nobody can kill you, you have already done that yourself. Nobody can take anything away from you; you have dropped all that which can be taken away from you. Now you are in nothingness, you *are* a nothingness. Hence the paradoxical phenomenon: that in this nothingness arises a great security, a great safety, a stability – because there is no more death possible.

With death, time disappears. With death all the problems that are created by death and by time disappear. In the wake of all these disappearances, what is left is a pure sky. This pure sky is *samadhi*, nirvana. Buddha is talking about this.

These sutras have been addressed to one of Buddha's greatest disciples, Sariputra. Why to Sariputra?

The first day I told you that there are seven planes, seven rungs of the ladder. The seventh is the transcendental: Zen, Tantra, Tao. The sixth is the spirituo-transcendental: Yoga. Up to the sixth, method remains important, "how" remains important. Up to the sixth, discipline remains important, ritual remains important, techniques remain important. Only when you reach to the seventh do you see that to be, nothing is needed.

Sariputra is addressed in these sutras because Sariputra was at the sixth center, the sixth rung. He was one of the greatest disciples of Buddha. Buddha had eighty great disciples; Sariputra is one of the chief amongst those eighty. He was the most knowledgeable man around Buddha. He was the greatest scholar and pundit around Buddha. When he had come to Buddha, he himself had five thousand disciples.

When he had come to Buddha for the first time he had come to argue, to debate with and defeat Buddha. He had come with his five thousand disciples – to impress. And when he stood before Buddha, Buddha laughed:

Buddha said to him, "Sariputra, you know much, but you do not know at all. I can see you have accumulated great knowledge, but you are empty. You have come to discuss and debate and to defeat me, but if you *really* want to discuss with me, you will have to wait at least one year."

Sariputra said, "One year? For what?"

Buddha said, "You will have to remain silent for one year; that will be the price to be paid. If you can remain silent for one year then you can discuss with me, because what I am going to say to you will come out of silence. You need a little experience of it. And I see, Sariputra, you have not even tasted a single moment of silence. You are so full of knowledge, your head is heavy. I feel compassion for you, Sariputra. You have been carrying such a load for many lives. You are not a brahmin only in this life, Sariputra, you have been a brahmin for many lives. And for many lives you have carried the Vedas and the scriptures. It has been your style for many lives.

"But I see a possibility. You are knowledgeable, but yet the promise is there. You are knowledgeable, but your knowledge has not completely blocked your being; there are a few windows still left. I would like, for one year, to clean those windows, and then there is a possibility of our meeting and talking and being. Be here for one year."

This was strange. Sariputra had been traveling all over the country, defeating people. That was one of the things in India: knowledgeable people used to travel all over the country and defeat others in great debates and discussions, marathon debates. And that was thought to be one of the greatest things to do. If somebody had become victorious all over the country and he had defeated all the scholars, that was a great ego satisfaction. That man was thought to be bigger than kings, emperors. That man was thought to be greater than the rich people.

Sariputra was traveling. And naturally, you cannot declare yourself the victorious one if you have not defeated Buddha. So he had come for that. So he said, "Okay, if I have to wait for one year, I will wait." And for one year he was sitting there in silence with Buddha. In one year, the silence settled in him.

And after one year Buddha asked him, "Now we can discuss and you can defeat me, Sariputra. I will be immensely happy to be defeated by you."

And Sariputra laughed and touched Buddha's feet and said, "Initiate me. In this one year's silence, listening to you, there have been a few moments when the insight has happened to me. Although I had come as the antagonist, I thought, 'While I am here sitting for one year, why not listen to this man, to what he is saying?' So out of curiosity I started listening. But sometimes those moments came and you penetrated me, and you touched my heart, and you played on my inner organ, and I have heard the music. You have defeated me without defeating me."

Sariputra became Buddha's disciple, and his five thousand disciples also became Buddha's disciples. Sariputra was one of the very well-known scholars of those days. These sutras are addressed to Sariputra.

Here, O Sariputra, form is emptiness and the very emptiness is form; emptiness does not differ from form, form does not differ

*from emptiness; whatever is form, that is emptiness, whatever is
emptiness, that is form; the same is true of feelings, perceptions,
impulses, and consciousness.*

Here, O Sariputra... What does Buddha mean by "here"?
He means his space. He says, "From the vision of my world,
from the transcendental standpoint, the space where I exist
and the eternity where I exist..."

*Here, O Sariputra, form is emptiness and the very empti-
ness is form...* This is one of the most important assertions.
The whole Buddhist approach depends on this: that the manifest is the unmanifest; that the form is nothing but the form
of emptiness itself, and the emptiness is also nothing but the
form, the possibility of the form. The statement is illogical and
obviously appears to be nonsense. How can form be emptiness? They are opposites. How can emptiness be form? They
are polarities.

One thing has to be understood before we can enter into
the sutra rightly: Buddha is not logical, Buddha is dialectical.

There are two approaches towards reality: one is logical.
Of that approach, Aristotle is the father in the West. It simply
moves in a line, a clear-cut line. It never allows the opposite;
the opposite has to be discarded. This approach says *A* is *A*
and never not *A*. *A* cannot be not *A*. This is the formulation
of Aristotelian logic – and it looks perfectly right, because we
have all been brought up with that logic in the schools, col-
leges, universities. The world is dominated by Aristotle: *A* is *A*
and never not *A*.

The second approach towards reality is dialectical. In the
West that approach is associated with the names of Heraclitus,
Hegel. The dialectical process says: life moves through polarities, through opposites – just as a river flows through two
banks which oppose each other, but those opposing banks
keep the river flowing between them. This is more existential.
Electricity has two poles, positive and negative. If Aristotle's
logic is of existence, then electricity is very, very illogical. Then existence itself is illogical, because it produces
new life out of the meeting of a man and a woman, which

are opposites – yin and yang, male and female. If existence followed an Aristotelian logic, a linear logic, then homosexuality would have been the norm and heterosexuality would have been perversion. Then man would love man and woman would love woman. Then opposites could not meet.

But existence is dialectical. Everywhere, opposites are meeting. In you, birth and death are meeting. Everywhere, opposites are meeting – day and night, summer and winter. The thorn and the flower, they are meeting; they are on the same branch, they come out of the same source. Man and woman, youth and old age, beauty and ugliness, body and soul, the world and godliness – all are opposites. This is a symphony of the opposites. Opposites are not only meeting but creating a great symphony – only opposites *can* create a symphony. Otherwise life would be a monotony, not a symphony. Life would be a boredom. If there were only one note continuously being repeated, it would be bound to create boredom. There are opposite notes: thesis meeting with the antithesis, creating a synthesis; and in its own turn, synthesis again becomes a thesis, creates an antithesis, and a higher synthesis evolves. That's how life moves.

This approach of Buddha's is dialectical, and it is more existential, more true, more valid.

A man loves a woman, a woman loves a man – then something else has to be understood too. Now biologists say, and psychologists agree, that man is not only man, he is woman too. And woman is not simply woman, she is man too. So when a man and a woman meet, there are not two persons meeting but four persons meeting. The man is meeting with the woman, but the man has a hidden woman in himself; so has the woman a hidden man in herself; they are also meeting. The meeting is on double planes. It is more intricate, more complex, more intertwined. A man is both man and woman. Why? – because he comes out of both. Something has been contributed to you by your father and something has been contributed to you by your mother, whosoever you are. A man flows in your blood and a woman too. You have to be both because you are the meeting of the polar opposites. You are a synthesis! It is impossible to deny one and just be the other. That's what has been done.

Aristotle has been followed literally, in every way, and that has created many problems for man – and such problems which seem to be unsolvable if Aristotle is to be followed. A man has been taught to be just a man: never to show any feminine traits, never to show any softness of the heart, never to show any receptivity, always be aggressive. Man has been taught never to cry, never weep – because tears are feminine. Women have been taught never to be in any way like the male: never to show aggression, never show expression, to always remain passive, receptive. This is against reality, and this has crippled both. In a better world, with better understanding, a man will be both, a woman will be both – because sometimes a man needs to be a woman. There are moments when he needs to be soft – tender moments, love-moments. And there are moments when a woman needs to be expressive and aggressive – in anger, in defense, in rebellion. If a woman is simply passive, then she will automatically turn into a slave. A passive woman is bound to become a slave – that's what happened down the ages. And an aggressive man, emphatically aggressive and never tender, is bound to create wars, neurosis in the world, violence.

Man has been fighting, continuously fighting; it seems that man exists on the earth just to fight. In three thousand years there have been five thousand wars! War continues somewhere or other, the earth is never whole and healthy without war. There is never a moment without war. Either it is in Korea, or it is in Vietnam, or it is in Israel, or India, Pakistan, or in Bangladesh; somewhere the massacre has to continue. Man has to kill. To remain man, he has to kill. Seventy-five percent of energy is put into war effort, into creating more bombs, hydrogen bombs, neutron bombs, and so on and so forth. It seems that man's whole purpose here on earth is war. The war heroes are respected the most. The war politicians become the great names in history: Adolf Hitler, Winston Churchill, Joseph Stalin, Mao Zedong – these names are going to remain. Why? – because they fought great wars, they destroyed. Whether in aggression or in defense is not the point, but these were the warmongers. And nobody ever knows who was aggressive – whether Germany was aggressive or not depends on who writes the history. Whosoever wins will write the history, and he will prove the other was the aggressor. History would be totally different if Adolf Hitler had been victorious. Yes, the Nuremberg trials would have been there, but the Americans and English and French generals and politicians would have been on trial. And history would have been written by Germans; naturally they would have a different vision.

Nobody knows what is true. One thing is certain: that man puts his whole energy into war effort. The reason? – the reason is that man has been taught to be just man, his woman has been denied. So no man is whole. And so is the case with woman – no woman is whole. She has been denied her male part. When she was a small child she could not fight with boys, she could not climb the trees; she had to play with dolls, she had to "play house." This is a very, very distorted vision.

Man is both, so is woman – and both are needed to create a real, harmonious human being. Existence is dialectical; and opposites are not only opposites, they are complementaries too.

Buddha says: "*Here O Sariputra...* In my world, Sariputra, in my space, in my time, Sariputra, at the seventh rung of the ladder, in this state of no-mind, in this state of *samadhi*, in this state of nirvana, enlightenment ...*form is emptiness...* Man is woman and woman is man, and life is death and death is life. Opposites are not opposites, Sariputra; they are interpenetrating each other, they exist through each other." To show this basic insight Buddha says: "Form is formlessness, and formlessness is form; the unmanifest becomes manifest, and the manifest again becomes unmanifest. They are not different, Sariputra, they are one." The duality is only apparent. Deep down it is all one.

...emptiness does not differ from form, form does not differ from emptiness; whatever is form, that is emptiness, whatever is emptiness, that is form; the same is true of feelings,

perceptions, impulses and consciousness. "The whole of life and the whole existence consists of polar opposites, but only on the surface are they different. These opposites are like my two hands: I can oppose them with each other, I can even manage a kind of conflict, a fight between them. But my left hand and my right hand are both my hands. Within me, they are one. That is exactly the case."

Why is Buddha saying this thing to Sariputra? – because if you understand this your worries will disappear. Then there is no worry. Life is death, death is life. To be is a way towards not to be, and not to be is a way towards to be. It is the same game. Then there is no fear, then there is no problem. With this insight a great acceptance arises.

Here, O Sariputra, all dharmas are marked with emptiness; they are not produced or stopped, not defiled or immaculate, not deficient or complete.

Buddha says: "All dharmas are full of emptiness." That nothingness exists at everything's core: that nothingness exists in a tree, that nothingness exists in a rock, that nothingness exists in a star.

Now scientists will agree: they say that when a star collapses it becomes a black hole, nothingness. But that nothingness is not just nothingness; it is immensely powerful, it is very full, overflowing.

The concept, the hypothesis of a black hole, is of immense value in understanding Buddha. A star exists for millions and trillions of years, but one day it has to die. Everything that is born has to die. Man exists for seventy years, then what happens? Exhausted, tired, he disappears, he falls back into the original unity. So it is going to happen to everything sooner or later. The Himalayas will disappear one day, so too will this earth disappear one day, so will this sun disappear one day.

But when a great star disappears, to where will it disappear? It collapses within itself. It is such a big mass; it collapses. Just as if a man walking – an old man – falls on the street and collapses, if you leave the man there, sooner or later his body will disappear, disintegrate into the mud, into the earth. If you leave it there for many years, then the bones will also disappear into dust. The man was there one day, walking, living, loving, fighting, and now all has disappeared into a black hole. So it happens with a star: when a star collapses into itself it becomes a black hole. Why is it called a black hole? – because now there is no mass, there is only pure emptiness, what Buddha calls *shunyata*. And the *shunyata*, the pure emptiness, is so powerful that if you come under the impact of it, near it, in its vicinity, you will be pulled, pulled into the emptiness, and you will also collapse and disappear.

For space travel this is going to be a future problem, because there are many stars which have become black holes. And you cannot see it because it is nothing, it is just absence. You cannot see it, and you can come across it. If a spaceship comes near it, under its gravitation it will simply be pulled in. Then there is no way to get out of it, it is impossible to find a way to get out of it. The pull is so big it will be simply pulled in, and it will disappear and collapse. And you will never hear about the spaceship, where it went, what happened to it, what happened to the space travelers.

This black hole is very, very like Buddha's concept of emptiness. All forms collapse and disappear into blackness, and then when they have rested for a long time, they bubble up – again a star is born. This goes on: life and death, life and death – this goes on. This is the way existence moves.

First it becomes manifest, then becomes tired, goes into unmanifestation, then again revives its energy through rest, relaxation, again becomes manifest. The whole day you work, you become tired; in the night you disappear in your sleep into a black hole. You put your lights out, you slip under your blanket, you close your eyes; then within moments consciousness is gone. You have collapsed withinwards. There are moments when even dreams are no longer there; then sleep is the deepest. In that deep sleep you are in a black hole, you are dead. For the time being you are in death, resting in death. And then in the morning you are back again, full of juice and gusto and life, again rejuvenated. If you have a really good, deep sleep without dreams, the morning is so fresh, so vital, so radiant, you are again young. If you know how to sleep deeply, you know how to revive yourself again and again. By the evening again you are collapsing, tired, exhausted by the day's activities.

The same happens to everything. Man is a miniature of the whole existence. What happens to man happens to the whole existence on a bigger scale, that's all. Every night you disappear into nothingness, every morning you come into form. Form, no-form, form, no-form; this is how life moves, these are the two steps.

Here, O Sariputra, all dharmas are marked with emptiness; they are not produced or stopped... And Buddha is saying nothing has to be done, only understanding is needed. This is a radical statement. It can transform your whole life if you can see it as an insight.

...they are not produced or stopped... Nobody is producing these forms, and nobody is stopping these forms. Buddha does not believe in a God as manipu-lator, as a controller, as a creator, no. That would be a duality, an unnecessary hypothesis. Buddha says it is happening on its own; it is natural, nobody is doing it. It is not that, as it says in the Bible, first God thinks "Let there be light," so there is light. And then one day he says "Now, let there be no light," and the light disappears. Why bring this God in? And why give him such ugly work? And he will have to do it forever and forever: "Let there be light, let there be no light, let there be light... Now let this man be there, now let him die" – just think of him and his boredom! Buddha relieves him, he says it is unnecessary.

It is just natural. Trees bring seeds, then seeds bring trees, and trees again bring seeds. What is a seed? The disappearance of the tree; the tree has moved into no-form. You can carry a seed in your pocket, you can carry a thousand seeds in your pocket, but you cannot carry a thousand trees in your pocket. The trees have form, bulk, mass; the seed has nothing. And if you look into the seed you will find nothing. If you had not seen, not known that a seed becomes a tree, and somebody gives you a seed and says, "Look, this seed is very, very magical – it can become a big tree, and there will be many fruits for many years, and great foliage and flowers and greenery, and birds will come and make nests there," you will say, "What are you talking about? Out of this small pebble? Do you think I am stupid or something? How can it happen? It can't happen."

But you know it happens, that's why you don't take any note of it. A miracle is happening. The small seed is carrying the whole blueprint of the tree, of the leaves – the shape and the size and the number – and the branches, and the form of the branches, and the length and the height of the tree, and the life, and how many fruits and how many flowers will come out of it, and how many seeds finally this one seed is going to produce. Scientists say that even a single seed is enough to make the whole earth green. It has immense potentiality. Not only the whole earth – one single seed can fill all the planets with greenery, because one seed can produce millions of seeds, then each seed will produce millions, and so on and so forth. The whole existence can become green out of a single seed. That nothingness is very potential, very powerful, immense, enormous, vast!

Buddha says nobody is producing it and nobody is stopping it. Buddha says there is no need to go to a temple and to pray and tell God, "Do this, don't do that" – there is nobody.

And what is his message? He says, "Accept it. It is so. It is in the nature of things. It is just natural, things come and go."

In this acceptance, in this *tathata,* in this suchness, all worries disappear; you are freed from worries. Then there is no problem. And nothing can be stopped, and nothing can be changed, and nothing can be produced. Things are as they are and things will be as they will be, so there is nothing for you to do. You can just watch these things happening. You can participate in these things. Be. In that being there is silence, in that being there is joy. That being is freedom.

These are:

...*not defiled or immaculate...* This existence is neither impure nor pure. There is nobody who is a sinner and nobody who is a saint.

Buddha's insight is utterly revolutionary: he says nothing can be impure and nothing can be pure; things are just as they are. It is all mind games that we play around, and we create the idea of purity – and then comes impurity. We create the idea of the saint – and then in comes the sinner. You want sinners to disappear? They can disappear only when your saints have disappeared, not before that. They exist together. You want immorality to disappear? – then morality has to go. It is morality that creates immorality. It is the moral ideals that create condemnation for a few people who cannot follow them, who cannot go with them. And you can make anything immoral – just create an idea: this is moral. You can make a holy cow out of anything, and then it becomes a problem.

Buddha says nothing is ever defiled and nothing is ever immaculate. Purity, impurity are mind attitudes. Can you tell about a tree whether it is moral or immoral? Can you say about an animal that he's a sinner or a saint? Try to see this ultimate vision: there is no sinner, no saint, nothing moral, nothing immoral. In this acceptance, where is the possibility of worrying? There is nothing to improve either! And there is no goal, because there is no value. This journey is a journey without any goal. It is a pure journey; it is a play, a *leela*. And there is nobody behind it, doing it. All is happening, and there is nobody doing it. If the doer is there then the problem arises – then pray to the doer, then persuade the doer, then become friends with the doer. Then you will be benefitted, and those who are not friends with the doer will be deprived – they will suffer in hell. That's what Christians, Hindus, Mohammedans think. Mohammedans think those who are Mohammedans are going to heaven and those who are not, poor fellows, they are going to hell. And the same is the case with Christians and Hindus: the Hindus think those who are not Hindus have no chance; the Christians think those who don't come through the church, those who don't pass through the church, are going to suffer eternal hell: not limited, unlimitedly, forever.

Buddha says there is no sinner, no saint; nothing is pure, nothing is impure, things are as they are. Just try to persuade a tree, ask the tree, "Why are you green? Why are you not red?"

And if the tree listens to you, she will become neurotic – "Why am I not red? Why? Really, the question is relevant. Why am I green?" Condemn the green and praise the red, and sooner or later you will find the tree on some psychiatrist's couch being analyzed, helped. First you create the problem, and then comes the savior. It is a beautiful business.

Buddha cuts the very root. He says you are the way you are. There is nothing to improve, nowhere to go. And this is my whole approach too: you are as perfect as you can be, more is not possible. The "more" will only create trouble for you. The idea of "more" will drive you mad. Accept nature, live naturally, simply, spontaneously, moment-to-moment, and there is holiness – because you are whole, not because you have become a saint.

...*not defiled or immaculate, not deficient or complete.* Nothing is complete and nothing is incomplete; these values are meaningless. Says Buddha: "Here, O Sariputra, where I exist, nothing is good, nothing is bad. Here, where I exist, *samsara* and nirvana are the same. There is no distinction between this world and that world. There is no distinction between the profane and the sacred. Here, where I exist, all distinctions have disappeared, because distinctions are made by thought. When thought disappears, distinctions disappear."

Sinners are created by thought, and saints are created by thought. Good and bad are created by thought. It is thought that makes distinctions. Buddha says: "When knowledge disappears, thought disappears. There is no duality. It is all oneness."

There is a famous saying of Sosan:

> *In the higher realms of true suchness*
> *there is neither self nor other than self.*
> *When direct identification is sought,*
> *we can only say "not two."*
> *One in all, all in one:*
> *if this is realized,*
> *no more worry about your not being perfect.*

One in all, all in one; if this is realized, no more worry about your not being perfect. There is no perfection, no imperfection. See it, and see it right now! Don't come later on and ask me how to do it. There is no "how" either. "How" brings knowledge, and knowledge is the curse.

Without the distorting media of thought you fall into unity with the whole. Without thought functioning between you and the real, all distances disappear, you are bridged. And that's what man is constantly hankering for. You are feeling uprooted, uprooted from the whole. That is your misery. And you are uprooted because of this distorting media of thought. Drop this distorting media of thought, drop these mediums, look into reality as it is, with no idea in your mind, with no idea of how it should be. Look with innocence. Look with not-knowing and all worries disappear. In that disappearing of the worries you become a buddha.

You are a buddha! But you are missing because you are carrying distorting mediums around you. You have perfect eyes and you are wearing glasses. Those glasses are distorting, they are coloring, they are making things as they are not. Throw away the glasses! That's what it means when we say "Throw away the mind." Negate the mind and there is silence – and in that silence you are divine. You have never been anything else, you have always been that. But the recognition comes back, the realization comes back. You suddenly see the point: you were trying to put legs on a snake. There was no need in the first place – the snake is perfectly perfect! Without legs, he moves perfectly. Just out of compassion you were trying to put legs on it. If you succeed you will kill the snake. It is fortunate that you can never succeed.

You are trying to become knowledgeable and that's why you are losing your perception, your knowing, your capacity to see. That's what I mean by "putting legs on a snake." Knowing is your nature. There is no need to have knowledge to know. In fact, knowledge is the hindrance, knowledge is the curse.

Negate knowledge and be – and you are a buddha, and you have always been a buddha.

Enough for today.

CHAPTER 4

understanding: the only law

The first question:

Osho,
I come from a family where there are four suicides on the
maternal side, including my grandmother. How does this
affect one's death? What helps to overcome this perversion of
death which runs as a theme through the family?

The phenomenon of death is one of the most mysterious and so is the phenomenon of suicide. Don't decide from the surface what suicide is. It can be many things. My own understanding is that people who commit suicide are the most sensitive people in the world, very intelligent. Because of their sensitivity, because of their intelligence, they find it difficult to cope with this neurotic world.

The society is neurotic. It exists on neurotic foundations. Its whole history is a history of madness, of violence, war, destruction. Somebody says, "My country is the greatest country in the world" – now this is neurosis. Somebody says,

"My religion is the greatest and the highest religion in the world" – now this is neurosis. And this neurosis has gone to the very blood and to the bones, and people have become very, very dull, insensitive. They *had* to become, otherwise life would be impossible.

You have to become insensitive to cope with this dull life around you; otherwise you start falling out of tune. If you start falling out of tune with the society, the society declares you mad. The society is mad, but if you are not in adjustment with it, it declares you mad. So you either have to go mad, or you have to find a way out of the society; that's what suicide is. Life becomes intolerable. It seems impossible to cope with so many people around you – and they are *all* insane. What will you do if you are thrown into an insane asylum?

It happened to one of my friends:

He was in a mental asylum, put there by the court for nine months. After six months – he was mad, so he could do it – he found a big bottle of phenol in the bathroom and he drank it. For fifteen days he suffered diarrhea and vomiting, and because of that diarrhea and vomiting he came back into the world. His system was purified, the poison disappeared. He was telling me that those next three months were the most difficult – "The first six months were beautiful because I was mad, and everybody was also mad. Things were going simply beautifully, there was no problem. I was in tune with the whole madness around me."

When he drank phenol, and those fifteen days of diarrhea and vomiting, somehow by an accident his system got purified, his stomach got purified. He could not eat for those fifteen days – the vomiting was too much – so he had to fast. He rested in bed for fifteen days. That rest, that fasting, that purifying helped – it was an accident – and he became sane. He went to the doctors, told them "I have become sane"; they all laughed.

They said, "Everybody says so." The more he insisted, the more they insisted: "You are mad, because every madman says so. Simply go and do your work. You cannot be released before the court's order."

"Those three months were impossible," he said, "night-marish!" Many times he thought about suicide. But he is a man of strong will. And it was only a question of three months, he could wait. It was intolerable! – somebody was pulling his hair, somebody was pulling his leg, somebody would simply jump upon him. All that had been going on for six months, but he had also been part in it. He was also doing the same things; he was a perfect member of that mad society. But for three months it was impossible because he was sane and everybody was insane.

In this neurotic world, if you are sane, sensitive, intelligent, either you have to go mad, or you have to commit suicide – or you have to become a sannyasin. What else is there?

The question is from Jane Ferber; she is Bodhicitta's wife. She has come to me in the right time. She can become a sann-yasin and avoid suicide.

In the East suicide does not exist so much, because san-nyas is an alternative. You can respectfully drop out; the East accepts it. You can start doing your own thing; the East has respect for it. Hence, the difference between India and America is of times five: for one Indian committing suicide, five Americans commit suicide. And the phenomenon of sui-cide is a growing phenomenon in America. Intelligence is growing, sensitivity is growing, and the society is dull. The society does not provide an intelligent world – then what to do? Just go on suffering unnecessarily?

Then one starts thinking, "Why not drop it all? Why not finish it? Why not give the ticket back to God?" In America, if sannyas becomes a great movement, the rate of suicide will start falling, because people will have a far better and more creative alternative of dropping out. Have you seen that hippies don't commit suicide? It is the square world, the conventional world where suicide is more prevalent. The hippie has dropped out. He is a kind of sannyasin – not yet fully alert to what he is doing but on the right way; moving, groping, but in the right direction. The hippie is the beginning of sannyas. The hippie is saying, "I don't want to be a part of this rotten game, I don't

want to be a part of this political game. I see things, and I
would like to live my own life. I don't want to become anybody's slave. I don't want to be killed on any war front. I don't
want to fight – there are far more beautiful things to do."

But for millions there is nothing; the society has taken
away all possibilities for their growth. They are stuck. People
commit suicide because they are feeling stuck and they don't
see any way out. They come to a cul-de-sac, and the more
intelligent you are, the sooner you will come to that cul-de-sac,
that impasse. Then what are you supposed to do? The society
does not give you any alternative; the society does not allow
an alternative society.

Sannyas is an alternative society. It looks strange that in
India the suicide rate is the lowest in the world. Logically it
should be the highest, because people are suffering, people
are miserable, starving. But this strange phenomenon happens everywhere: poor people don't commit suicide. They
have nothing to live for, they have nothing to die for. Because
they are starved they are occupied with their food, shelter,
money, things like that. They cannot afford to think about suicide, they are not yet that affluent. America has everything,
India has nothing.

Just the other day I was reading where somebody has
written: "Americans have a smiling Jimmy Carter, Johnny Cash
and Bob Hope. And Indians have a dry, dull, dead Morarji
Desai, no cash, and very little hope."

But still people don't commit suicide: they go on living,
they enjoy life. Even beggars are thrilled, excited. There is
nothing to be excited about, but they are hoping.

Why is it happening so much in America? – the ordinary problems of life have disappeared, the mind is free to
rise higher than the ordinary consciousness. The mind can rise
beyond body, beyond mind itself. The consciousness is ready
to take wings and the society does not allow it. Out of ten
suicides, about nine are sensitive people. Seeing the meaning-
lessness of life, seeing the indignity that life imposes, seeing
the compromises that one has to make for nothing, seeing all
the taciturnity, looking around and seeing this – "a tale told by

an idiot, signifying nothing" – they decide to get rid of the body. If they could have wings in the body, they would not decide so. Suicide has another significance too; it has to be understood. In life everything seems to be common, imitative. You can't have a car that others don't have. Millions of people have the same car as you have. Millions of people are living the same life as you are living, watching the same film, the same movie, the same TV as you are, reading the same newspaper as you do. Life is too common, nothing unique is left for you to do, to be. Suicide seems to be a unique phenomenon: only you can die for yourself, nobody else can die for you. Your death will be *your* death, nobody else's. Death is unique!

Look at the phenomenon: death is unique – it defines you as an individual, it gives you individuality. The society has taken your individuality; you are just a cog in the wheel, replaceable. If you die nobody will miss you, you will be replaced. If you are a professor in the university, another will be the professor in the university. Even if you are the president of a country, another will be the president of the country – immediately, the moment you are no longer. You are replaceable.

This hurts – that your worth is not much, that you will not be missed, that one day you will disappear and soon those people who will remember you will also disappear. Then, it will be almost as if you had never been. Just think of that day. You will disappear. Yes, for a few days people will remember: your lover will remember you, your children will remember you, maybe a few friends. By and by, their memory will become pale, faint, will start disappearing. But maybe while those people with whom you had a certain kind of intimacy are alive, you may be remembered once in a while. But once they are also gone, then you simply disappear, as if you had never been here. Then there is no difference whether you have been here or have not been here.

Life does not give you unique respect. It is very humiliating. It drives you into such a hole where you are just a cog in the wheel, a part in the vast mechanism. It makes you anonymous.

Death, at least, is unique. And suicide is more unique than

death. Why? – because death comes, and suicide is something that you do. Death is beyond you: when it will come, it will come. But death you can manage, you are not a victim. Suicide you can manage. With death you will be a victim, with suicide you will be in control. Birth has already happened – now you cannot do anything about it, and you had not done anything before you were born – it was an accident.

There are three things in life which are vital: birth, love, and death. Birth has happened; there is nothing to do about it. You were not even asked whether you wanted to be born or not. You were a victim. Love also happens; you cannot do anything about it, you are helpless. One day you fall in love with somebody, you cannot do anything about it. If you want to fall in love with somebody you cannot manage, it is impossible. And when you fall in love with somebody, if you don't want – if you want to pull yourself away – that too seems to be difficult. Birth is a happening, so is love. Now only death is left about which something can be done: you can be a victim or you can decide on your own.

A suicide is one who decides, who says, "Let me at least do one thing in this existence where I was almost accidental: I will commit suicide. At least there is one thing I can do!" Birth is impossible to do; love cannot be created if it is not there; but death... Death has an alternative. Either you can be a victim or you can be decisive.

This society has taken all dignity from you. That's why people commit suicide – because committing suicide will give them a sort of dignity. They can say to existence, "I have renounced your world and your life. It was not worth anything!" The people who commit suicide are almost always more sensitive than the others who go on dragging, living. And I'm not saying to commit suicide, I am saying there is a higher possibility. Each moment of life can be so beautiful, individual, non-imitative, non-repetitive. Each moment can be so precious! Then there is no need to commit suicide. Each moment can bring such blessing, and each moment can define you as unique – because you *are* unique! Never before has there been a person like you, and never again will there be.

But the society forces you to become part of a big army. The society never likes a person who goes his own way. The society wants you to be part of the crowd: be a Hindu, be a Christian, be a Jew, be an American, be an Indian – but be part of a crowd; any crowd, but be part of a crowd. Never be yourself. And those people who want to be themselves are the salt of the earth. They are the most valuable people on the earth. The earth has a little dignity and fragrance because of these people. Then they commit suicide.

Sannyas and suicide are alternatives. This is my experience: you can become a sannyasin only when you have come to the point where, if not sannyas, then suicide. Sannyas means, "I will try to become an individual while alive! I will live my life in my own way. I will not be dictated to, dominated. I will not function like a mechanism, like a robot. I will not have any ideals, and I will not have any goals. I will live in the moment, and I will live on the spur of the moment. I will be spontaneous, and I will risk all for it!"

Sannyas is a risk.

Jane, I would like to say to you: I have looked into your eyes; the possibility of suicide is there too. But I don't think you will have to commit suicide – sannyas will do! You are more fortunate than the four people in your family who committed suicide. In fact, every intelligent person has the capacity to commit suicide, only idiots never commit. Have you ever heard of any idiot committing suicide? He does not care about life; why should he commit suicide? Only a rare intelligence starts feeling the need to do something, because life as it is lived is not worth living. So, either do something and change your life – give it a new shape, a new direction, a new dimension – or why go on carrying this nightmarish burden, day-in day-out, year-in year-out? And it will continue... Medical science is helping you to continue it even longer – a hundred years, a hundred and twenty years. And now those people are saying that a man can easily live to nearabout three hundred years. Just think, if people have to live for three hundred years the suicide rate would go very high – because then even mediocre minds would start thinking that it is pointless.

Intelligence means seeing deeply into things. Has your life any point? Has your life any joy? Has your life any poetry in it? Has your life any creativity in it? Do you feel grateful that you are here? Do you feel grateful that you were born? Can you thank existence? Can you say with your whole heart that it is a blessing? If you cannot, then why do you go on living? Either make your life a blessing – or why go on burdening this earth? Disappear. Somebody else may occupy your space and may do better. This idea comes to the intelligent mind naturally. It is a very, very natural idea when you are intelligent. Intelligent people commit suicide. And those who are even more intelligent than the intelligent people take sannyas. They start creating a meaning, they start creating a significance, they start living. Why miss this opportunity?

Heidegger has said: "Death isolates me and makes of me an individual." It is my death, not that of the multitude to which I belong. Each of us dies his own death; death cannot be repeated. I can take an examination twice, or thrice; compare my second marriage with my first, and so on and so forth. I die only once. I can get married as many times as I like, I can change my jobs as many times as I like, I can change my town as many times as I like, but I die only once. Death is so challenging because it is at once certain and uncertain. That it will come is certain, when it will do so is uncertain.

Hence there is great curiosity about death, about what it is. One wants to know about it. And there is nothing morbid about this contemplation of death. Accusations of that kind are merely the device of the impersonal "they" – the crowd – to prevent one escaping its tyranny and becoming an individual. What is necessary is to see our life as being towards death. Once this point has been reached, there is a possibility of deliverance from the banality of everyday life and its servitude to anonymous powers. He who has so confronted his death is stabbed awake thereby. He perceives himself now as an individual distinct from the mass, and is prepared to take over responsibility for his own life. In this way, we decide for authentic against inauthentic existence. We emerge from the mass and become ourselves at last.

Even to contemplate death gives you an individuality, a form, a shape, a definition – because it is *your* death. It is the only thing left in the world that is unique. And when you think about suicide it becomes even more personal; it is your decision.

Remember, I am not saying that you should go and commit suicide. I am saying that your life, as it is, is leading you towards suicide. Change it.

And contemplate death. It can come any moment, so don't think that it is morbid to think about death. It is not, because death is the culmination of life, the very.crescendo of life. You have to take note of it. It is coming – whether you commit suicide or it comes... But it is coming. It has to happen. You have to prepare for it, and the only way to prepare for death – the right way – is not to commit suicide; the right way is to die each moment to the past. That's the right way. That's what a sannyasin is supposed to do: die each moment to the past, never carry the past for a single moment. Each moment, die to the past and be born in the present. That will keep you fresh, young, vibrant, radiant; that will keep you alive, throbbing, excited, ecstatic.

A man who knows how to die each moment to the past knows how to die, and that is the greatest skill and art. So when death comes to such a man, he dances with it, he embraces it! – it is a friend, it is not the enemy. It is existence coming to you in the form of death. It is total relaxation into existence. It is again becoming the whole, again becoming one with the whole.

So don't call this perversion. You say: "I come from a family where there are four suicides on the maternal side, including my grandmother." Don't condemn those poor people, and don't think for a single moment that they were perverts.

"How does this affect one's death? What helps to overcome this perversion of death which runs as a theme through the family?" Don't call it a perversion; it is not. Those people were simply victims. They could not cope with the neurotic society, and they decided to disappear into the unknown. Have compassion for them, don't condemn. Don't abuse them, don't use names – don't call it a perversion or anything like that. Have compassion for them and love for them.

There is no need to follow them, but feel for them. They must have suffered a lot. One does not decide very easily to drop life: they must have suffered intensely, they must have seen the hell of life. One never decides easily for death, because to survive is a natural instinct. One goes on surviving in all kinds of situations and conditions. One goes on compromising – just to survive. When somebody drops his life it simply shows it is beyond his capacity to compromise; the demand is too much. The demand is *so* much that it is not worth it; only then does one decide to commit suicide. Have compassion for those people.

If you feel that something is wrong then something is wrong in the society, not in those people. The society is perverted! In a primitive society nobody commits suicide. I have been to primitive tribes in India: for centuries they have not known of anybody committing suicide. They don't have any record of anybody ever having committed suicide. Why? The society is natural, the society is not perverted. It does not drive people to unnatural things. The society is accepting. It allows everybody his way, his choice to live his life. That is everybody's right. Even if somebody goes mad, the society accepts it; it is his right to go mad. There is no condemnation. In fact, in a primitive society, mad people are respected like mystics – and they have a kind of mystery around them. If you look into a madman's eyes and into the eyes of a mystic, there is some similarity – something vast, something undefined, something nebulous, something like a chaos out of which stars are born. The mystic and the madman have some similarity.

All madmen may not be mystics, but all mystics are mad. By "mad" I mean they have gone beyond mind. The madman may have fallen below mind, and the mystic may have gone beyond mind, but one thing is similar – both are not in their minds. In a primitive society even the madman is respected, tremendously respected. If he decides to be mad, that's okay. Society takes care of his food, of his shelter. Society loves him, loves his madness. Society has no fixed rule; then nobody commits suicide because freedom remains intact.

When society demands slavery and goes on destroying your freedom and crippling you from every side and paralyzing your soul and deadening your heart, one comes to feel it is better to die than to compromise.

Don't call them perverts. Have compassion for them; they suffered a lot, they were victims. And try to understand what happened to them; that will give you an insight into your own life. There is no need to repeat it, because I give you an opportunity to be yourself. I open a door for you. If you are understanding you will see the point of it, but if you are not understanding then it is difficult. I can go on shouting and you will hear only that which you can hear, and you will hear only that which you want to hear – that which you want to hear.

A psychologist friend has come: he has written a long question. He says: "Why do you go on saying drop the ego? Nobody has ever been able to drop the ego." Now how does he know that nobody has ever been able to drop the ego? He says it has not succeeded. How do you know? It *has* succeeded, although it has succeeded only with very rare and few people. But it has succeeded, and it has succeeded only with rare people because only those rare people allowed it to succeed. It can succeed with everybody, but people don't allow it to succeed. They are not ready to lose their egos.

He is a psychologist, and he says, "Osho, I see in you too a great ego." As a psychologist he says, "I see a great ego in you." Then you have not seen me at all. Then you have seen something which is your projection. The ego goes on projecting itself. The ego goes on creating its own reality around itself, its own reflections.

Now, if you can see so deeply into me why have you come here? You can see deeply into yourself; if you have such great insight, what is the point in coming here? – it is pointless. And if you have decided already that the ego cannot be dropped, that it is not possible, then you have taken a decision without even trying.

I am not saying the ego can be dropped. I am saying the ego exists not. How can you drop something which doesn't exist? And Buddha has not said that the ego has to be dropped, he is saying the ego has to be only looked into – and you don't find it, hence it disappears.

What can you do then – when you go inside your being and you don't find any ego, you find silence there: no self dominating, no center like an ego there? Dropping the ego does not mean that you have to *drop* it. Dropping the ego is only a metaphor. It simply means that when you go in, you look in and you don't find anything, the ego disappears. In fact, even to say "disappears" is not right, because it was not there in the first place. It is a misunderstanding.

Now, rather than going into yourself you are looking at me. And you think you have looked into me! And because you are a psychoanalyst or a psychologist, then you decide. Your decision will become a barrier, because the ego does not exist in me. And I would like to declare: the ego does not exist in you! Even to this psychologist friend I will say: the ego does not exist in him. The ego exists not. It is a nonexistential idea, just an idea.

It is like when you see a rope in the dark and you think it is a snake, and you start running, and you are out of breath, and you stumble upon a rock and you get a fracture, and by the morning you come to know that it was only a rope. But it worked tremendously! The snake was not there, but it affected your reality. A misunderstanding is as real as understanding. It is not true, but it is real. That is the difference between reality and truth. A snake seen in a rope is real, because its results, its consequences are going to be real. If you have a weak heart it can be very dangerous seeing a snake in a rope: you can run so fast that you can have heart failure. It can affect your whole life. And it looks so ridiculous; it was just a rope.

What I am saying, or what Buddha is saying is: just take a lamp and go inside. Have a good look at whether the snake exists or not. Buddha has found it does not exist in him. I have found it does not exist in me. And the day I found it does not exist in me, I looked around into everybody's eyes and I have never found it. It is an unfounded idea. It is a dream.

But if you are too full of the dream, you can even project

it on me and I cannot do anything about it. If you project, you project. It is as if you are wearing glasses, colored glasses, green glasses, and the whole world looks green. And you come to me and you say, "Osho, you are wearing a green robe." What can I do? I can only say, "Just take off your glasses." And you say, "Nobody has ever been able to take off his glasses. It has never happened!" Then it is difficult.

But it is not a problem for me; it is going to be a problem for you. I feel sorry for you, because if this is your idea then you will suffer your whole life – because ego creates suffering. An unreal idea, thought to be real, creates suffering. What is suffering really? Suffering is when you have some ideas which don't correlate with the truth. Then there is suffering.

For example, you think stones are food and you eat them; then you suffer, then you have a great stomachache. But if it is real food then you don't suffer, then you are satisfied. Suffering is created by ideas which don't go with reality; bliss is created when you have ideas which go with reality. Bliss is a coherence between you and the truth; suffering is a dichotomy, a division between you and the truth. When you are not moving with truth you are in hell; when you are moving with truth you are in heaven – that's all. And that is the whole thing to be understood.

Now this man comes from faraway America. Listening to my tapes, he started feeling for me. He has come here, but if this is his way of looking at things he will miss. And remember, it is not a problem for me. If you think I am a great egoist, thank you – it is not a problem for me. This is your idea, and you are perfectly entitled to have ideas. But if you are so certain about it, what is going to happen?

He says, "I have been to many holy saints of many religions, and they were all egoists." You must be wearing the same glasses everywhere. You go on creating your own reality, which is not true. That's why Buddha insists so much on nothingness, on no-mind – because when the mind has no thoughts you cannot project anything. Then you have to see that which is. When you don't have any ideas, when you are simply empty, a mirror mirroring, then whatsoever comes in front of you is mirrored. And it is mirrored as it is. But if you have ideas, then you distort. Thoughts are the media for distortion.

If you can see ego in me, you are really doing a miracle. But it is possible... And you can enjoy. But it is only you who will be harmed by your idea, nobody else. If this idea persists, then there will be no possibility of being bridged with me. At least for these few days that you are here, put your ideas aside. And one thing is certain: your psychology has not helped you, otherwise you would not need to be here at all.

Just the other day he was sitting in front of me and talking about his problems. And sometimes I wonder... He has so many problems, and he is a group leader. What will he be doing with people? What kind of help can come from him? And he has such a fat body and he cannot even change that; and he goes on stuffing himself. And these were his problems. And he was so afraid that he was insisting again and again to Laxmi that he needed a private interview, because, "I cannot say things before people." Why? People will be seeing that you are fat. It doesn't matter whether you say it or not. Everybody has eyes and they can see that you are fat, and that you go on stuffing. How will you avoid the cafeteria people? They will know.

He wanted to have a private interview so that he could tell his problems, and the problem was fatness – "I go on eating and I cannot stop; what should I do?" Your psychology has not even been of that much help, and you think your psychology is capable of knowing me, of seeing me? Don't be deceived by your own games.

And you have not been to any holy men. I am not saying that they were not holy; I am simply saying that you may have been there, but you have not been with them. If you cannot be with me, how can you be with them? You have not been with any holy man. Wherever you went, you went with your psychology, with all the knowledge that you have gathered around yourself. And it is of no use to you. It is worthless! You go on advising people. You will create the same kinds of traumas, complexes, in other people too. A therapist can be of help only when his advice is not only for others, but when his advice is his life, when he has lived it and has seen its truth.

You say that the teaching of the ages to drop the ego, drop the mind, has not worked. It has worked. It has worked for me; that's why I say it has worked. I know it has not worked for you. But there is nothing wrong in the teaching, something is wrong in you; that's why it is not working in you. It has worked in millions of people. And sometimes it happens that your neighbor may be an enlightened being and you may not be able to see.

It happened...

A seeker came from America. He had heard there was a great Sufi mystic in Dhaka, in Bangladesh, so he came rushing – as Americans come. He came rushing: he simply jumped on Dhaka! He caught hold of a taxi driver and said, "Take me to this mystic!"

The taxi driver laughed. He said, "You are really interested? Then you have found the right man. If you had asked any other taxi driver, nobody would have known. I know this man. I have lived with this man for almost fifty years."

"Fifty years? How old is he?" the American asked.

The taxi driver said, "He is also fifty years old."

He thought, "This man seems to be crazy!" He tried other taxi drivers, but nobody knew the man so he had to come back to this crazy man.

He said, "I had told you that nobody knows him. Come with me and I will take you." And he took him – and Dhaka is an old city and small streets and tiny – and he went zigzag here and there, for hours. And the American was feeling very happy, because the goal was coming closer and closer and closer. After three, four hours, they stopped before a small house, a very poor man's house. And the taxi driver said, "Wait, and I will arrange for the master."

Then a woman came and she said, "The master is waiting for you." And the man went in, and the taxi driver was sitting there.

And he said, "Come on, my son, what do you have to ask?"

The American could not believe it. He said, "You are the master?"

He said, "I am the master, and I have lived with this man for fifty years; nobody else knows about it." And it turned out that he was the master.

But you have your ideas: "How can a taxi driver be a master?" Just think of me as a taxi driver. You will not believe – will you? Will this psychologist friend believe? It will be impossible.

You have ideas. Because of your ideas you go on missing many things that are around. The earth is never empty of masters. There are people everywhere, but you can't see! And when you want to see them you go to the Vatican because you have some idea that the pope must be enlightened. In fact, how can an enlightened person be a pope? No enlightened person will agree to that nonsense. He may prefer to be a taxi driver.

Please drop your ideas while you are here, for these few days. Open yourself, don't be prejudiced from the very beginning: "This has never happened." This *has* happened! It has happened in me. Just look into my eyes, just feel me, and this can happen in you. There is nothing that is hindering it except these ideas, this knowledge. That's why I say knowledge is a curse. Get rid of your knowledge and you will get rid of your pathology.

The second question:

Osho,
I am a weakling. Yet I have the feeling that I can, for the first
time, relax into my weakness here. Must I be strong and
courageous?

There is no must here. All shoulds, musts, oughts, have to be dropped. Only then do you become a natural being.

And what is wrong in being weak? Everybody is weak. How can the part be strong? – the part has to be weak. And we are tiny parts, drops in this vast ocean. How can we be strong? – strong against whom, strong for what? Yes, you have been taught, I know, to be strong, because you have been taught to be violent, aggressive, warring. You have been taught to be strong because you have been taught to be competitive, ambitious, egoistic. You have been taught all kinds of aggressiveness because you have been brought up to rape others, to rape nature. You have not been brought up to love.

Here, the message is love – so what do you need strength for? The message here is surrender. The message here is acceptance, total acceptance of whatsoever is the case.

Weakness is beautiful. Relax into it, accept it, enjoy it. It has its own beauties, its own joys.

"I am a weakling..." Please, don't even use that word *weakling*, because it has a condemnatory note in it. Say "I am a part," and the part is bound to be helpless. In itself the part is bound to be impotent. The part is potent only with the whole. Your strength is in being with truth; there is no other strength. Truth is strong, we are weak. Existence is strong, we are weak. With it we are also strong; against it, without it, we are weak. Fight the river, try to go upstream and you will be proved a weakling. Float with the river and go downstream – don't even swim, be in a let-go and let the river take you wherever it is going – and then there is no weakness. When the idea of being strong is dropped there is no weakness left. They both disappear together. And then, suddenly, you are neither weak nor strong. In fact, you are not; existence is – neither weak nor strong.

You say: "Yet I have the feeling that I can for the first time relax into my weakness here." A good feeling; don't lose track of it! A right feeling: relax – that's my whole teaching. Relax into your being, whoever you are. Don't impose any ideals. Don't drive yourself crazy; there is no need. Be – drop becoming. We are not going anywhere, we are just being here. And this moment is so beautiful, is such a benediction; don't bring any future into it, otherwise you will destroy it. Future is poisonous. Relax and enjoy. If I can help you to relax and enjoy, my work is done. If I can help you to drop your ideals, ideas about how you should be and how you should not be, if I can take away all the commandments that have been given to you, then my work is done. And when you are without any commandments, and when you live on the spur of the moment – natural, spontaneous, simple, ordinary – there is great celebration, you have arrived home.

Now don't bring it again: "Must I be strong and courageous?" For what? In fact it is weakness that wants to be strong. Try to understand it; it is a little bit complex but let us go into it. It is weakness that wants to be strong, it is inferiority that wants to be superior, it is ignorance that wants to be knowledgeable – so that it can hide in knowledge, so that you can hide your weakness in your so-called power. Out of inferiority comes the desire to be superior. That is the whole substratum of politics in the world, power-politics. It is only inferior people who become politicians: they have a power urge, because they know they are inferior. If they don't become the president of a country or the prime minister of a country, they cannot prove themselves to others. In themselves they feel weak; they drive themselves to power.

But how, by becoming a president, can you be powerful? Deep down you will know that your weakness is there. In fact it will be felt more, even more than before, because now there will be a contrast. On the outside there will be power, and in the inside there will be weakness – more clear, like a silver lining in a black cloud. That's what happens: inside you feel poor and you start grabbing, you become greedy, you start possessing things, and you go on and on and on, and there is no end to it. And your whole life is wasted in things, in accumulation.

But the more you accumulate, the more penetratingly you feel the inner poverty. Against the riches it can be seen very easily. When you see this – that weakness tries to become strong – it is absurd. How can weakness become strong? Seeing it, you don't want to become strong. And when you don't want to become strong, weakness cannot stay in you. It can stay only with the idea of strength – they are together, like negative-positive poles of electricity. They exist together. If you drop this ambition to be strong, one day suddenly you will find weakness has also disappeared. It cannot keep a hold in you. If you drop the idea of being rich, how can you go on thinking yourself poor? How will you compare, and how will you judge that you are poor? Against what? There will be no possibility to measure your poverty. Dropping the idea of richness, of being rich, one day poverty disappears.

When you don't hanker for knowledge and you drop knowledgeability, how can you remain ignorant? When knowledge disappears, in the wake of it, like its shadow, ignorance disappears. Then a man is wise. Wisdom is not knowledge; wisdom is the absence of both knowledge and ignorance.

These are three possibilities: you can be ignorant, you can be ignorant and knowledgeable, and you can be without ignorance and knowledge. The third possibility is what wisdom is. That's what Buddha calls *prajnaparamita* – the wisdom beyond, the transcendental wisdom. It is not knowledge.

First, drop this desire for strength, and watch. One day you will be surprised, you will start dancing: the weakness has disappeared. They are two aspects of the same coin: they live together, they go together. Once you have penetrated to this fact in your being, there is a great transformation.

The third question:

Osho,
Why and how are people coming to you from the four
corners of the earth?

If one tells the truth, he's sure to be found out sooner or later – that's why.

If you have uttered the truth, it is impossible for people not to come. They are hankering for it, they are thirsty for it, they are hungry for it; and they have remained hungry for many lives. Once a ripple of truth arises anywhere, a song, something starts happening in the unconscious of those who are hungry. They may be anywhere on the planet. We are connected in the unconscious; in the deepest realm of our being we are one. If one man becomes a buddha, then everybody's unconscious is thrilled. You may not know consciously, but everybody's unconscious is thrilled. It is like a spider's web: you touch it from anywhere and the whole web starts trembling. We are one in our base. We are like a solid strong tree, standing solitary in the field – big, huge, with great foliage. Leaves are millions, branches are many, but it all depends on a solid trunk, and they all are rooted in one soil. If one leaf turns enlightened, the whole tree will know it unconsciously: "Something has happened."

Those who are consciously searching for truth will be the first to start moving. The unconscious will have the ripples.

A friend has just written: he was sitting somewhere in California... And it can happen more easily in California than anywhere else. California is the future; the most potential consciousness is happening there. California is the most vulnerable, so it can happen only in California. It cannot happen in Russia – things are very dull and dead.

A friend went to visit a woman. They were eating and drinking, and suddenly he looked into the eyes of the woman and there was immense power. Maybe the alcohol, the drinking, the music, the aloneness of these two persons, the loving atmosphere, triggered something. He saw immense power in the eyes of the woman, and he got caught in those eyes, almost magnetized, hypnotized. And he started looking, and when he started looking the woman started swaying, something started moving, something in the unconscious. And after a few minutes the woman started saying, "Rauneesh, Rauneesh, Rauneesh" – and she had not known me at all, had not ever heard about me. When she came back, the man said, "You were repeating a certain name – Rauneesh – it seems to be very strange. I have never heard it."

And the woman said, "I have never heard it. I don't know." They both went to a bookstall to search for the name. Of course, it was not Rauneesh, it was Rajneesh. And he looked into my books, and that's what he had been searching for, for many, many years. Next month he will be coming here. Now how does it happen? Something in the depth of the woman...

It is easier for a woman to receive messages, because she is closer to the unconscious than man. Man has gone far away from the unconscious. He has become too much hung up in the head, in the conscious. The woman still lives by hunches. Something started stirring in her unconscious with the man looking into her eyes. And the man is a conscious searcher; the woman is not. The woman had never been looking for a master. She is not coming. She must have explained it away as just a coincidence or something. She has never been interested in any search, but her unconscious was more receptive. Being a woman, and then alcohol, and this man looking immensely magnetized by her eyes – all these things worked, something surfaced. And this man's conscious was looking. Hearing this word he was hooked. He got hooked with the word; he could not forget it. He had to go to the bookstalls to find out, to the library, here and there, ask friends what this word was.

It is not a miracle. It is a simple process of how things happen.

You ask me: "How and why are people coming to you from the four corners of the earth?" Distance is not the question; search, hunger, thirst is the question. If somebody is in search, sooner or later he will come to know about me – sometimes accidentally – and he will start having a pull towards me. Millions are searching, and the more people there are around me, and the more people start getting deeper into their beings, the more will become the pull of this place. Then it will not be only I pulling them, not only I stirring their depths – the whole place here will start pulling. It can become a magnetic center.

It depends on you, on how far you start moving into your being, how far you fall in tune with me, how deep your surrender is.

The last question:

Osho,
What to do with fear? I am feeling very tired being led
around by it. Can it be mastered or killed? How?

It cannot be killed, it cannot be mastered, it can only be understood. *Understanding* is the key word here. And only understanding brings mutation, nothing else. If you try to master your fear it will remain repressed, it will go deep into you. It will not help, it will complicate things. It is surfacing, you can repress it – that's what mastery is. You can repress it; you can repress it so deeply that it disappears from your consciousness completely. Then you will never be aware of it, but it will be there in the basement, and it will have a pull. It will manage, it will manipulate you, but it will manipulate you in such an indirect way that you will not become aware of it. But then the danger has gone deeper. Now you cannot even understand it.

So fear has not to be mastered, it has not to be killed. It cannot be killed either, because fear contains a kind of energy and no energy can be destroyed. Have you seen that in fear you can have immense energy? – just as you can have in anger; they are both two aspects of the same energy phenomenon. Anger is aggressive and fear is nonaggressive, passive. Fear is anger in a negative state; anger is fear in a positive state. When you are angry have you not seen how powerful you become, how great an energy you have? You can throw a big rock when you are angry; ordinarily you cannot even shake it. You become thrice, four times bigger when you are angry. You can do certain things you cannot do without anger.

Or, in fear, you can run so fast that even an Olympic runner will feel jealous. Fear creates energy; fear *is* energy, and energy cannot be destroyed. Not a single iota of energy can be destroyed from existence. This has to be remembered constantly, otherwise you will do something wrong. You cannot destroy anything, you can only change its form. You cannot destroy a small pebble; a small atom of sand cannot be destroyed, it will only change its form. You cannot destroy a drop of water. You can turn it into ice, you can evaporate it, but it will remain. It will remain somewhere, it cannot go out of existence.

You cannot destroy fear, either. Down the ages people have been trying to destroy fear, trying to destroy anger, trying to destroy sex, trying to destroy greed, this and that. The whole world has been continuously working, and what is the result? Man has become a mess. Nothing is destroyed, all is there; only things have become confused. There is no need to destroy anything because nothing can be destroyed in the first place.

Then what has to be done? You have to understand fear. What is fear? How does it arise? From where does it come? What is its message? Look into it – and without any judgment; only then will you understand. If you already have an idea that fear is wrong, that it should not be – "I should not be afraid" – then you cannot look. How can you confront fear? How can you look into the eyes of fear when you have already decided that it is your enemy? Nobody looks into the eyes of the enemy. If you think it is something wrong you will try to bypass it, avoid it, neglect it. You will try not to come across it, but it will remain. This is not going to help.

First drop all condemnation, judgment, evaluation. Fear is a reality. It has to be faced, it has to be understood. And only through understanding can it be transformed. In fact, it *is* transformed through understanding. There is no need to do anything else; understanding transforms it.

What is fear? First: fear is always around some desire. You want to become a famous man, the most famous man in the world – then there is fear. What if you cannot make it? – fear comes. Now fear comes as a by-product of desire: you want to become the richest man in the world. What if you don't suc-ceed? You start trembling; fear comes. You possess a woman: you are afraid that tomorrow you may not be able to possess, she may go to somebody else. She is still alive, she can go. Only dead women won't go; she is still alive. You can possess only a corpse – then there is no fear, the corpse will be there. You can possess furniture, then there is no fear. But when you try to possess a human being fear comes. Who knows, yes-terday she was not yours, today she is yours. Who knows – tomorrow she will be somebody else's. Fear arises. Fear is arising out of the desire to possess, it is a by-product; because you want to possess, hence the fear. If you don't want to possess, then there is no fear. If you don't have the desire that you would like to be this and that in the future, then there is no fear. If you don't want to go to heaven then there is no fear, then the priest cannot make you afraid. If you don't want to go anywhere then *nobody* can make you afraid.

If you start living in the moment, fear disappears. Fear comes through desire. So basically, desire creates fear.

Look into it. Whenever there is fear, see from where it is coming – what desire is creating it – and then see the futility of it. How can you possess a woman or a man? It is such a silly, stupid idea. Only things can be possessed, not persons.

A person is a freedom. A person is beautiful because of freedom. The bird is beautiful on the wing in the sky: you encage it – it is no longer the same bird, remember. It looks like it, but it is no longer the same bird. Where is the sky? Where is the sun? Where are those winds? Where are those clouds? Where is that freedom on the wing? All have disappeared. This is not the same bird.

You love a woman because she is a freedom. Then you encage her: then you go to the law court and you get married, and you make a beautiful, maybe a golden, cage around her, studded with diamonds, but she is no longer the same woman. And now fear comes. You are afraid, afraid because the woman may not like this cage. She may hanker for freedom again. And freedom is an ultimate value, one cannot drop it.

Man consists of freedom, consciousness consists of freedom. So sooner or later the woman will start feeling bored, fed up. She will start looking for somebody else. You are afraid. Your fear is coming because you want to possess – but why in the first place do you want to possess? Be nonpossessive, and then there is no fear. And when there is no fear, much of your energy that gets involved, caught up, locked up in fear, is available, and that energy can become your creativity. It can become a dance, a celebration.

You are afraid to die? Buddha says: "You cannot die, because in the first place, you are not." How can you die? Look into your being, go deep into it. See, who is there to die? – and you will not find any ego there. Then there is no possibility of death. Only the idea of ego creates the fear of death. When there is no ego there is no death. You are utter silence, deathlessness, eternity – not as you, but as an open sky, uncontaminated by any idea of "I," of self – unbounded, undefined. Then there is no fear.

Fear comes because there are other things. You will have to look into those things, and looking into them will start changing things.

So please don't ask how it can be mastered or killed. It is not to be mastered, it is not to be killed. It cannot be mastered and it cannot be killed; it can only be understood. Let understanding be your only law.

Enough for today.

the fragrance of nothingness

*Therefore, O Sariputra, in emptiness there is no form, nor
feeling, nor perception, nor impulse, nor consciousness; no eye,
ear, nose, tongue, body, mind; no forms, sounds, smells, tastes,
touchables or objects of mind; no sight-organ element, and so
forth, until we come to: No mind-consciousness element; there is
no ignorance, no extinction of ignorance, and so forth, until we
come to: There is no decay and death, no extinction of decay and
death. There is no suffering, no origination, no stopping, no path.
There is no cognition, no attainment and no non-attainment.*

Nothingness is the fragrance of the beyond. It is the opening
of the heart to the transcendental. It is the unfoldment of the
one-thousand-petaled lotus. It is man's destiny. Man is complete only when he has come to this fragrance, when he has
come to this absolute nothingness inside his being, when this
nothingness has spread all over him, when he is just a pure
sky, unclouded.

This nothingness is what Buddha calls nirvana. First we
have to understand what this nothingness actually is, because

it is not just empty – it is full, it is overflowing. Never for a single moment think that nothingness is a negative state, an absence, no. Nothingness is simply no-thingness. Things disappear, only the ultimate substance remains. Forms disappear, only the formless remains. Definitions disappear, the undefined remains.

So nothingness is not as if there is nothing. It simply means there is no possibility of defining what is there. It is as if you move all the furniture from your house outside. Somebody comes in and he says, "Now, here is nothing." He had seen the furniture before; now the furniture is missing and he says, "Here there is no longer anything. Nothing is." His statement is valid only to a certain extent. In fact, when you remove the furniture, you simply remove obstructions in the space of the house. Now pure space exists, now nothing obstructs. Now there is no cloud roaming in the sky; it is just a sky. It is not just nothing, it is purity. It is not only absence, it is a presence.

Have you ever been in an absolutely empty house? You will find that emptiness has a presence; it is very tangible, you can almost touch it. That's the beauty of a temple or a church or a mosque – pure nothing, just empty. When you go into a temple, what surrounds you is nothingness. It is empty of everything, but not just empty. In that emptiness something is present – but only present for those who can feel it, who are sensitive enough to feel it, who are aware enough to see it.

Those who can see only things will say, "What is there? Nothing." Those who can see nothing will say, "All is here, because nothing is here."

The identity of "yes" and "no" is the secret of nothingness. Let me repeat it; it is very basic to Buddha's approach: nothingness is not identical with no, nothingness is the identity of yes *and* no, where polarities are no longer polarities, where opposites are no longer opposites.

When you make love to a woman or to a man, the point of orgasm is the point of nothingness. At that moment the woman is no longer a woman and the man is no longer a man. Those forms have disappeared. That polarity between man and woman is no longer there, that tension is no longer there; it is utterly relaxed. They have both melted into each other. They have unformed themselves, they have gone into a state which cannot be defined. The man cannot say "I," the woman cannot say "I"; they are no longer "I's," they are no longer egos – because egos are always in conflict, the ego exists through conflict, it cannot exist without conflict. In that moment of orgasm there are no longer any egos. Hence the beauty of it, hence the ecstasy of it, hence the *samadhi-like* quality of it.

It happens only for a moment but even that moment, a single moment of it, is more valuable than your whole life – because in that moment you come closest to the truth. Man and woman are no longer separate; this is a polarity. Yin and yang, positive and negative, day and night, summer and winter, life and death – these are polarities. When yes and no meet, when opposites meet and are no longer opposites, when they go into each other and dissolve into each other, there is orgasm. Orgasm is the meeting of yes and no. It is not identical with no; it is beyond both yes and no.

In a sense it is beyond both; in a sense it is both together, simultaneously. The merger of the negative and the positive is the definition of nothingness. And that is the definition of orgasm too, and that is the definition of *samadhi* too. Let it be remembered.

The identity of yes and no is the secret of emptiness, nothingness, nirvana. Emptiness is not just empty; it is a presence, a very solid presence. It does not exclude its opposites; it includes it, it is full of it. It is a full emptiness, it is an overflowing emptiness. It is alive, abundantly alive, tremendously alive. So never for a single moment let dictionaries deceive you, otherwise you will misunderstand Buddha.

If you go to the dictionary and look for the meaning of *nothingness*, you will miss Buddha. The dictionary only defines the ordinary nothingness, the ordinary emptiness. Buddha is talking about something very extraordinary. If you want to know it you will have to go into life, into some situation where yes and no meet – then you will know it. Where the body and the soul meet, when the world and godliness meet, where opposites are no longer opposites – only then will you have a taste of it. The taste of it is the taste of Tao, of Zen, of Hasidism, of Yoga.

The word *yoga* is also meaningful. It means coming together. When a man and woman meet, it is a yoga: they come together, they really come close, they start overlapping and then they disappear into each other. Then they don't have centers any more. The conflict of the opposites has disappeared and there is utter relaxation.

This relaxation happens only momentarily between a man and a woman. But this relaxation can happen with the total, with the whole, in a nontemporal way. It can happen in an eternal way. In love you have only a drop of its ecstasy. In ecstasy you have the whole ocean of love.

This nothingness can be achieved only if there are no thought-clouds in you. Those are the clouds that are hampering your inner space, obstructing your inner space. Have you watched the sky? In summer it is so clean and clear, so crystal clear – not a speck of a cloud. And then come the rains, and thousands of clouds come, and the whole earth is surrounded with clouds. The sun disappears, the sky is no longer available. This is the state of the mind: the mind is constantly clouded. It is the rainy season of your consciousness; the sun is no longer available, the light is hidden, hindered, and the purity of space and the freedom of space are no longer available. Everywhere you find yourself defined by the clouds.

When you say, "I am a Hindu," what are you saying? You are getting caught by a cloud, the thought that you are a Hindu. When you say, "I am a Mohammedan" – or a Christian or a Jaina – what are you saying? You are becoming identified with a thought-cloud, you are losing your purity. That's why I say a religious man is neither Hindu nor Mohammedan nor Christian – he cannot be. He's a summertime of consciousness, he has no clouds: the sun is there, bright, unhindered, and there is infinite space around him, there is silence around him. You will not find the vibe of the cloudy consciousness.

When you say, "I am a Communist," what are you saying? You are saying that you have been reading Karl Marx, Lenin, Stalin, Mao; that you have become too attached to *Das Kapital*; that you have become identified with the idea of class struggle – the poor and the rich and the conflict; that you have become too attracted, hypnotized by a dream, an utopia: that someday in the future a classless society can be created; that you have become too obsessed with this utopia and you are ready to do anything for it. Even if you have to kill millions of people you are ready – for their own sakes, for their own good. This is a cloudy state.

When you say "I am an Indian," it is again the same. When you say "I am a Chinese," it is again the same. If you really want to be religious you will have to slowly, slowly drop these identities. No idea should ever possess you. No book should be your Bible. No Veda should define you, no Gita should confine you. You should not allow any philosophy, theology, dogma, theory, hypothesis to overcrowd you. You should not allow any smoke around your flame of consciousness. Only then are you religious.

If you ask a religious man who he is he can only say, "I am a nothingness," because nothingness is not an idea, it is not a theory. It simply indicates a state of purity.

Remember, perception has nothing to do with knowledge. In fact, when you perceive through knowledge you don't perceive rightly. All knowledge creates projections. Knowledge is a bias, knowledge is a prejudice. Knowledge is conclusion – you have concluded even before you have gone into it.

For example, if you come to me with a conclusion already in your mind – it may be for me, it may be against me, that doesn't matter – if you come to me with a conclusion then you come with a cloud. Then you will go on looking at me through your cloud, and naturally your cloud will throw shadows on me. If you have come with the idea, "This is the right man," then you will find something which goes on supporting your idea. If you have come with the idea, "This is a wrong man, dangerous, evil," then you will go on finding something which supports your idea.

Whatsoever idea you bring is self-perpetuating, it goes on finding proofs for itself. And the man who has come with a prejudice will go with his prejudice strengthened. In fact, he has never come to me.

To come to me one needs to be unclouded, with no prejudice for or against, with no a priori judgment. You just come to see what is there, you don't bring any opinion. You have heard many things but you don't believe any. You simply come to see with your own eyes, you come to feel with your own heart. That is the quality of a religious man.

If you want to know truth you will have to drop all kinds of knowledge that you have gathered down the ages, in many, many lives. Whenever somebody comes to truth with knowledge he cannot see it, he is blind. Knowledge blinds you. If you want to have clear eyes, drop knowledge. Perception has nothing to do with knowledge.

Truth and knowledge don't go together. Knowledge cannot contain the immensity of life and existence. Knowledge is so tiny, so small, and existence is so vast, so enormous – how can it contain existence? It cannot. And if you force existence into your patterns of knowledge you will destroy the beauty of it and you will destroy the truth of it. Once existence is converted into knowledge it is no longer existence. It is as if a person is carrying a map of India and thinks that he is carrying India. No map can contain India.

The picture of the moon is not the moon. The word *God* is not God; the word *love* is not love either. No word can contain the mysteries of life. And knowledge is nothing but words and words and words. Knowledge is a great illusion. That's why Buddha says: "Allow nothingness to settle in you."

Nothingness means a state of not-knowing, a state where no cloud floats in your consciousness. When your consciousness is unclouded, then you are nothing. Nothing goes perfectly well with truth – *only* nothing goes perfectly well with truth. Knowledge cannot contain the mystery of being; knowledge is against the mysterious. "The mysterious" means that which is not known, that which cannot be known, that which is basically, intrinsically, essentially unknowable – not only unknown, but unknowable. How can the unknowable be reduced to knowledge? Knowledge goes on collecting pebbles on the shore and goes on missing the diamonds. Knowledge is mediocre, borrowed, never authentic, never original. To know truth you need an insight, original insight. You need eyes which can see through and through; you need transparent vision.

So only when the mind is entirely naked of knowledge, empty of knowledge, does it come to know. When there is no knowledge, there is knowledge, because when there is no knowledge there is knowing. When the mind is entirely naked of knowledge, nude, silent, non-functioning; when the mind is in waiting, with no idea for what, just a pure waiting, expectant but not knowing for what, waiting for the guest but with no idea, waiting for the knock of the guest with an open door but with no idea who this guest is... How can you know it beforehand?

If you carry a blueprint of God you will go on missing God – because you have not known him before. Yes, others have known, but whatsoever they have said are only maps. I can give you only a map. All knowledge is a map. Don't start worshipping the map, don't start creating a temple around the map. That's how temples have been created. One temple is devoted to the Vedas, another to the Bible, another to the Koran – these are maps! These are not the real country, they are only charts. When I say something to you, I have to use words. Words reach you, you jump upon the words, you start hoarding the words – the mind is a great hoarder – and then you start thinking that you know.

This is not the way to know. The way to know is to discard all knowledge. And discard it in a single blow! Don't go slowly, gradually. If you see the point it can happen in this very moment. In fact, to see the point is to let it happen. You need not do anything in particular, you need not even drop knowledge. Just seeing the point – that knowledge cannot make you a knower, in fact it will hinder you – the revolution. Seeing this – the transformation.

So when the mind is naked, is silent, is nonfunctioning, is

111

in utter waiting, then there comes truth. Then there *is* truth. It need not come from anywhere, it has always been there. But you were so full of knowledge, hence you went on missing it.

Nothingness can know truth because in nothingness intelligence functions totally. *Only* in nothingness does intelligence function totally. That's why – you see the miracle! – children are so intelligent and old people, by and by, become so dull. Children learn things so fast! The older you become, the more difficult it becomes to learn. If you are old and you want to learn Chinese, you will take thirty years; and a child learns within two or three years.

Now scientists say that a child can learn at least four languages very easily if he is just exposed to four languages – very easily! This is the minimum. The maximum has not yet been decided: how many languages a child can learn together if he's exposed to them. It happens: if the family is multilingual it happens very easily. If the town is multilingual it happens very easily. In Mumbai it happens easily: the child will learn Hindi, English, Marathi, Gujarati, very easily. The child needs only to be exposed. He is so intelligent that he immediately sees the point of it and learns it. The older you become, the more difficult.

It is very difficult, they say, to teach an old dog new tricks. It need not be so. If you remain a nothingness, then it need not be so – because then you remain a child your whole life.

Socrates is a child even when he is dying, because he is still vulnerable, open, ready to learn; ready to learn even from death. When he is lying on the bed and the poison is being prepared – at six o'clock he will be given the poison, as the sun will be setting – he is so excited, like a child. His disciples are crying and weeping, and he is so excited. He gets up again and again and goes out to inquire of the man who is preparing the poison: "How long will it take?" – his eyes are so curious. And the man is going to die! – this is no time to be so curious. The man is going to have his last breath within minutes, and he is so excited, so ecstatic. One disciple asks, "For what are you getting so excited? You are going to die!" And Socrates says, "I have known life, and I have learned much from life. Now I would like to know death and learn from death. That's why I'm excited."

Even death becomes a great experience to one who is innocent. Socrates is innocent. The West has not produced another man comparable to Socrates. Socrates is the Buddha of the West.

You can always remain capable of learning if you remain a child. What creates dullness in you, stupidity, mediocrity? Knowledge. You accumulate knowledge; you become less and less capable of knowing.

Renounce knowledge. I teach you renunciation of knowledge. I don't teach you renunciation of the world; that is stupid, foolish, meaningless. I teach you renunciation of knowledge. And a strange thing happens...

I have come across people who have renounced the world. In the Himalayas I met a Hindu fakir – very old, he must have been ninety years old or even more. For seventy years he had been a sannyasin, for seventy years he had lived outside society. He had renounced society, he had not been back to the plains for seventy years. When he was just a young man of twenty he went to the Himalayas, and he had not gone back to the country again. He had never been in a crowd again, but he was still a Hindu. He still thought of himself as a Hindu.

I told him, "You renounce society but you have not renounced your knowledge, and the knowledge was given by the society. You are still a Hindu. You are still in the crowd – because to be a Hindu is to be in a crowd. You are still not an individual; you have not become a nothing yet."

The old man understood. He started crying. He said "Nobody has said this to me."

You can renounce the society, you can renounce wealth, you can renounce the wife, the children, the husband, the family, the parents – it is easy, nothing much in it. The real thing is to renounce knowledge. These things are outside you, you can escape from them – but where and how will

you escape from something that is inside you, that is clinging there? That will go with you. You can go to a Himalayan
cave and you remain a Hindu, you remain a Mohammedan,
you remain a Christian. Then you will not be able to see the
beauty and truth of the Himalayas. You will not be able to see
that virginity of the Himalayas. A Hindu cannot see it, a Hindu
is blind.

To be a Hindu means to be blind; to be a Mohammedan
means to be blind. You may use different instruments to
become blind, that doesn't matter. One is blind because of
the Koran, another is blind because of the Bhagavad Gita, and
somebody else is blind because of the Bible – but eyes are full
of knowledge.

Buddha says: "Nothingness allows intelligence to function."

The word *buddha* comes from *buddhi* – it means intelligence: when you are a nothing, when nothing confines you,
when nothing defines you, when nothing contains you, when
you are just an openness, then there is intelligence. Why? –
because when you are nothing fear disappears, and when fear
disappears you function intelligently. If fear is there you cannot
function intelligently. Fear cripples you, paralyzes you.

You go on doing things because of fear; that's why you
cannot become a buddha, which is your birthright. You are
virtuous because of fear, you go to the temple because of
fear, you follow a certain ritual because of fear, you pray to
God because of fear. And a man who lives through fear cannot be intelligent. Fear is poison to intelligence. How can you
be intelligent if there is fear? The fear will go on pulling you in
different ways. It will not allow you to be courageous, it will
not allow you to step into the unknown, it will not allow you to
become an adventurer, it will not allow you to leave the fold,
the crowd. It will not allow you to become independent, free;
it will keep you a slave. And we are slaves in so many ways.
Our slavery is multidimensional: politically, spiritually, religiously, we are slaves in every way, and the fear is the root
cause of it.

You don't know whether God exists or not, and still you
pray? This is very unintelligent, this is foolish. To whom are

you praying? You don't know whether God is or not. You don't have any trust, because how can you have any trust? – you have not known yet. So just out of fear you go on clinging to the idea of God. Have you seen it? – when there is much fear you remember God more. When somebody is dying, you start remembering.

I have known a follower of J. Krishnamurti. He is a very renowned scholar, known all over the country. And for at least forty years he has been a Krishnamurti follower, so he does not believe in God, he does not believe in meditation, he does not believe in prayer.

Then one day it happened that he fell ill, he had a heart attack. By chance I was in the same town. His son phoned me and said, "My father is in a very dangerous situation. If you can come it will be a great solace to him. These may be his last moments."

So I rushed. When I went into the room, he was lying down on the bed with closed eyes chanting, "Rama, Rama, Rama."

I could not believe it! For forty years he had been saying, "There is no God, and I don't believe..." And what happened to this old man? I shook him up and asked, "What are you doing?"

He said, "Don't disturb me. Let me do what I want to do."

But I said, "This is so much against Krishnamurti."

He said, "Forget about Krishnamurti! I am dying and you are talking about Krishnamurti!"

"But what about your forty years, wasted? And you had never believed that a *japa* – a chant – could help, or a prayer could help."

He said, "Yes, that's true. I had never believed, but now I am facing death. There is great fear in me. Maybe – who knows – God is, and within minutes I will be encountering him. If he is not, then there is no problem; nothing is lost by my repeating, 'Rama, Rama.' If he is, something is gained. At least I can say to him, 'At the last moment I had remembered you.'"

Have you seen it? – whenever you are in misery you start

remembering God more. When you are in danger you remember God. When you are happy and everything is going smoothly, you forget all about God. Your God is nothing but your fear projected.

Buddha says: "Out of fear there is no possibility of intelligence." And fear is there for a very fundamental reason – because you think you are. That's why there is fear. The ego brings fear as a shadow. The ego itself is illusory, but the illusion casts a big shadow on your life. Because you think "I am," hence there is fear: "Maybe if I do something wrong I will be thrown in hell, then I will suffer." If you think "I am," then naturally you think to make some provisions for the future life, for the other world – do something good, accumulate a little *punya*.

You know, the name of this town – Pune – comes from *punya*, virtue. Accumulate a little virtue, accumulate something in your account, in your bank balance so you can show God: "Look, I have been a really good boy. I have done these things: fasted so many days, have never looked at anybody's woman with any evil eye, have never been a thief, have donated so much money to this temple and to that church. I was always behaving as I was expected to behave." One starts accumulating virtue just in case it is needed in the other world.

But this is out of fear. Your good people, your bad people are all living out of fear. An intelligent person lives without fear. But to live without fear you will have to see into the fact of your ego. If there is no ego, if "I am not," then where can fear exist? Then, "I cannot be thrown into hell because I am not in the first place, and I cannot be rewarded in heaven because I am not in the first place. I am not, only God is, so how can I be a sinner or a saint? If only God is, then what is there for me to fear? I am not born, because I am not in the first place; and I will not die, because I am not in the first place. So there is no birth, no death. I am not separate, I am one with this existence. As a wave I may disappear, but as the ocean I will live. And the ocean is the reality, the wave is just arbitrary."

Nothingness knows no fear, no greed, no ambition, no violence. Nothingness knows no mediocrity, no stupidity, no idiocy.

Nothingness knows no hell, no heaven. And because there is no fear, there is intelligence. This is one of the greatest statements to be remembered: intelligence is when fear is not. Then action has a totally different quality to it. When you act out of your nothingness the action has a totally different quality to it. It is divine, it is godly. Why? – because when you act out of nothingness it is not a reaction, when you act out of nothingness it is not a plan, when you act out of nothingness it is not rehearsed. When you act out of nothingness it is spontaneous, then you live moment to moment. You are a nothingness: a situation arises and you respond to it. If you are an ego you never respond, you always react.

Let it be explained to you. When you are an ego you always react. For example, if you think you are a very, very good man, you think you are a saint, and then something happens – somebody insults you – now, will you be responding to this insult or reacting? If you think you are a saint you will think thrice about how to react, what to do so you can save your sainthood too; otherwise this man can destroy it just by insulting you. You cannot be spontaneous, you have to look back, you have to ponder over it. And time is passing. It may even be a single moment, but time is passing. It cannot be spontaneous, it cannot be in the moment. And you act out of the past. You think, "This is too much. If I become angry" – and anger is coming – "if I become angry my sainthood will be lost. That is too much to pay for this." You start smiling. To save your sainthood you smile.

This smile is false; it is not coming from you, it is not coming from your heart. It is just there, painted on the lips. It is pseudo. You are not smiling, it is only your mask that is smiling. You are deceiving. You are a hypocrite. You are pseudo. You are phony. But you have saved your sainthood: you acted out of the past, out of your particular image and idea of your being. This was a reaction.

The man of spontaneity does not react, he responds. What is the difference? He just allows the situation to function over him, and he allows the response to come out, whatsoever it is.

The man who lives out of the past is predictable, and the man who lives moment to moment is unpredictable. And to be predictable is to be a thing. To be unpredictable is to be freedom – that is the dignity of man. The day you are unpredictable... Nobody knows, not even you; remember, not even you... If you already know what you will do, then it is no longer response. You are already ready, it is rehearsed.

For example, you are going for an interview. You rehearse: you think what is going to be asked and how you are going to answer it. It happens every day, it is so clear-cut.

Every evening I see people – both kinds of people are there: when somebody has come here readymade, has thought over what he is going to say to me, has prepared it already; the script is ready, he has just to replay it, he has decided everything about what he is going to ask. And I can see the difficulty of the person, because when he comes in front of me, when he sits by the side of me, it is a different situation. A change starts happening. The climate, the presence, his love for me, my love for him, others' presence, the trust that is there very tangibly, the love that is flowing, a meditative state – and it is absolutely different than he had been thinking before. Now whatsoever he has prepared looks irrelevant; it does not fit. He becomes fidgety, restless – "What to do?" And he does not know how to act spontaneously, how to act out of this situation.

He comes in front of me but I see the phoniness of it. His question does not come from his heart. It is just from the throat, it has no depth. His voice has no depth. He himself is not certain whether he wants to ask it anymore or not, but he has prepared it, maybe for days. So the mind goes on saying, "Ask it. You have prepared it." And he sees the irrelevance of it. Maybe it has already been answered. Maybe in answering somebody else I have answered it. Maybe the very situation is such that his mind has changed and it is no longer meaningful.

But he acts out of the past: that is reacting. It will look awkward. He feels embarrassed if he has nothing to ask. And he cannot cry because he is a phony person, and he cannot simply say, "Hello," and he cannot say, "I would like just to sit in front of you for one minute, and I have nothing to say." He cannot act out of this moment. He cannot be herenow; he feels embarrassed. He has to ask, otherwise what will people think? – "Then why, in the first place, had you asked for *darshan* if you had nothing to ask?" So he asks. He is no longer behind it. It is a rotten old question which no longer has meaning – but he asks.

Sometimes – you may have seen – to a few people I go on answering and take a long time, and to a few people I answer in a very short way. Whenever I see that somebody is phony, his question is phony, is a prepared question, then it is meaningless to answer him. Just out of respect for him I talk a little bit to him, but I am no longer interested. And the phony questioner is also not interested in what I am saying – because he is no longer interested even in his question, so how can he be interested in the answer?

But there are other people... By and by the phoniness disappears and sannyasins become more and more true, authentic. Then somebody simply sits there and laughs. That's what is coming in that moment. He does not feel embarrassed, he does not feel that it is out of place. It is not. The prepared script is out of place.

Facing a nothingness, you have to be nothing. Only then can there be a meeting, because only similars can meet. Then there is great joy, then there is great beauty. Then there is dialogue. Maybe not a single word is uttered, but there is dialogue. Sometimes somebody comes and simply sits and starts swaying, closes his eyes, goes inwards – that is the way to come towards me. He goes inside himself and simply jumps into me and allows me to jump into him, or simply touches my feet, or simply looks into my eyes. Or sometimes a great question also arises, but it is in the moment – then it is true, then it has immense power, then it comes from your very deepest core. It has relevance.

When you act out of nothingness, you respond; it is no longer a reaction. It has truth, it has validity in it, authenticity. It is existential. It is immediate, spontaneous, simple, innocent. And this action does not create any karma.

Remember, the word *karma* means action, a particular action. Not all actions create karma, remember. Buddha lived after his enlightenment for forty-two years. He was not sitting all the time under the *bodhi* tree doing nothing. He did a thousand and one things, but karma was not created. He acted but it was no longer reaction, it was response.

If you respond out of nothingness it leaves no residue, it leaves no traces on you, karma is not created. You remain free. You go on acting and you remain free. It is as if a bird flies into the sky, leaving no traces, no footprints. The man who lives in the sky of nothingness leaves no footprints, leaves no karma, no residue. His act is total. And when the act is total, it is finished, it is complete. A complete act does not hang around you like a cloud; only incomplete acts hang around you.

Somebody insulted you – you wanted to hit him but you didn't. You saved your sainthood, you smiled and blessed the man and went home. Now it is going to be difficult: now the whole night you will dream that you are hitting the man. You may even kill him in your dreams. For years it will hang around you; it is incomplete. Anything incomplete is dangerous. When you are phony everything becomes incomplete. You love a woman but not enough to make it complete. Even while making love you are not entirely there; maybe you are still rehearsing. Maybe you have been reading sex manuals which are available. Maybe you have been reading Vatsyayana's *Kama Sutra*, or Masters and Johnson or the *Kinsey Report*, and you have been learning how to make love. And you are ready, knowledgeable! Now this woman is just an opportunity to practice your knowledge. So you are practicing your knowledge, but it is going to be incomplete because you are not in it. And then it is unsatisfying, then you feel frustrated – and the cause is your knowledge.

Love is not something to be practiced. Life need not be practiced; life has to be lived, in utter innocence. Life is not a drama – you need not prepare, you need not go into a rehearsal for it. Let it come as it comes, and be spontaneous.

But how can you be spontaneous if the ego is there? Ego is

a great actor, ego is a great politician; ego goes on manipulating you. The ego says, "If you really want to act in a polished way preparation is needed. If you really want to act in a cultured way you have to rehearse it." The ego is a performer, and because of this performer you go on missing the joy, the celebration, the blessing of life.

Buddha says: "When action comes out of nothing it creates no karma." Then it is so total that its very totality... The circle is complete and finished. You never look backwards. Why do you go on looking backwards? – because there are things incomplete. Whenever something is complete you don't look back. It is finished. The full point has been achieved, there is nothing more to do about it. Act out of nothingness and your action is total, and the total action leaves no memory – no psychological memory, I mean. The memory is left in the brain, but there is no psychological hang-up. And a man who has no hang-ups is my definition of a sannyasin.

When an act is utterly complete, you are free of it. When an act is total, you slip out of it – like a snake slips out of the old skin and the old skin is left behind. Only incomplete acts become karma, remember it. But to have a complete act, it has to come out of nothingness.

There are three levels of awareness: awareness of the self, awareness of the world, and awareness of the intervening fantasy between the self and the world. Fritz Perls called this intermediate level the DMZ – demilitarized zone – and it functions to keep us from being totally in touch with ourselves and with our world. The DMZ contains our prejudices, the prejudgments through which we view the world and other people and ourselves. If we look at the world through our biases, we cannot see the truth of it. We cannot see that which is. We create an illusion; that's what Hindus call *maya*.

If we look outside with judgments, a priori prejudices, then we create a world of our own, which is *maya*, illusion, a projection. If we look at ourselves through these judgments and knowledge and opinions, we create another illusion – the ego. Then we cannot see what reality is there inside us. We cannot see what is out there, and we cannot see what is in here.

When the outside is missed we create illusion, *maya*; when the inside is missed we create the ego, *ahankar*. And both of these things happen through the DMZ – the demilitarized zone.

Gurdjieff used to call this zone the "zone of the buffers." DMZ is a beautiful name for it. The bigger the DMZ is, the more pathological the person is, the more neurotic. The smaller the DMZ is, the healthier, psychologically sane a person is. And when the DMZ completely disappears and there is no thought intervening between you and the world – not a single thought – that's what Buddha means by nothingness. Then the person is utterly sane, holy, whole.

Before we enter the sutra, a few things about this ego. The illusion of the self has to be understood.

The first thing: the ego is not a reality, it is just an idea. You don't come with it when you come into the world, you don't bring it with you. It is not part of your being. When a child is born he does not bring the ego into the world. The ego is something that he learns, it is not part of genetics.

Gordon Alport calls the self *proprium,* and it can be defined by considering the adjective form *propriate,* as in the word *appropriate. Proprium* refers to something that belongs to or is unique to a person. The self is created because each nothingness is unique, each nothingness has its own way of flowering. Because of this uniqueness there is the possibility of creating an ego.

I love in my way, you love in your own way. I behave in my way, you behave in your own way. There is a difference between people, but only a difference in ways. The roseflower flowers in one way and the marigold in another, but both flower. The flowering is the same, the nothingness is the same. But each nothingness functions in a unique way. Because of this there is a possibility to create the ego.

There are seven doors from where the ego enters, seven doors from where we learn the ego. Those doors have to be understood, because if you understand them you will be able to drop the ego – because those doors, understood perfectly well, can be closed. Then the ego is no longer created. Seen rightly, understood perfectly well – that the ego is just a shadow – it starts disappearing on its own.

The first door Alport calls "the bodily self." We are not born with a sense of self. The child in the mother's womb has no sense of the self. He is one with the mother; he is utterly one, joined, bridged with the mother. The mother is his whole existence, his cosmos. He does not know that he is separate. The separation comes when the child comes out of the womb, when his bridge with the mother is cut and the child has to breathe on his own. In fact, the breathing is not something that the child is going to do. How can he do? He cannot even breathe yet, so he is not yet there. The breathing happens. It is not that the child is doing it, it is a happening. It comes out of nothingness: the child starts breathing. Those few seconds are very, very valuable, critical, dangerous. The parents, the doctor, the nurses who are looking after the birth are all in a great waiting: whether the child is going to breathe or not.

The child cannot be forced, the child cannot be persuaded, and the child cannot do anything on its own. If it is going to happen, it is going to happen. It may not happen, it may happen. Sometimes children never breathe, then we think they are born dead.

It is miraculous how the child breathes the first breath: he has never done it before, he cannot be prepared for it. He does not know that the mechanism to breathe exists. The lungs have not functioned ever before, but the breath comes and the miracle starts. But the breath is coming out of nothingness, remember. Later on you will start saying, "I am breathing." That is absurd. You are not breathing: breathing is happening. Don't create the idea of "I," don't say, "I am breathing." Nobody is breathing. It is not within your capacity to do or not to do.

You can try: stop breathing for a few seconds and you will know that it is also difficult to stop. Within seconds a great rush comes from nowhere and you start breathing again. Or stop the breathing outside; try for a few seconds and suddenly you see a great rush. It is beyond you. The breathing wants to come in.

It is "nothing" that is breathing in you, or you can call it

God – it makes no difference, it is the same. Nothing or God, they mean the same. *Nothing* in Buddhism means exactly what *God* means in Christianity, Judaism, Hinduism. God is a nothing.

We are not born with a sense of self. It is not part of our genetic endowment. The infant is not able to distinguish between self and the world around it. Even when the child has started breathing, it takes months for him to become aware that there is a distinction between his inside and the outside. Gradually, through increasingly complex learning and per-ceptual experiences, a vague distinction develops between something "in me" and other things "out there."

This is the first door from which the ego enters: the distinc-tion that there is something "in me." For example: the child feels hunger, he can feel it coming from inside. And then the mother slaps the child, and he can feel it is coming from the outside. Now a distinction is bound to be felt by and by, that there are things which come from inside, and there are things which come from outside. When the mother smiles he can see the smile is coming from there, and then he responds, he smiles. Now he can feel the smile is coming from within, somewhere inside. The idea of inside and outside arises. This is the first experience of the ego.

In fact there is no distinction between the outside and the inside. The inside is part of the outside and the outside is part of the inside. The sky inside your house and the sky outside your house are not two skies, remember; they are one sky. And so is it the case with you there and me here. We are not two; we are two aspects of the same energy, two aspects of the same coin. But the child starts learning the ways of the ego.

The second door is self-identity. The child learns its name, realizes that the reflection in the mirror today is of the same person as the one seen yesterday, and believes that the sense of me or self persists in the face of changing experiences. The child goes on knowing that everything changes. Sometimes he is hungry, sometimes he is not hungry; sometimes he is sleepy and sometimes he is awake; and sometimes he is angry, and sometimes he is loving – things go on changing. One day it is a beautiful day, another day it is dark and dismal. But he stands before the mirror...

Have you watched a small baby sitting before a mirror? He tries to catch hold of the child inside the mirror because he thinks the child is "there outside." If he cannot catch hold, then he goes around and looks at the back of the mirror – maybe the child is hiding there? But by and by he starts knowing that it is he who is reflected. And then he starts feeling a kind of continuity: yesterday it was the same face, today it is also the same face in the mirror. When children look for the first time into the mirror they become fascinated with the mirror. They don't leave it. They go again and again to the bathroom to look at who they are.

Everything goes on changing. One thing seems to be unchanging: the self-image. The ego has another door from where it is entering: the self-image.

The third door is self-esteem. This is concerned with the child's feeling of pride as a result of learning to do a thing on its own: doing, exploring, making. When a child learns anything – for example he has learned a word, *daddy*; then he goes on saying, "Daddy, daddy," the whole day. He does not miss a single opportunity when he can use the word. When the child starts learning to walk, he tries the whole day. He falls again and again, he stumbles, he is hurt, but again he stands – because it gives pride: "I can also do something! I can walk! I can talk! I can carry things from here to there!"

The parents are very worried because the child is a disturbance. He starts carrying things. They can't understand: "Why? For what? Why have you taken that book from there?" The child is not interested in the book at all. It is all nonsense for him. He cannot conceive why you go on looking in this thing continuously – "What are you searching for there?" But his interest is different: he can carry a thing.

The child starts killing animals. An ant, and he will immediately jump on it and kill it. He can do something! He is enjoying doing; he can become very destructive. If he finds a clock, he will open it – he wants to know what is inside. He becomes an explorer, an inquirer.

He enjoys doing things because that gives a third door to his ego: he feels proud, he can do. He can sing a song, then he is ready to sing the song to anybody. If any guest comes he is present, waiting for somebody to give a hint so he can sing the song. Or he can dance, or he can do a mime, or something! Whatsoever it is, he wants to do something to show that he is not just helpless, that he can also do. This doing brings ego in.

The fourth is self-extension, belonging, possession. The child speaks of *my* house, *my* father, *my* mother, *my* school. He starts increasing the field of "mine." *Mine* becomes his key word. If you take his toy – he is not much interested in the toy; he is more interested in, "The toy is mine, you cannot take it!" Remember, he is not much interested in the toy. When nobody is interested he will throw the toy in the corner and will escape to play outside. But once somebody wants to take it, he does not want to give it. It is his – "mine."

"Mine" gives a sense of "me"; "me" creates "I." And remember, these doors are not only for children, they remain that way your whole life. When you say *my* house, you are being childish. When you say *my* wife, you are being childish. When you say *my* religion, you are being childish. When a Hindu starts fighting with a Mohammedan about religion, they are children. They don't know what they are doing. They have not really become mature and grown up. Children are constantly arguing, "My daddy is the greatest daddy in the world!" And so the priests go on fighting, "My concept of God is the best, the most powerful, the real! Others are just so-so."

These are very childish attitudes, but they linger around you for your whole life. You are very interested in your name. When I change people's names, a few people are very stubborn; they don't want it. A few people write letters to me: "I want to take sannyas, but please, don't change my name." Why? *My* name! It seems to be something like a great wealth. And there is nothing in the name. But for thirty years, forty years, your ego has survived with that name. It is very difficult for the ego to close a door. That's why the name is changed: so that you can see that the name is arbitrary, it can be changed any day. And that's why I change your name without any fuss about it.

In other religions the name is also changed. If you become a Jaina monk they will make much fuss about it – a great procession and celebration; somebody is becoming a monk! Now he will become very attached to this new name. So much celebration and so much festivity, and so much honor and respect; so much fuss about it, then the whole point is lost. I simply change it as a matter of fact, just to give you an idea that it is nothing; it is arbitrary, it can be changed very easily. You can be called A, you can be called B, you can be called C – it doesn't matter. In fact you are nameless; that's why it doesn't matter. Any name will do, it is only utilitarian.

The fifth door is self-image. This refers to how the child sees himself. Through interaction with parents, through praise and punishments, he learns to have a certain image of himself – good or bad.

The child is always looking at how the parents react to him. If he is doing a certain thing, do they praise it or do they punish him? If he feels punished he thinks, "I have done something wrong. I am bad." If he does something good and is praised, he thinks, "I am good, I am appreciated." He starts trying to do more and more good, so that he is appreciated. Or, if the parents are really very difficult and impossible people, and their demands are such that the child cannot fulfill them, then he takes the other route, he starts doing all that they call "bad." He reacts and rebels.

These are the two ways – the door is the same: either you praise him and he feels good that he is somebody; or if you don't praise him easily then he says, "Okay, then I will show you." Then too he will make his presence felt. He will start destroying things, he will start smoking, he will start doing things which you don't like. And he will say, "Now you see? You have to take note of me; you have to notice me. You have to know that I am somebody and I am here, and you cannot just neglect me." The good guy and the bad guy are born this way, the saint and the sinner.

The sixth is self as reason. The child learns the ways of

reason, logic, argument. He learns that he can solve problems. Reason becomes a great support to his self – that's why
people argue. That's why educated people think that they are
somebodies. Uneducated? – you feel a little embarrassed. You
have a great degree – you are a PhD or a DLitt – and you go
on showing, exhibiting your certificate: you are a gold med-
alist, you have topped the university, and this and that. Why?
– because you are showing that you have become a rational
being, well-educated, educated in the best of universities,
educated by the best of professors: "I can argue better than
anybody else." Reason becomes a great support.

And the seventh is *propriate* striving, life-goal, ambition,
becoming: what and who one is through what or who one
wants to become. Future concern, dreams and long-range
goals appear – the last stage of the ego. Then one starts thinking about what to do in the world to leave a mark in history,
to leave a signature here on the sands of time. To become a
poet? To become a politician? To become a mahatma? To
do this or to do that? Life is running fast, slipping fast, and
one has to do something, otherwise soon one will become
nothing and nobody will ever know that you had existed. One
wants to become an Alexander or a Napoleon. If it is possible,
one wants to become a good guy, famous, well-known, a saint,
a mahatma.

If it is not possible, then too one wants to become somebody. Many murderers have confessed in the courts that they
had not murdered somebody because they were interested in
murdering him, but they just wanted their names on the front
page of the newspapers.

A man murdered somebody from behind. He came and
stabbed him, and he had not even seen the man before. He
was absolutely unknown to him; they were not acquainted,
there was no friendship, no enmity. He had never met him.
And this time also, he had not seen the face of the man whom
he had murdered. He had not seen him, he simply murdered
him from behind. The man was sitting on the beach looking at
the waves, and this man came and killed him.

The court was puzzled, but the man said, "I was not interested in the man whom I killed. He was irrelevant, anybody
would have done. I had gone there to kill somebody. If this
man had not been there, then somebody else..." But why?
And he said, "Because I wanted my photo and my name on
the front page of the newspapers. My desire is fulfilled. I am
talked about all over the country, I am happy. Now I am ready
to die. If you sentence me to death I can die happily: I was
known, I was famous."

If you cannot become famous, you try to become noto-
rious. If you cannot become Mahatma Gandhi, you would
like to become Adolf Hitler – but nobody wants to remain a
nobody.

These are the seven doors through which the illusion of the
ego strengthens, becomes stronger and stronger. And these
are the seven doors – if you understand – through which the
ego has to be sent out again. Slowly, slowly from each door
you have to look deep into your ego and say goodbye to it.
Then nothingness arises.

The sutra:

*Therefore, O Sariputra, in emptiness there is no form, nor
feeling, nor perception, nor impulse, nor consciousness; no eye,
ear, nose, tongue, body, mind; no forms, sounds, smells, tastes,
touchables or objects of mind; no sight-organ element, and so
forth, until we come to: No mind-consciousness element; there
is no ignorance, no extinction of ignorance, and so forth, until
we come to: There is no decay and death, no extinction of decay
and death. There is no suffering, no origination, no stopping,
no path. There is no cognition, no attainment and no non-
attainment.*

A tremendously revolutionary statement.

Therefore, O Sariputra...

First we have to understand the word *therefore*. *Therefore* is perfectly relevant in a syllogism, in a logical argument. There has been no argument preceding it, and Buddha says: *Therefore, O Sariputra...*

Scholars have been very worried about why he uses *therefore*. *Therefore* is part of a syllogism: All men are mortal. Socrates is a man, therefore Socrates is a mortal. It is part of logic. But there has been no proposition, no argumentation, and suddenly Buddha says: *Therefore...* Why?

The scholars cannot understand it, because there had been no argument on the surface. But there has been a dialogue between the eyes of Buddha and Sariputra. There has arisen an understanding. Listening to Buddha talking about emptiness, nothingness, Sariputra has risen to that level of nothingness.

It can arise in you here, you can feel it, its wings fluttering around you.

Looking into his eyes Buddha feels, sees that Sariputra has understood: now the argument can go further. On the surface there has been no argument. There has been no debate, discussion, but there has been a dialogue. The dialogue is between these two energies: Buddha and Sariputra. There has been a unity, they have been bridged. In that bridge, in that moment of bridging, Sariputra has looked into Buddha's emptiness. Now Buddha says to Sariputra, "Therefore... You have looked, Sariputra, now I can go further into it, into more detail. Now I can say a few things to you which would not have been possible before."

Therefore, O Sariputra, in emptiness there is no form, nor feeling, nor perception...

Because there is nobody to feel, so how can there be feeling? When the ego is not there, there is no feeling, no knowledge, no perception. No form arises because the sky is completely cloudless. You can see a form in a cloud. Have you not seen sometimes? – a cloud looks just like an elephant, and then it changes into a horse and then into something else, and it goes on changing. It takes so many forms.

But have you ever seen any form arising in the pure sky? No form ever arises.

...there is no form, nor feeling, nor perception, nor impulse...

And when there is nobody inside, how can impulse arise? How can desire arise?

...nor consciousness...

When there is no content, when there is no object, the subject also disappears. That consciousness which is always of the object is no longer found there.

...no eye, no ear, no nose, no tongue, no body, no mind...

Buddha says, "Everything disappears into that nothingness, Sariputra. And now you can understand, Sariputra; therefore I am saying it. You have seen it. You have looked into me. You have been on the very verge of it. You have peeped into the abyss, the eternal, the abysmal depth."

...no forms, sounds, smells, tastes, touchables or objects of mind;
no sight-organ element, and so forth...
...No mind-consciousness element...

When you are in that state you cannot even say "I am in this state of nothingness" because if you say this you have come back.

...until we come to...

If you say, "I have experienced nothingness," that means you have come back to the world of form. The mind has started functioning again. In that moment you are not separate from nothingness, so how can you say, "I am experiencing nothingness?" Nothingness is not like an object: it is not separate from you, you are not separate from it. The observer is the observed there; the object is the subject there. The duality has disappeared.

...there is no ignorance...

...Buddha says. There is no knowledge, there is no ignorance either, because ignorance can only be when you think in terms of knowledge. It is comparison with knowledge. When you call a man ignorant what do you mean? You are comparing him with somebody who is knowledgeable. But there is no knowledge so there cannot be any ignorance.

...there is no ignorance, no extinction of ignorance...

And Buddha says: "Remember, I am not saying that ignorance disappears. Ignorance has never been there; it was a shadow of knowledge, it was a shadow of the mind addicted to knowledge."

When you bring a light into a dark room, what do you say? – that the darkness disappears, goes out from the room, escapes from the room, runs away? No, you cannot say that – because darkness does not exist in the first place. How can it go out? Light comes and darkness is not found, because darkness was just the absence of light.

So there is no ignorance, and no extinction of ignorance. There is no knowledge and there is no non-knowledge. One simply is innocent of all – knowledge, ignorance; just innocent, virgin. To be free of knowledge and to be free of ignorance is to be virgin, to be pure.

There is no decay and death...

...Because there is nobody to die. And remember, there is no extinction of decay and death. And Buddha is not saying that death disappears, because death has never been there in the first place. To say that death has disappeared would be wrong. Buddha is very, very perfect in his assertion, very careful. He has not uttered a single word which can be refuted by anybody who knows reality. He has not compromised. He has not compromised with the listener. He has said the most perfect thing that can possibly be said.

There is no suffering...

Now he comes to the ultimate revolutionary statement.

You must have heard about the four noble truths of Buddha. The first noble truth is suffering: that everybody is suffering, that the whole existence is *dukkha*, suffering, pain, misery, agony.

And the second noble truth is: its origination is in craving – *tanha*, desire. Suffering exists: the first noble truth – *arya satya*; the second noble truth is that suffering has a cause and the cause is in desire. We suffer because we desire.

And the third noble truth is: this desiring can be stopped. It is possible – *nirodha*; it can be stopped. By looking deep into desiring it can be stopped, and when desiring stops suffering disappears. And the fourth noble truth is: there is an eightfold path that leads to the stoppage, *nirodha*, of desiring, and consequently of suffering.

This is Buddhism's most fundamental philosophy, and in this statement Buddha denies that too! He says:

There is no suffering, no origination, no stopping, and no path.

Nobody has ever stated such a revolutionary thing. Buddha reaches the uttermost peak of revolution; everybody else falls short.

Now, scholars have always been worried that this is contradictory. Buddha teaches that there is suffering, and then one day he says, "There is no suffering." He teaches that there is a cause for why suffering is, and then one day he says, "There is no origination." He teaches that there is a possibility – *nirodha* – that it can be stopped, and one day he says, "There is no stopping." And he says – and the whole of Buddhism depends on that saying – that there is an eightfold path, *astangik marga*: right vision, right exercise, right meditation, right *samadhi*, and so on and so forth; the eight-limbed path which leads you to the ultimate truth. And now one day he says, "There is no path. The reality is a pathless reality." Why this contradiction? The first statement is made to those who do not know that they are not. The first statements are made to ordinary people, full of ego. *This* statement is made to Sariputra in a particular space, in a particular state.

Therefore, O Sariputra... Now I can say this to you. I could not have said it before, you were not ready. Now you have looked into me, and looking into me you have seen what nothingness is. You have had a taste of it. *Therefore,* Sariputra: *Tasmat,* Sariputra! Now it is possible to say to you that there is no suffering, that it is a dream; people are suffering in dream. And there is no causation – people are desiring in a dream. And there is no stopping – people are exercising, doing methods, meditating, Yoga, etcetera, in a dream. And the whole path exists in the dream. Now it can be said to you because you are awake, Sariputra. Your eyes are opened; now you see the ego does not exist.

And to get out of the ego is to get out of sleep. To get out of the ego is to get out of darkness. To get out of the ego is to be free. In that freedom it can be said that there is no path. It is like a dream.

In dream you are suffering, and when you are suffering in a dream, it is so real. And you are searching: "Why am I suffering?" And then you come across a great sage – in the dream – and the sage says, "You are suffering because you are desiring. You are so much infatuated with money; that's why you are suffering. Drop this desire and the suffering will disappear." You understand it, it is very logical. You know it, you have experienced it yourself that whenever you desire, suffering comes. The more desire is there, the more suffering. The greater the desire, the bigger the suffering. You understand it. Then you ask, "Then how to stop it?" And the great sage says, "Stand on your head, do Yoga, do chaotic meditation, do Kundalini, do Nadabrahma, do encounter group and do Leela and do Primal Therapy and all." The great sage says, "Do these things; these will help. You will become more understanding of your desire, and you will be able to drop the desire."

So the sage gives you a well-formulated eightfold path. He says, "This is the way." One day, when you are really awake... And remember, these things help you to awaken. Now even if you stand on your head in a dream there is a possibility your dream will be broken. Try! Try tonight! When you are in a dream, just stand on your head in the dream, and suddenly you will see that you are awake. Do Kundalini in a dream – you will be awake. And if you are not, at least your husband will be awake, the neighbors will be awake, something is going to happen.

All methods are just to wake you. But when you are awake...

Therefore, Sariputra...

And now Buddha can say this to Sariputra; he is awake. He can say, "Now I can tell you the truth – that nobody exists, neither the disciple nor the master, nor the dream, nor the suffering, nor the sage, nor the cause, nor the stopping. There is no path."

This is the ultimate statement of truth.

But this can be made only at the highest stage, at the seventh rung of the ladder. Sariputra reached to that rung on this day. That's why "Therefore – *tasmat* – Sariputra."

Enough for today.

CHAPTER 6

don't be too sane

The first question:

Osho,
What is the difference between the emptiness of the
child before the formation of the ego and the awakened
childlikeness of a buddha?

There is a similarity and there is a difference. Essentially the child is a buddha, but his buddhahood, his innocence, is natural, not earned. His innocence is a kind of ignorance, not a realization. His innocence is unconscious – he is not aware of it, he is not mindful of it, he has not taken any note of it. It is there but he is oblivious. He is going to lose it. He *has* to lose it. Paradise will be lost sooner or later; he is on the way towards it. Every child has to go through all kinds of corruption, impurity – the world.

The child's innocence is the innocence of Adam before he was expelled from the Garden of Eden, before he had tasted the fruit of knowledge, before he became conscious. It is animal-like. Look into the eyes of any animal – a cow, a dog – and there is purity, the same purity that exists in the eyes of a buddha, but with one difference.

The difference is vast too: a buddha has come back home; the animal has not yet left home. The child is still in the Garden of Eden, is still in paradise. He will have to lose it because to gain one has to lose. Buddha has come back home – the whole circle. He went away, he was lost, he went astray, he went deep into darkness and sin and misery and hell. Those experiences are part of maturity and growth. Without them you don't have any backbone, you are spine-less. Without them your innocence is very fragile; it cannot stand against the winds, it cannot bear storms. It is very weak, it cannot survive. It has to go through the fire of life – a thousand and one mistakes committed, a thousand and one times you fall, and you get back on your feet again. All those experiences slowly, slowly ripen you, make you mature; you become a grown-up.

Buddha's innocence is that of a mature person, utterly mature. Childhood is nature unconscious; buddhahood is nature conscious. The childhood is a circumference with no idea of the center. The buddha is also a circumference, but rooted in the center, centered. Childhood is unconscious anonymity; buddhahood is conscious anonymity. Both are nameless, both are formless, but the child has not yet known the form and the misery of it. It is like you have never been in a prison, so you don't know what freedom is. Then you have been in the prison for many years, or many lives, and then one day you are released... You come out of the prison doors dancing, ecstatic! And you will be surprised that the people who are already outside, walking on the street, going to their work, to the office, to the factory, are not enjoying their freedom at all – they are oblivious, they don't know that they are free. How can they know? They don't know the contrast because they have never been in prison; the background is missing.

It is as if you write with a white chalk on a white wall – nobody will ever be able to read it. What to say about anybody else – even *you* will not be able to read what you have written.

I have heard a famous anecdote about Mulla Nasruddin:

In his village he was the only man who could write, so
people used to come if they wanted to write a letter or a docu-
ment, or anything. He was the only man who could write. One
day a man came. Nasruddin wrote the letter, whatsoever the
man dictated – and it was a long letter – and the man said,
"Please read it now because I want to be sure that everything
has been written and I have not forgotten anything, and you
have not messed up anything."

Mulla said, "Now, this is difficult. I know how to write but
I don't know how to read. And moreover, the letter is not
addressed to me so it will be illegal to read it too."

And the villager was convinced, the idea was perfectly
right, and the villager said, "Right you are – it is not addressed
to you."

If you write on a white wall even you yourself will not be
able to read it, but if you write on a blackboard it comes loud
and clear – you can read it. The contrast is needed. The child
has no contrast; he is a silver lining without the black cloud.
Buddha is a silver lining in the black cloud.

In the day there are stars in the sky; they don't go anywhere – they can't go so fast, they can't disappear. They are
already there, the whole day they are there, but in the night
you can see them because of darkness. As the sun sets they
start to appear. As the sun goes deeper and deeper below
the horizon, more and more stars bubble up. They have been
there the whole day, but because the darkness was missing it
was difficult to see them.

A child has innocence but no background. You cannot see
it, you cannot read it; it is not very loud. A buddha has lived
his life, has done all that is needed – good and bad – has
touched this polarity and that, has been a sinner and a saint.
Remember, a buddha is not just a saint; he has been a sinner
and he has been a saint. And buddhahood is beyond both.
Now he has come back home.

That's why Buddha said in yesterday's sutra: *Na jhanam,*

na praptir na-apraptih – "There is no suffering, no origination, no stopping, no path. There is no cognition, no knowledge, no attainment, and no non-attainment." When Buddha became awakened he was asked, "What have you attained?" And he laughed, and he said, "I have not attained anything – I have only discovered what has always been the case. I have simply come back home. I have claimed that which was always mine and was with me. So there is no attainment as such, I have simply recognized it." It is not a discovery, it is a rediscovery. And when you become a buddha you will see the point – nothing is gained by becoming a buddha. Suddenly you see that this is your nature. But to recognize this nature you have to go astray, you have to go deep into the turmoil of the world. You have to enter into all kinds of muddy places and spaces just to see your utter cleanliness, your utter purity.

The other day I told you about the seven doors – of how the ego is formed, how the illusion of the ego is strengthened. It will be helpful to go deeply into a few things about it.

These seven doors of the ego are not very clear-cut and separate from each other; they overlap. And it is very rare to find a person who has attained to his ego from all seven doors. If a person has attained the ego from all seven doors he has become a perfect ego. And only a perfect ego has the capacity to disappear, not an imperfect ego. When the fruit is ripe it falls; when the fruit is unripe it clings. If you are still clinging to the ego, remember, the fruit is not ripe; hence the clinging. If the fruit is ripe, it falls to the ground and disappears. So is the case with the ego.

Now a paradox: only a really evolved ego can surrender. Ordinarily you think that an egoist cannot surrender. That is not my observation, and not the observation of buddhas down the ages. Only a perfect egoist can surrender because only he knows the misery of the ego, only he has the strength to surrender. He has known all the possibilities of the ego and has gone into immense frustration. He has suffered a lot, and he knows enough is enough, and he wants any excuse to surrender it. The excuse may be godliness, the excuse may be a master, or any excuse, but he wants to surrender it. The burden is too much and he has been carrying it for long.

People who have not developed their egos can surrender, but their surrender will not be perfect, it will not be total. Something deep inside will go on clinging, something deep inside will still go on hoping: "Maybe there is something in the ego. Why are you surrendering?"

In the East, the ego has not been developed well. Because of the teaching of egolessness, a misunderstanding arose that if the ego has to be surrendered, then why develop it, for what? A simple logic: if it has to be renounced one day, then why bother? Then why make so much effort to create it? It has to be dropped! So the East has not bothered much in developing the ego. And the Eastern mind finds it very easy to bow down to anybody. It finds it very easy, it is always ready to surrender. But the surrender is basically impossible, because you don't yet have an ego to surrender.

You will be surprised: all the great buddhas in the East have been kshatriyas, from the warrior race – Buddha, Mahavira, Parshwanath, Neminath. All the twenty-four *tirthankaras* of the Jainas belong to the warrior race, and all the *avataras* of the Hindus belonged to the kshatriya race – Rama, Krishna – except one, Parashuram, who was, accidentally it seems, born to a brahmin family, because you cannot find a greater warrior than him. It must have been an accident – his whole life was a continuous war.

It is a surprise when you come to know that not a single brahmin has ever been declared a buddha, an *avatara*, a *tirthankara*. Why? The brahmin is humble; from the very beginning he has been brought up in humbleness, for humbleness. Egolessness has been taught to him from the very beginning, so the ego is not ripe, and unripe egos cling.

In the East people have very, very fragmentary egos, and they think it is easy to surrender. They are always ready to surrender to anybody. A drop of a hat and they are ready to surrender – but their surrender never goes very deep, it remains superficial.

Just the opposite is the case in the West: people who come from the West have very, very strong and developed egos.

Because the whole Western education is to create an evolved, well-defined, well-cultured, sophisticated ego, they think it is very difficult to surrender. They have not even heard the word surrender. The very idea looks ugly, humiliating. But the paradox is that when a Western man or woman surrenders, the surrender goes really deep. It goes to the very core of his being or her being, because the ego is very evolved. The ego is evolved; that's why you think it is very difficult to surrender. But if surrender happens it goes to the very core, it is absolute. In the East people think surrender is very easy, but the ego is not so evolved so it never goes very deep.

A buddha is one who has gone into the experiences of life, the fire of life, the hell of life, and has ripened his ego to its ultimate possibility, to the very maximum. And in that moment the ego falls and disappears. Again you are a child; it is a rebirth, it is a resurrection. First you have to be on the cross of the ego, you have to suffer the cross of the ego, and you have to carry the cross on your own shoulders – and to the very end. Ego has to be learned; only then can you unlearn it. And then there is great joy. When you are free from the prison you have a dance, a celebration in your being. You cannot believe why people who are out of prison are going so dead and dull and dragging themselves. Why are they not dancing? Why are they not celebrating? They cannot: they have not known the misery of the prison.

These seven doors have to be used before you can become a buddha. You have to go to the darkest realm of life, to the dark night of the soul, to come back to the dawn when the morning rises again, the sun rises again, and all is light. But it rarely happens that you have a fully developed ego.

If you understand me, then the whole structure of education should be paradoxical: first they should teach you the ego – that should be the first part of education, the half of it; and they should then teach you egolessness, how to drop it – that will be the latter half. People enter from one door or two doors or three doors, and get caught up in a certain fragmentary ego.

The first, I said, is the bodily self. The child starts learning slowly, slowly: it takes nearabout fifteen months for the child to learn that he is separate, that there is something inside him and something outside. He learns that he has a body separate from other bodies. But a few people remain clinging to that very, very fragmentary ego for their whole lives. These are the people who are known as materialists, Communists, Marxists. The people who believe that the body is all – that there is nothing more than the body inside you; that the body is your whole existence; that there is no consciousness separate from the body, above the body; that consciousness is just a chemical phenomenon happening in the body; that you are not separate from the body and when the body dies you die, and all disappears, dust unto dust; there is no divinity in you – they reduce man to matter.

These are the people who remain clinging to the first door; their mental age seems to be only fifteen months. The very, very rudimentary and primitive ego remains materialist. These people remain hung up with two things: sex and food. But remember, when I say materialist, Communist, Marxist, I do not mean that this completes the list. Somebody may be a spiritualist and may still be clinging to the first.

For example, Mahatma Gandhi: if you read his autobiography – he calls his autobiography *My Experiments with Truth* but if you go on reading his autobiography you will find the name is not right; he should have given it the name *My Experiments with Food and Sex*. Truth is nowhere to be found. He is continuously worried about food: what to eat, what not to eat. His whole worry seems to be about food, and then about sex: how to become a celibate – this runs as a theme, this is the undercurrent. Continuously, day and night, he is thinking about food and sex – one has to get free. Now, he is not a materialist: he believes in the soul, he believes in God. In fact, because he believes in God he is thinking so much about food – because if he eats something wrong and commits a sin, then he will be far away from God. He talks about God but thinks about food.

That is not only so with him, it is so with all the Jaina monks. He was under much impact from Jaina monks. He was born in Gujarat; Gujarat is basically Jaina, Jainism has the greatest impact on Gujarat. Even Hindus are more like Jainas in Gujarat than like Hindus. Gandhi is ninety percent a Jaina – born in a Hindu family, but his mind is conditioned by Jaina monks. They think continuously about food.

Then the second idea arises, of sex: how to get rid of sex. For his whole life, to the very end, he was concerned about how to get rid of sex. In the last year of his life he was experimenting with nude girls and sleeping with them, just to test himself; because he was feeling that death was coming close, he had to test himself to see whether there was still lust in him.

The country was burning, people were being killed: Mohammedans were killing Hindus, Hindus were killing Mohammedans; the whole country was on fire. And he was in the very middle of it in Novakali, but his concern was sex. He was sleeping with girls, nude girls; he was testing himself, testing whether his *brahmacharya,* his celibacy, was perfect or not.

But why this suspicion? – because of long repression. He had repressed his whole life. Now, in the very end, he had become afraid because at that age he was still dreaming about sex. So he was very suspicious: would he be able to face his God? Now, he is a spiritualist, but I will call him a materialist, and a very primitive materialist. His concern is food and sex.

Whether you are for it or against it doesn't matter; your concern shows where your ego is hanging. And I will include the capitalist in it also: his whole concern is how to gather money, hoard money because money has power over matter. You can purchase any material thing through money. You cannot purchase anything spiritual, you cannot purchase anything that has any intrinsic value; you can purchase only things. If you want to purchase love, you cannot purchase it; but you can purchase sex. Sex is the material part of love. Through money, matter can be purchased, possessed.

Now you will be surprised: I include both the Communist and the capitalist in the same category, and they are enemies, just as I include Charvaka and Mahatma Gandhi in the same category, and they are enemies. They *are* enemies, but their concern is the same. The capitalist is trying to hoard money, the Communist is against it. He wants that nobody should be allowed to hoard money except the state. But his concern is also money, he is also continuously thinking about money. It is not an accident that Marx had given the name *Das Kapital* to his great book on Communism – *The Capital*. That is the Communist Bible, but the name is *The Capital*. That is their concern: how to not allow anybody to hoard money so the state can hoard, and how to possess the state – so, in fact, basically, ultimately, you hoard the money.

Once I heard that Mulla Nasruddin had become a Communist. I know him and I was a little puzzled. This was a miracle! I know his possessiveness. So I asked him, "Mulla, do you know what Communism means?"

He said, "I know."

I said, "Do you know that if you have two cars and somebody hasn't a car, you will have to give one car?"

He said, "I am perfectly willing to give."

I said, "If you have two houses and somebody is without a house you will have to give one house?"

He said, "I am perfectly ready, right now."

And I said, "If you have two donkeys you will have to give one donkey to somebody else who has not?"

He said, "There I disagree. I cannot give, I cannot do that!"

But I said, "Why? – because it is the same logic, the same corollary."

He said, "No, it is not the same – I *have* two donkeys, I don't have two cars."

The Communist mind is basically a capitalist mind, the capitalist mind is basically a Communist mind. They are partners in the same game – the game's name is *The Capital, Das Kapital*.

Many people, millions of people, only evolve this primitive ego, very rudimentary. If you have this ego it is very difficult to surrender; it is very unripe.

The second door I call self-identity. The child starts growing an idea of who he is. Looking in the mirror, he finds the same face. Every morning, getting up from the bed, he runs to the bathroom, looks, and he says, "Yes, it is I. The sleep has not disturbed anything." He starts having the idea of a continuous self.

Those people who become too involved with this door, get hooked with this door, are the so-called spiritualists who think that they are going into paradise, heaven, *moksha,* but that *they* will be there. When you think about heaven, you certainly think of yourself that as you are here, you will be there too. Maybe the body will not be there, but your inner continuity will remain. That is absurd! That liberation, that ultimate liberation happens only when the self is dissolved and all identity is dissolved. You become an emptiness.

Therefore, O Sariputra... in nothingness there is no form, or *...form is emptiness and emptiness is form...* There is no knowledge because there is no knower; there is not even *vigyan,* no consciousness, because there is nothing to be conscious about and nobody to be conscious about it. All disappears.

That idea that the child has of self-continuity is carried by the spiritualists. They go on searching: from where does the soul enter into the body, from where does the soul go out of the body, what form does the soul have, planchettes and mediums, things like that – all rubbish and nonsense. The self has no form. It is pure nothingness, it is vast sky without any clouds in it. It is a thoughtless silence, unconfined, uncontained by anything.

That idea of a permanent soul, the idea of a self, continues to play games in your mind. Even if the body dies, you want to be certain: "I will live." Many people used to come to Buddha... Because this country has been dominated by this second kind of ego, people believe in the permanent soul, eternal soul, atman, they would come to Buddha again and again and ask, "When I die, will something remain or not?" And Buddha would laugh and he would say, "There is nothing right now, so why bother about death? There has never been anything from the very beginning." This was inconceivable to the Indian mind.

The Indian mind is predominantly hooked with the second type of ego. That's why Buddhism could not survive in India.

Within five hundred years, Buddhism disappeared. It found better roots in China because of Lao Tzu. Lao Tzu had created really a beautiful field for Buddhism there. The climate was ready; it was as if somebody had prepared the ground, only the seed was needed. And when the seed reached China it grew into a great tree. But it disappeared from India. Lao Tzu had no idea of any permanent self, and in China people have not bothered much about it.

There are these three cultures in the world: one culture, called the materialist – very predominant in the West; another culture, called the spiritualist – very predominant in India; and China has a third kind of culture, neither materialist nor spiritualist. It is Taoist: live the moment and don't bother for the future, because to bother about heaven and hell and paradise and *moksha* is basically to be continuously concerned about yourself. It is very selfish, it is very self-centered. According to Lao Tzu, according to Buddha too, and according to me also, a person who is trying to reach heaven is a very, very self-centered person, very selfish. And he does not know a thing about his own inner being – there is no self.

The third door was self-esteem: the child learns to do things and enjoys doing them. A few people get hooked there: they become technicians, they become performers, actors, they become politicians, they become the showmen. The basic theme is the doer; they want to show the world that they can do something. If the world allows them some creativity, good; if it does not allow them creativity, they become destructive.

Did you know that Adolf Hitler wanted to enter an art school? He wanted to become a painter, that was his idea. Because he was refused, because he was not a painter, because he could not pass the entrance examination in art school – that rejection was very hard for him to accept – his creativity turned sour. He became destructive. But basically he wanted to become a painter, he wanted to do something. Because he was not found capable of doing it, as revenge, he started being destructive.

The criminal and the politician are not very far away, they

are cousin-brothers. If the criminal is given the right opportunity he will become a politician, and if the politician is not
given the right opportunity to have his say, he will become a
criminal. They are border cases. Any moment, the politician
can become a criminal and the criminal can become a politician. And this has been happening down the ages, but we
don't yet have that insight to see into things.

The fourth door was self-extension. The word *mine* is the
key word there. One has to extend oneself by accumulating
money, by accumulating power, by becoming bigger and
bigger and bigger: the patriot who says, "This is my country,
and this is the greatest country in the world." You can ask the
Indian patriot: he goes on shouting from every nook and corner that this is *punya bhumi* – this is the land of virtue, the
purest land in the world.

Once a so-called saint came to me, a Hindu monk, and he
said, "Don't you believe that this is the only country where so
many buddhas were born, so many *avataras*, so many *tirthankaras* – Rama, Krishna and others. Why? – because this is the
most virtuous land."

I told him, "The fact is just the opposite: if in the neighborhood you see that in somebody's house a doctor comes
every day – sometimes a *vaidya,* a physician, a *hakim,* an
acupuncturist, and the naturopath, and this and that – what
do you understand by it?"

He said, "Simple! That that family is ill."

That is the case with India: so many buddhas needed,
the country seems to be utterly ill and pathological. So many
healers, so many physicians... Buddha has said, "I am a physician." And you know that Krishna has said, "Whenever
there is darkness in the world, and whenever there is sin in
the world, and whenever the law of the cosmos is disturbed,
I will come back." So why had he come that time? It must
have been for the same reason. And why so many times to
India?

But the patriot is arrogant, aggressive, egoistic. He goes

on declaring, "My country is special, my religion is special, my church is special, my book is special, my guru is special" – and everything is nothing. This is just ego claiming.

A few people get hooked with this "mine" – the dogmatist, the patriot, the Hindu, the Christian, the Mohammedan.

The fifth door is self-image. The child starts looking into things, experiences. When the parents feel good with the child, he thinks, "I am good." When they pat him he feels, "I am good." When they look with anger, they shout at him and they say, "Don't do that!" he feels, "Something is wrong in me." He recoils.

A small child was asked in school on the first day he entered, "What is your name?"

He said, "Johnny Don't."

The teacher was puzzled. He said, "Johnny Don't? I never heard of such a name!"

He said, "Whenever, whatsoever I am doing, this is my name – my mother shouts, 'Johnny *don't!*' My father shouts, 'Johnny *don't!*' So I think this is my name. 'Don't' is always there. What I am doing is irrelevant."

The fifth is the door from where morals enter: you become a moralist; you start feeling very good, "holier than thou." Or, in frustration, in resistance, in struggle, you become an immoralist and you start fighting with the whole world, to show the whole world.

Fritz Perls, the founder of Gestalt Therapy, has written about one of his experiences that proved very fundamental to his life's effort. He was a psychoanalyst practicing in Africa. The practice was very good because he was the only psycho-analyst there. He had a big car, a big bungalow with a garden, a swimming pool – and everything that a mediocre mind wants to have, the middle-class luxuries. And then he went to Vienna to attend a world psychoanalyst's conference. Of course, he was a successful man in Africa, so he was thinking that Freud would receive him, there would be great welcome.

Freud was the father-figure for the psychoanalysts, so he wanted to be patted by Freud.

He had written a paper and had worked for months on it, because he wanted Freud to know who he was. He read the paper; there was no response. Freud was very cold, other psychoanalysts were very cold. His paper was almost unnoticed, uncommented on. He felt very shocked, depressed, but still he was hoping that he would go to see Freud, and then something might happen. And he went to see Freud. He was just on the steps, had not even entered the door, and Freud was standing there. And he said to Freud, just to impress him, "I have come from thousands of miles." And rather than welcoming him, Freud said, "And when are you going back?" That hurt him very much: "This is the welcome? – 'When are you going back?'" And that was the whole interview – finished! He turned away, continuously repeating, like a mantra in his head: "I will show you, I will show you, I will show you!" And he tried to show him: he created the greatest movement against psychoanalysis – gestalt.

This is a childish reaction. Either the child is accepted – then he feels good, then he is ready to do anything the parents want; or, if again and again he is frustrated, then he starts thinking in terms of, "There is no possibility that I can receive their love, but still I need their attention. If I cannot get their attention the right way, I will get their attention the wrong way. Now I will smoke, I will masturbate, I will do harm to myself and to others, and I will do all kinds of things that they say 'Don't do,' but I will keep them occupied with me. I will show them."

This is the fifth door, the self-image. Sinner and saint are hooked there. Heaven and hell are the ideas of people who are hooked there. Millions of people are hooked. They are continuously afraid of hell and continuously greedy for heaven. They want to be patted by God, and they want God to say to them, "You are good, my son. I am happy with you." They go on sacrificing their lives just to be patted by some fantasy somewhere beyond life and death. They go on doing a thousand and one tortures to themselves just in order that God can say, "Yes, you sacrificed yourself for me."

It seems as if God is a masochist or a sadist, or something like that. People torture themselves with the idea that they will be making God happy. What do you mean by this? You fast and you think God will be very happy with you? You starve yourself and you think God will be very happy with you? Is he a sadist? Does he enjoy torturing people? And that is what saints, so-called saints, have been doing: torturing themselves and looking at the sky. Sooner or later God will say, "Good boy, you have done well. Now come and enjoy the heavenly pleasures. Come here! Wine flows here in rivers, and roads are of gold, and palaces are made of diamonds. And the women here never age, they remain stuck at sixteen. Come here! You have done enough, you have earned, now you can enjoy!" The whole idea behind sacrifice is this. It is a foolish idea, because *all* ego ideas are foolish.

The sixth is the self as reason. It comes through education, experience, reading, learning, listening: you start accumulating ideas, then you start creating systems out of ideas, consistent wholes, philosophies. This is where the philosophers, the scientists, the thinkers, the intellectuals, the rationalists are hooked. This is becoming more and more sophisticated: from the first, the sixth is very sophisticated.

The seventh is *propriate* striving: the artist, the mystic, the utopian, the dreamer – they are hooked there. They are always trying to create a utopia in the world. The word *utopia* is very beautiful: it means that which never comes. It is always coming but it never comes; it is always there but never here. But there are moon-gazers who go on looking for the faraway, the distant, and they are always moving in imagination. All the egos of the great poets, imaginative people are involved in becoming. There is somebody who wants to become God; he is a mystic.

Remember, *becoming* is the key word on the seventh, and the seventh is the last of the ego. The most mature ego comes there. That's why you will feel, you will see a poet – he may not have anything, he may be a beggar, but in his eyes, on his nose, you will see a great ego. The mystic may have renounced the whole world and may be sitting in a Himalayan cage, in a Himalayan cave. You go there and look at him: he may be sitting there naked – but such a subtle ego, such a refined ego. He may even touch your feet, but he is showing, "Look how humble I am!"

There are seven doors. When the ego is perfect, all these seven doors have been crossed; then that mature ego drops on its own accord. The child is before these seven egos, and the buddha is after these seven egos. It is a complete circle.

You ask me: "What is the difference between the emptiness of the child before the formation of the ego and the awakened childlikeness of a buddha?" This is the difference. Buddha has moved into all these seven egos – seen them, looked into them, found that they are illusory, and has come back home, has become a child again. That's what Jesus means when he says, "Unless you become like small children, you will not enter into my kingdom of God."

The second question:

Osho,
I am just curious. Have you read the book Zorba the Greek
by Kazantzakis? I love it so much. Is not Zorba exactly the
way you want us to be? At least that is how I understand
your teaching.

I have been Zorba the Greek for many lives. I need not read the book; that is my autobiography. And that's what I would like you to be.

Take life joyfully, take life easily, take life relaxedly, don't create unnecessary problems. Ninety-nine percent of your problems are created by you because you take life seriously. Seriousness is the root cause of problems. Be playful, and you will not miss anything – because life is God. Forget about God; just be alive, be abundantly alive. Live each moment as if this is the last moment. Live it intensely; let your torch burn from both sides together. Even if it is only for one moment, that is enough. One moment of intense totality is enough to give you the taste of God. You can live in a lukewarm way, the bourgeois way, the middle-class way. You can go on living, dragging yourself for millions of years – you will only collect dust from the roads and nothing else. One moment of clarity, totality, spontaneity, and you burn like a flame. Just one moment is enough. One moment will make you eternal; you will enter from that moment into eternity. That's my whole message for my sannyasins: live it in such way that you need not repent, ever.

A friend has sent me a newspaper cutting:

An old woman, eighty-five years old, was asked by a journalist that if she had to live again, how would she live?

The old woman said – there is a great insight in it, remember it – "If I had my life to live over, I would dare to make more mistakes next time. I would relax, I would limber up. I would be sillier than I have been this trip. I would take fewer things seriously. I would take more chances. I would take more trips. I would climb more mountains and swim more rivers. I would eat more ice cream and less beans. I would perhaps have more actual troubles, but I would have fewer imaginary ones.

"You see, I am one of those people who lived sensibly and sanely hour after hour, day after day. Oh, I have had my moments, and if I had it to do over again I would have more of them. In fact, I would try to have nothing else – just moments, one after another, instead of living so many years ahead of each day. I have been one of those persons who never go anywhere without a thermometer, a hot water bottle, a raincoat and a parachute. If I had to do it again I would travel lighter than I have.

"If I had my life to live over, I would start barefoot earlier in the spring, and stay that way later into the fall. I would go to more dances. I would ride more merry-go-rounds. I would pick more daisies."

And that's my vision of a sannyasin too. Live this moment as totally as possible. Don't be too sane, because too much sanity leads to insanity. Let a little craziness exist in you. That gives zest to life, that makes life juicy. Let a little irrationality always be there. That makes you capable of playing, being playful; that helps you to relax. A sane person is utterly hung up in the head, he cannot get down from there. He lives upstairs. Live all over the place, this is your house! Upstairs, good, the ground floor, perfectly good – and the basement is beautiful too. Live all over the place, this is your house. And don't wait for next time, I would like to tell this old woman, because the next time never comes.

Not that you will not be born again; you will be born again, but then you will forget. Then you will start again from *ABC*. This old woman has been here before. She must have been here millions of times before. And I can say to you that *each* time, nearabout the age of eighty-five, she would have decided the same way: "Next time I'm going to do it differently." But next time you don't remember – that's the problem. You lose all memory of the past life. Then again you start from *ABC* and the same thing happens.

So I would not say to you to wait for the next time. Take hold of *this* moment! This is the only time there is, there is no other time. Even if you are eighty-five you can start living. And what is there to lose when you are eighty-five? If you go barefoot on the beach in the spring, if you collect daisies – even if you die in that, nothing is wrong. To die barefoot on the beach is the right way to die. To die collecting daisies is the right way to die. Whether you are eighty-five or fifteen doesn't matter. Take hold of this moment. Be a Zorba.

You ask: "I am just curious. Have you read the book *Zorba the Greek*? I love it so much." Only loving it won't help. *Be* it! Sometimes it happens that you love the opposite of what you are. You enjoy the opposite of what you are because it releases fantasies in you. It gives you a vision of how you would like to be: that's the appeal of a Zorba.

But loving the book will not help. That's what people have been doing down the ages. People love the Bible, and don't become Jesus, and they love the *Heart Sutra* – they repeat it, they chant it every day. Millions of people in the East repeat the *Heart Sutra* five times a day: in China, in Japan, in Korea, in Vietnam they go on repeating it. It is a small sutra; it can be repeated within minutes. They love it, but they don't *become* it!

Be a Zorba. Remember, loving books is not going to help, only being helps.

"I love it so much. Is not Zorba exactly the way you want us to be?" Not exactly, because I would not like many Zorbas in the world. Not *exactly,* because that would be ugly and monotonous and boring. Be a Zorba in your own way – not *exactly.*

Never try to imitate anybody, never be an imitator; that is suicide. Then you will never be able to enjoy. You will always remain a carbon copy, you will never be the original. And all that happens in life – truth, beauty, good, liberation, meditation, love – happens to the original, never to the carbon copy. Beware – not *exactly;* that is dangerous. If you simply start following Zorba and start doing things as he is doing them you will get into trouble. That's how people have done it.

Look at the Christians, look at the Hindus: they have been trying to do it *exactly.* Nobody can be a Buddha again. Existence does not permit any repetition. Existence does not allow secondhand people, it loves firsthand people. It loved Buddha. It loved so much that it is finished. Now there is no need for Buddha. It would not be a love affair anymore. It would be like going to the same movie that you have seen before, it would be like reading the same book that you have read many times before. Existence is not dull and stupid, it never allows anybody to repeat anybody else: Christ only once, Buddha only once – and so are you only once! And you are alone, there is nobody else like you. Only you are you. This I call reverence for life. This is really self-respect.

Learn from Zorba, learn the secret, but never try to imitate. Learn the climate, appreciate, go into it, sympathize with it, participate with Zorba, and then go on your own. Then be yourself.

The third question:

Osho,
Will you please speak about what is common between
prayer and meditation, and also the difference between
them?

The question is from Mark Nevejan.

P.S. You don't know me because I have not yet met you
personally. Arup knows me a little bit.

Arup does not know herself, how can she know you? – not even a little bit! You have not met me, that is true. But I know you, because I know myself. The day I came to know myself, I have come to know everybody because it is the same noth- ingness flowering in different ways.

I know you, Mark. You may not know me. How can you know me? – you don't know yourself. But I know you. I may not know your form, but I know you – and you are not the form.

Therefore, O Sariputra... Form is emptiness, emptiness is form. I know the truth in you; I may not know the personality around you. That's why I can help you – because I know you. That's why I can take you to the beyond – because I know you. If I don't know you I cannot take you beyond.

And you ask: "Will you please speak about what is com- mon between prayer and meditation, and also the difference between them?" I was just going to speak about it yesterday, but there were so many questions and I could not answer you.

Mark has written another question today:

Dear Summertime of Consciousness and Freedom,
The other day I asked you a question about what is common
and different in prayer and meditation. In the meantime,
I have been reading in your book I Am the Gate, *and found*
the answer. Thank you for the response.
Dutch Cloudy Sky called Mark Nevejan.

You will not be called Mark Nevejan for long! I think it is

going to be today, because I don't wait for tomorrow. I will find you a beautiful name. It will not be cloudy; it will not be a cloudy Dutch sky. It will be an Indian summer sky with no clouds.

It will happen many times that you ask a question, and if you look for it, you will find it. Patience is needed, because when I'm answering others' questions, they are yours too. Just patience is needed. When I answer one question, I answer many: the asked ones and the unasked ones, and the ones that will be asked in the future, and the ones that will never be asked.

Good, Mark, that you waited one day and didn't get angry. A few people get very angry. They write me angry letters: "I have been asking questions and you don't answer me." They are not listening to me, they are only searching for *their* question. That is their ego, the question is not important – "My question has to be answered." And whenever I see that somebody has asked a question in which "my" is more important, I never answer.

Mukta is sitting there. She goes on writing questions and questions again and again: "Osho, why do you never answer my questions?" The day she drops her "my," she will start finding answers.

I am continuously answering! But when you are too attached with *your* question, and you are simply waiting for when *your* question is being answered, you will miss all the answers that have been showering on you. It happens many times that when I answer a question, the questioner himself cannot receive it but others receive it more easily, because they are not worried, it is not their question, so they are sitting silently. They are not excited about it, they are not tense about it, it is nothing personal. They can relax and enjoy the answer. When it is your question you are tense and you are afraid. And I never miss a chance – if I can hit you, I hit!

The fourth question:

Osho,
I have heard you say repeatedly that we should remain in

the world, in the marketplace. Yet most of the people I meet
here are planning to live with you in Gujarat, only returning
to the West to gather enough money to do so. A large
community is being planned. Please comment.
You emphasize the importance of being with a living master,
but that after a connection is made you are always with us.
Why does everyone want to live in your community instead
of staying in the world? It certainly would be wonderful, but
what about the marketplace?

It is going to be the greatest marketplace that you have
ever seen. Don't be worried about that! It is going to be the
very world – more intense, of course, than you can find it
anywhere; more chaotic of course. And nobody is planning
it, remember, it is coming up of out nothing. *Therefore, O*
Sariputra...!

The fifth question:

Osho,
What chance is there for your ideal society in the face of the
politicians and the priests and the vested interests of capital?

First, I am not interested in any ideal society. For that matter, I am not even interested in any ideal individual. The word
ideal is a dirty word to me. I have no ideals. Ideals have driven
you mad. It is ideals that have made this whole earth a big
madhouse.

An ideal means you are not that which you should be.
It creates tension, anxiety, anguish. It divides you, it makes
you schizophrenic. And an ideal is in the future and you are
here. How can you live unless you are the ideal? First be the
ideal, then start living – and that never happens. That cannot happen in the very nature of things. Ideals are impossible;
that's why they are ideals. They drive you crazy and make
you insane. And condemnation arises, because you always
fall short of the ideal. Guilt is created. In fact, that is what
the priests and the politicians have been doing – they want

to create guilt in you. To create guilt they use ideals; that is the simple mechanism. First give an ideal, then guilt comes automatically.

I say to you that two eyes are not enough, you need three eyes; open your third eye! Read Lobsang Rampa – open your third eye! And now you try hard, this way and that, and you stand on your head, and you do a mantra – and the third eye does not open. Now you start feeling guilty: something is missing, you are not the right person. You become depressed. You rub the third eye hard, and it doesn't open.

Beware of all this nonsense. These two eyes are beautiful. And if you have only one eye, that is perfect. Because Jesus says, "When two eyes become one, then the whole body is full of light." But I'm not saying that you should try to make one eye out of two. Just accept yourself as you are. God has made you perfect, he has not left anything incomplete in you. And if you feel incompletion is there, then that is part of perfection. You are perfectly imperfect. God knows better: that only in imperfection is there growth, only in imperfection is there flow, only in imperfection is something possible. If you were just perfect you would be dead like a rock. Then there would be nothing happening, then nothing could happen. If you understand me, I would like to tell you: God is also perfectly imperfect, otherwise he would have been dead long ago. He would not have waited for Friedrich Nietzsche to declare that God is dead.

What would this God be doing if he were perfect? Then he could not do anything, then he could not have any freedom to do. He could not grow; there would be nowhere to go. He would be simply stuck there. He could not even commit suicide, because when you are perfect you don't do things like that.

Accept yourself as you are.

I am not interested in any ideal society, not at all. I am not interested even in ideal individuals. I am not interested in idealism at all!

To me the society does not exist, there are only individuals. The society is just a functioning structure, utilitarian. You cannot come across society. Have you ever come across society? Have you ever come across humanity? Have you ever come across Hinduism, Islam? No, you always come across the individual, the concrete, the solid individual.

But people have been thinking how to improve society, how to make an ideal society. And these people have proved calamities. They have been a great mischief. Because of their ideal society they have destroyed people's respect for themselves, and they have created guilt in everybody. Everybody is guilty, nobody seems to be happy the way he is. You can create guilt for anything, and once guilt is created, you become powerful. The person who creates guilt in you becomes powerful over you – remember this strategy – because then only can he redeem you of guilt. Then you have to go to him. The priest first creates guilt, then you have to go to the church. Then you have to go and confess, "I have committed this sin," and he forgives you in the name of God. First in the name of God he created guilt, then he forgives you in the name of God.

Listen to this story:

Calvin was caught committing a grave sin by his mother, and immediately was sent to confession.

"Father," said Calvin, "I played with myself."

"Why did you do that?" the priest was really angry and shouted.

"I had nothing better to do," said Calvin.

"For penance, do five Our Fathers and five Hail Marys."

A week later Calvin's mother caught him again, and once more he was sent to confession.

"Father, I played with myself."

"Why did you do that?"

"I had nothing better to do," said Calvin.

"For penance, do ten Our Fathers and five Hail Marys."

The following week, Calvin was guilty again. "Back you go," said his mother. "And take this chocolate cake for the good Father."

While waiting on a long line Calvin finished the cake. In the confessional he said, "Father, Mom sent you a chocolate cake, but I ate it all up while I was waiting."

"Why did you do that?" asked the priest.

"I had nothing better to do."
"Why didn't you play with yourself then?"

The priest is not interested in what you are doing; he has his vested interest – his chocolate cake. And then you can go to hell! Then you do whatsoever you want, but where is the chocolate cake?

They create guilt, then they forgive you in the name of God. They make you sinners and then they say, "Now come to Christ, he is the savior." Nobody is there who can save you, because in the first place you have not committed any sin. You need not be saved.

This is the message of Buddha: you are already there. You are already saved. The savior need not come, you are not guilty. There is no suffering, Sariputra, no origination of suffering, no stopping of it, and there is no path to it. It is not attained, it is not non-attained. It is already the case, it is your very nature.

I am not interested in any ideal society. Please drop that dream; it has created great nightmares in the world. Remember, nothing can happen now politically. Politics is dead. Whether you vote right or left, do it without illusions. It is necessary to renounce the idea that any system can be a savior. No system can be a savior – Communism, Fascism, Gandhism. No society can save you, and no society can be an ideal society. And there is no savior – Christ, Krishna or Rama. You have just to drop that nonsense that you are carrying about guilt and your being a sinner.

Put your whole energy into living; withdraw your energy from guilt. Put your energy into dancing, celebrating. And then you are ideal, here and now – not that you have to become ideal.

Ideology, as such, has lost its truth. In fact it was never there in the first place. And the power to persuade is also gone. Few serious minds believe any longer that one can set down blueprints, and through social engineering bring about a new utopia of social harmony. We are living in the age of utter freedom. We have come of age. Humanity is no longer childish, it is more mature. We are living in a very Socratic period, because people are asking all the important questions of life. Don't start hankering and longing for some future ideal, idea, perfection. Drop all ideals and live herenow.

My commune is not going to be an ideal society. My commune is going to be a herenow commune.

Enough for today.

CHAPTER 7

full emptiness

*Therefore, O Sariputra, it is because of his non-attainmentness
that a bodhisattva, through having relied on the perfection of
wisdom, dwells without thought-coverings. In the absence of
thought-coverings he has not been made to tremble, he has
overcome what can upset, and in the end he attains to nirvana.*

*All those who appear as buddhas in the three periods of time
fully awake to the utmost, right and perfect enlightenment
because they have relied on the perfection of wisdom.*

What is meditation? This whole *Heart Sutra* is about the
innermost core of meditation. Let us go into it.

The first thing: meditation is not concentration. In concentration there is a self concentrating and there is an object
being concentrated upon. There is duality. In meditation there
is nobody inside and nothing outside. It is not concentration.
There is no division between the in and the out. The in goes on
flowing into the out, the out goes on flowing into the in. The
demarcation, the boundary, the border, no longer exists. The in
is out, the out is in; it is a nondual consciousness.

Concentration is a dual consciousness: that's why concentration creates tiredness; that's why when you concentrate you feel exhausted. And you cannot concentrate for twenty-four hours, you will have to take holidays to rest. Concentration can never become your nature. Meditation does not tire, meditation does not exhaust you. Meditation can become a twenty-four hour thing – day in, day out, year in, year out. It can become eternity. It is relaxation itself.

Concentration is an act, a willed act. Meditation is a state of no will, a state of inaction. It is relaxation. One has simply dropped into one's own being, and that being is the same as the being of all. In concentration there is a plan, a projection, an idea. In concentration the mind functions out of a conclusion: you are doing something. Concentration comes out of the past.

In meditation there is no conclusion behind it. You are not doing anything in particular, you are simply being. It has no past to it, it is uncontaminated by the past. It has no future to it, it is pure of all future. It is what Lao Tzu has called *wei-wu-wei*, action through inaction. This is what Zen masters have been saying: "Sitting silently doing nothing, the spring comes and the grass grows by itself." Remember, "by itself" – nothing is being done. You are not pulling the grass upwards; the spring comes and the grass grows by itself. That state – when you allow life to go on its own way, when you don't want to direct it, when you don't want to give any control to it, when you are not manipulating, when you are not enforcing any discipline on it – that state of pure undisciplined spontaneity is what meditation is.

Meditation is in the present, pure present. Meditation is immediacy. You cannot meditate, but you can be in meditation; you cannot be in concentration, but you can concentrate. Concentration is human, meditation is divine.

Concentration has a center in you; it comes from that center. Concentration has a self in you. In fact the man who concentrates much starts gathering a very strong self. He starts becoming more and more powerful, he starts becoming more and more of an integrated will. He will look more collected, more one piece.

The man of meditation does not become powerful: he becomes silent, he becomes peaceful. Power is created out of conflict; all power is out of friction. Out of friction comes electricity. You can create electricity out of water: when the river falls from a mountainside there is friction between the river and the rocks, and the friction creates energy. That's why people who are seeking power are always fighting. Fight creates energy. It is always through friction that energy is created, power is created. The world goes into war again and again because the world is too dominated by the idea of power. You cannot be powerful without fighting.

Meditation brings peace. Peace has its own power, but that is an altogether different phenomenon. The power that is created out of friction is violent, aggressive, male. The power – I am using the word because there is no other word – the power that comes out of peace, is feminine. It has a grace to it. It is passive power, it is receptivity, it is openness. It is not out of friction; that's why it is not violent.

Buddha is powerful, powerful in his peace, in his silence. He is as powerful as a roseflower, he's not powerful like an atom bomb. He's as powerful as the smile of a child – very fragile, very vulnerable; but he's not as powerful as a sword. He is as powerful as a small earthen lamp, the small flame burning bright in the dark night. It is a totally different dimension of power. This power is what we call divine power. It is out of non-friction.

Concentration is a friction: you fight with your own mind. You try to focus the mind in a certain way, towards a certain idea, towards a certain object. You force it, you bring it back again and again. It tries to escape, it runs away, it goes astray, it starts thinking of a thousand and one things, and you bring it again and you force it. You go into a self-fight. Certainly power is created; that power is as harmful as any other power, that power is as dangerous as any other power. That power will again be used to harm somebody, because the power that comes out of friction is violence. Something out of violence is going to be violent, it is going to be destructive. The power that comes out of peace, non-friction, non-fight, non-manipulation, is the power of a roseflower, the power of a small lamp, the power of a child smiling, the power of a woman weeping, the power that is in tears and in the dew-drops. It is immense but not heavy; it is infinite but not violent.

Concentration will make you a man of will. Meditation will make you an emptiness. That's what Buddha is saying to Sariputra. *Prajnaparamita* exactly means meditation, the wisdom of the beyond.

You cannot bring it but you can be open to it. You need not do anything to bring it into the world – you cannot bring it; it is beyond you. You have to disappear for it to come. The mind has to cease for meditation to be. Concentration is mind effort; meditation is a state of no-mind. Meditation is pure awareness, meditation has no motive in it.

Meditation is the tree that grows without a seed: that is the miracle of meditation, the magic, the mystery. Concentration has a seed in it: you concentrate for a certain purpose, there is motive, it is motivated. Meditation has no motive. Then why should one meditate if there is no motive?

Meditation comes into existence only when you have looked into all motives and found them lacking, when you have gone through the whole round of motives and you have seen the falsity of it. You have seen that motives lead nowhere, that you go on moving in circles; you remain the same. The motives go on and on leading you, driving you, almost driving you mad, creating new desires, but nothing is ever achieved. The hands remain as empty as ever. When this has been seen, when you have looked into your life and seen all your motives failing...

No motive has ever succeeded, no motive has ever brought any blessing to anybody. The motives only promise; the goods are never delivered. One motive fails and another motive comes in and promises you again and you are deceived again. Being deceived again and again by motives, one day you suddenly become aware – suddenly you see into it, and that very seeing is the beginning of meditation. It has no seed in it, it has no motive in it. If you are meditating for something, then you are concentrating, not meditating. Then you are still in the world – your mind is still interested in cheap things, in trivia. Then you are worldly. Even if you are meditating to attain to godliness, you are worldly. Even if you are meditating to attain to nirvana, you are worldly – because meditation has no goal.

Meditation is an insight that all goals are false. Meditation is an understanding that desires don't lead anywhere. Seeing that... And this is not a belief that you can get from me or from Buddha or from Jesus. This is not knowledge; you will have to see it. You can see it right now! You have lived, you have seen many motives, you have been in turmoil, you have thought about what to do, what not to do, and you have done many things. Where has it all led you? Just see into it! I'm not saying agree with me, I'm not saying believe in me. I'm simply making you alert to a fact that you have been neglecting. This is not a theory, this is a simple statement of a very simple fact. Maybe because it is so simple, that's why you go on without looking at it. Mind is always interested in complexities, because something can be done with a complex thing. You cannot do anything with a simple phenomenon.

The simple is overlooked, the simple is neglected, the simple is ignored. The simple is so obvious you never look into it. You go on searching for complexities – the complexity has a challenge in it. The complexity of a phenomenon, of a problem, of a situation, gives you a challenge. In that challenge comes energy, friction, conflict: you have to solve this problem, you have to prove that you can solve this problem. When a problem is there you are thrilled by the excitement, that there is a possibility to prove something. But what I am stating is a simple fact, it is not a problem. It gives you no challenge, it is simply there. You can look at it or you can avoid it. And it doesn't shout; it is so simple. You cannot even call it a still, small voice within you; it does not even whisper. It is simply there – you can look, you may not look.

See it! And when I say, "See it," see it right now, immediately. There is no need to wait. And be quick when I say, "See it"! Do see it, but quickly, because if you start thinking, if you don't see it quickly, immediately, in that split second the mind comes in and the mind starts brooding, and the mind starts bringing thoughts, and the mind starts bringing prejudices. And you are in a philosophical state – many thoughts. Then you have to choose what is right and what is wrong, and speculation has started. You missed the existential moment.

The existential moment is right now. Just have a look, and that is meditation – that look is a meditation. Just seeing the facticity of a certain thing, of a certain state, is meditation. Meditation has no motive, hence there is no center to it. And because there is no motive and no center, there is no self in it. You don't function from a center in meditation, you act out of nothingness. The response out of nothingness is what meditation is all about.

Mind concentrates: it acts out of the past. Meditation acts in the present, out of the present. It is a pure response to the present, it is not reaction. It acts not out of conclusions, it acts seeing the existential.

Watch in your life: there is a great difference when you act out of conclusions. You see a man, you feel attracted – a beautiful man, looks very good, looks innocent. His eyes are beautiful, the vibe is beautiful. But then the man introduces himself and he says, "I am a Jew" – and you are a Christian. Something immediately clicks and there is distance: now the man is no longer innocent, the man is no longer beautiful. You have certain ideas about Jews. Or, he is a Christian and you are a Jew; you have certain ideas about Christians – what Christianity has done to Jews in the past, what other Christians have done to Jews, how they have tortured Jews down the ages...and suddenly he is a Christian – and something immediately changes.

This is acting out of conclusions, prejudices, not looking at this man – because this man may not be the man that you think a Jew has to be: each Jew is a different kind of man, each Hindu is a different kind of man, so is each Mohammedan. You cannot act out of prejudices. You cannot act by categorizing people. You cannot pigeonhole people; nobody can be pigeonholed. You may have been deceived by a hundred Communists, and when you meet the hundred and first Communist, don't go on believing in the category that you have made in your mind: that Communists are deceptive – or anything. This may be a different type of man, because no two persons are alike.

Whenever you act out of conclusions, it is mind. When you look into the present and you don't allow any idea to obstruct the reality, to obstruct the fact, you just look into the fact and act out of that look, *that* is meditation.

Meditation is not something you do in the morning and you are finished with it, meditation is something that you have to go on living every moment of your life. Walking, sleeping, sitting, talking, listening – it has to become a kind of climate. A relaxed person remains in it. A person who goes on dropping the past remains meditative. Never act out of conclusions; those conclusions are your conditionings, your prejudices, your desires, your fears, and all the rest of it. In short, you are there!

You means your past. *You* means all your experiences of the past. Don't allow the dead to overrule the living, don't allow the past to influence the present, don't allow death to overpower your life – that's what meditation is. In short, in meditation you are not there. The dead is not controlling the living.

Meditation is a kind of experience which gives you a totally different quality to live your life. Then you don't live like a Hindu, or a Mohammedan, Indian or German; you simply live as consciousness. When you live in the moment and there is nothing interfering, attention is total because there is no distraction – distractions come from the past and the future. When attention is total the act is total. It leaves no residue. It goes on freeing you, it never creates cages for you, it never imprisons you. And that is the ultimate goal of Buddha; that's what he calls nirvana.

Nirvana means freedom – utterly, absolute, unobstructed. You become an open sky. There is no border to it, it is infinite. It is simply there. And then there is nothingness all around you, within and without. Nothingness is the function of a meditative state of consciousness. And in that nothingness is benediction. That nothingness itself is the benediction.

Now the sutras:

Therefore, O Sariputra, it is because of his non-attainmentness that a bodhisattva, through having relied on the perfection of wisdom, dwells without thought-coverings. In the absence of thought-coverings he has not been made to tremble, he has overcome what can upset, and in the end he attains to nirvana.

Remember, that "therefore" is always an indication that Buddha is going on looking into Sariputra's nothingness – as he goes on feeling that his energies are relaxing, that his energies are no longer in turmoil, that he is not brooding but listening, that he is not thinking but is just there with Buddha, present, open, available. That "therefore" indicates to that unfoldment of Sariputra's being. Buddha is seeing more and more petals are opening so he can go a step further, so he can take Sariputra a little deeper. Sariputra is available.

This "therefore" is not logical, this "therefore" is existential. Looking into Buddha, Sariputra is unfolding. And looking into Sariputra, Buddha is ready to take him a little further towards the beyond. Each statement is going deeper and higher.

Therefore, O Sariputra, it is because of his non-attainment-ness that a bodhisattva, through having relied on the perfection of wisdom, dwells without thought-coverings. Each single word has to be meditated upon – not concentrated on, mind you, but meditated upon; listened to, looked into, not contemplated, not thought about. These things are higher than thought, bigger than thought. Thought is silly in these realms.

First he says: ...*it is because of his non-attainmentness...* Meditation cannot be attained, because meditation cannot have a motive. When you attain something you attain through a motive. When you attain something you always have to work for the future and plan for the future. You cannot attain anything right now – except meditation. Let me repeat it: you cannot attain anything right now, except meditation. Why? If you want money you cannot attain it right now, you will have to work hard for it; legally, illegally, but you will have to work for it.

There are slow ways, you may become a businessman;

and there are faster ways, you may become a politician – but you will have to do something. Slow or fast, but time will be needed. Time is a must. Without time you cannot attain money. If there is no time, how can you attain in this very moment? Even if you want to rob a neighbor, even if you want to pick the pocket of the person who is sitting by your side, that will take time. Time is a must. If you want to become famous, time will be needed. If you want to become politically powerful, time will be needed.

Only meditation can be attained right now, this very moment, instantaneously. Why? – because it is your nature. Why? – because it is already there. You have not claimed it, that's right; but it remains there, unclaimed. You can claim it right now. Not even a single moment has to be lost.

...*it is because of his non-attainmentness*... Nirvana is nothing but meditation come to a full circle. God is nothing but the bud of meditation become a flower.

These are not attainments, these are your very realities. You can go on overlooking them for ages, neglecting them for ages, but you cannot lose them; they are there, just sitting inside you. Any day you close your eyes and look you will start laughing. You have been searching for this blessing, and searching in wrong places. You were searching for this security that comes out of nothingness, but you were searching in money, bank balances, this and that. And it never happened through that. It cannot happen through that. Nothing outside you can make your life secure. The outside is insecure; how can it make your life secure? The government cannot make your life secure because the government itself is insecure – a revolution may be coming. The bank cannot make your life secure because the bank may go bankrupt. Only banks can go bankrupt, what else? The woman that you love cannot make your life secure – she may fall in love with somebody else. The man that you love cannot make your life secure – he may die.

All these things remain there. So the more you have securities outside the more insecure you become, because then you are afraid of the bank going bankrupt. If you don't have any account you don't care; let it go bankrupt any day. But if you have a bank account there then you are worried. Then you have attained to one more insecurity: the possibility of the bank going bankrupt. Now you cannot sleep because you go on thinking about what is going to happen.

If you have put your trust in anything outside, it creates more insecurity. That's why the richer a person becomes, the more insecure. And I am not in favor of poverty, remember. I am not saying be poor. Poverty has nothing holy in it. And I am not saying that the poor person is secure; he has his insecurities. The rich man has his insecurities; of course the rich man's insecurities are more complex and the poor man's insecurities are simple, but the insecurities are there. And I'm not saying that to be poor is something very special, or that to be poor is something very important and significant, or that you can brag that you are poor.

To be poor has nothing to do with spirituality. Neither has being rich anything to do with spirituality. Those are irrelevant facts. The poor also looks outside as much as the rich. Maybe the poor has only a bullock cart and the rich has a Cadillac, but that doesn't matter. The bullock cart is as much outside as the Cadillac; both look outside. The rich may have many bank accounts, and the poor may have just a small purse or may have a little money saved, but that doesn't matter – both look outside.

Security is on the inward path, because there you come to know that there is nobody to die, that there is nobody to suffer, that there is nothing that can happen, that there is pure sky. Clouds come and go, and the sky abides. Lives come and go, forms come and go, but the nothingness abides.

This nothingness is already there. That's why Buddha says it can be attained only when you understand that it is nonattainable. It can be attained only when you understand the basic fact: that it is already there, that it is already the case.

This emptiness that is there is not in any way to be evolved, developed. It is fully there. Hence it can be attained in a single moment. Buddha calls it "full emptiness," because emptiness can only be full if it is there. If it is not full, that means something other than the emptiness is also there, and that something else will hamper, obstruct, and that something else will create a duality, and that something else will create a friction, and that something else will create tension, and that something else will create anxiety – you cannot be at ease with "something else."

Emptiness is there only when it is full, when all obstructions have been dropped, when you don't have anything inside, when nobody is there to be an observer to it. Buddha says: "This emptiness is not even an experience, because if you experience it that means you were there to experience it." It is you, so you cannot experience it. You can experience only something that is not you. Experience means duality – the observer and the observed, the knower and the known, the subject and the object, the seer and the seen. But there is only emptiness, nobody to see it, nobody to be seen, nothing as an object, nothing as a subject. This nondual emptiness is full. It is utterly full. Its fullness cannot be refined, its fullness cannot be added to. Nothing can be taken out of it because there is nothing, and nothing can be added to it; it is utterly full.

"Full emptiness" is not an experience, because there is no experiencer in it. Hence, Buddha says: "Spirituality is not an experience. God cannot be experienced." Those who say, "I have experienced God," either don't understand what they are saying or they are using a very, very inadequate language. You cannot experience God. In that experience you are not found. The experience is there, but the experiencer is not there – so you cannot claim it as an experience. So, whenever somebody asked Buddha, "Have you experienced God?" he kept quiet; he did not say a single word. He immediately changed the subject, he started talking about something else.

Whenever it was asked, his whole life, he consistently remained silent. Many people thought that he had not experienced God; that's why he kept quiet. But he's the only person who has not said anything – negative or positive. And it is not because he has not experienced. He has experienced, but it cannot be talked of as an experience; that's why he keeps quiet. That's why Jesus remained silent when Pontius Pilate asked, "What is truth?"

J. Krishnamurti makes a very subtle distinction between experience and experiencing, and that is a beautiful distinction: he says, "It is an experiencing, not an experience." It is a process, not a thing. It is alive, not dead. It is ongoing, not finished. You enter into God, and then it is an ongoing phenomenon: it goes on and on and on for eternity; you never come out of it. It is an experiencing, an alive process – like a river, like a flower opening and opening and opening, and going on opening. And there never comes any end to it.

To say that one has experienced God is stupid, cheap and silly. To say that one has attained *moksha,* nirvana, truth, is not very meaningful, because these are things which cannot be categorized as attainments.

So Buddha says: *Therefore, O Sariputra, it is because of his non-attainmentness...* When the mind has come to a stop and is no longer interested in attaining anything, then it attains buddhahood. When the mind has come to a full stop and is not going anywhere, it starts going inwards, it starts falling into one's own being, that abysmal abyss. Full emptiness is attained by a non-attainmentness. So don't become achievers, don't start thinking in terms of achievement – that you have to achieve this and that, that you have to attain godliness. These are games; the mind is again deceiving you. The name of the game changes but the game, the subtle game, remains the same.

...that a bodhisattva attains through non-attainmentness, through having relied on the perfection of wisdom... This is a very, very significant statement. Buddha says: "One should rely on nothing whatsoever." Now this is against the ordinary Buddhist religion, because the ordinary Buddhist religion has three fundamental refuges: *Buddham sharanam gachchhami, sangam sharanam gachchhami, dhammam sharanam gachchhami.* When the disciple comes to Buddha, he bows down to him, surrenders to him and says, "I take refuge in the Buddha – *buddham sharanam gachchhami.*" "I take refuge in the community of the Buddha – *sangam*

sharanam gachchhami." "I take refuge in the law taught by the Buddha – *dhammam sharanam gachchhami.*" And Buddha says here that one should not rely on anything; there is no refuge, nowhere any shelter.

This *Heart Sutra* has been called the soul of Buddhism, and the church of Buddha has been called the body. Those three refuges are for the very ordinary mind which is in search of some shelter, some prop, some support. These statements are for the highest soul – one who has come to the sixth, and is just hanging between the sixth and the seventh, just a little push...

Therefore, O Sariputra... It has been said that the first sermon of Buddha, which is called the *Sermon of the Turning of the Wheel of Religion, Dhamma Chakrapravatan Sutra* – that was his first sermon, near Varanasi – created the so-called ordinary religion, for the ordinary masses. In that sermon he declares, "Come and take refuge in Buddha; come and take refuge in the law taught by the Buddha; come and take refuge in the community, in the commune of the Buddha."

After twenty years he declares this second dispensation. He took twenty years to bring a few people to the highest possibility. This is called the second most important sermon. The first was in Saranath, near Varanasi, when he told people, "Come and take refuge in me. I have attained! Come and take refuge in me. I have reached! Come and partake of me. I have arrived! Come and follow me." That was for the ordinary mind; it is natural. Buddha could not have declared the *Heart Sutra*; the masses would not have been able to understand.

Then he worked for twenty years with his disciples. Now Sariputra is coming very close. Because of that closeness, he says:

Therefore, O Sariputra... "Now I can say it to you. I can say to you that having relied on the perfection of wisdom..." Only on one thing does one have to rely, and that is meditation. Only on one thing does one have to rely, and that is awareness, attentiveness. Only on one thing does one have to rely, that is one's own inner source, being. Everything else has to be dropped, all refuges.

Through having relied on nothing but the perfection of

meditation, what one has to do is not to rely on anything, worldly or otherwise, to let it all go, to give the resulting emptiness a free run, unobstructed by any for-or-against attitude, to stop relying on anything, to seek nowhere any refuge or support – that is the real renunciation.

Our separate self is a spurious reality which can maintain itself only by finding supports or props on which to lean or rely. To go for refuge to the three treasures is the central act of the Buddhist religion – refuge in the Buddha, refuge in the *sangha*, refuge in the *dhamma*. Here Buddha refutes that. It is not contradictory. He simply says that which you can understand. In my assertions you will find a thousand and one contradictions, because they have been in reference to different people. The more you will grow, different assertions will be made by me because my assertions are a response to you. I am not talking to the walls. I am talking to you, and I can give only that much which you can receive. The higher your consciousness, the deeper your consciousness, different things will be stated by me.

Naturally, those different statements will be very contradictory. If one goes for a logical consistency, he will not find any. You cannot find any logical consistency in Buddha's statements. That's why, the day Buddha died, Buddhism was divided into thirty-six schools. The exact day he died, and the disciples were divided into thirty-six schools.

What happened? – because he had been making so many statements to different people, because of their different consciousness and understanding, they all started quarreling and fighting. They said, "This has been said to me by Buddha!" Just think: the first five disciples, to whom he had said, "I have attained, now come to me and I will take you there"... If those first disciples met Sariputra and Sariputra said, "It is attained through a kind of non-attainmentness. One who declares that he has attained is wrong, because it cannot be attained," what would those first disciples have said? They would have said, "What are you talking about? We are the oldest disciples, the seniormost, and this was the first statement that Buddha has made to us: 'I have attained!' In fact we would have never followed him if he had not declared that. Because he declared it, we followed him. Our motive was clear: that he had attained, we also wanted to attain; that's why we followed him. And he said to us, 'I am your refuge. Come and take refuge in me. Let me be your shelter.' And what nonsense are you talking about? Buddha could not have said this. You must have misunderstood. Something has gone wrong, or you have fabricated it."

Now this statement, this *Heart Sutra*, was made in privacy. It was said to Sariputra, it was specifically addressed to Sariputra. It is like a letter. Sariputra cannot produce any proofs, because in those days tape recorders were not in existence. He can simply say, he can take an oath: "I am not saying anything untrue. Buddha has said to me, 'Rely only on your meditation and nothing else.'"

The mind that relies on something else is the spurious self, the ego. The ego cannot exist without props, it wants props. Something has to support it. Once all props have been removed, the ego falls to the ground and disappears. But only when the ego falls to the ground does that consciousness arise in you which is eternal, which is timeless, deathless.

Here, Buddha says: "There is no refuge, Sariputra. There is no remedy, Sariputra. There is nothing and nowhere to go. You are already there."

If you reach into this full-emptiness unprepared, it will give you a great trembling. If you are thrown into it by somebody... For example, sometimes people come to me with deep love and respect; they say, "Osho, why don't you push me a little harder?" If you are not ready for it and you are pushed into it, it is not going to help. It may hinder your progress for many lives to come. Once you have gone into that nothingness unprepared you will be so shocked, so frightened, so scared to death, that never again, for at least a few lives, will you come to any person who talks about nothingness, who talks about godliness. You will avoid. That fear will become a seed in you.

No, you cannot be pushed unprepared. You can be pushed only slowly, slowly, only in the same proportion as you are prepared.

Have you heard the famous statement of Søren Kierkegaard, the Danish philosopher, the founder of modern exis-
tentialism? He says, "Man is a trembling, constant trembling."
Why? – because death is there. Why? – because the fear is
there: "One day I may not be."

This is true about the ordinary mind: everybody is trembling. The problem is always, "To be or not to be." Death is
always hanging there. You cannot conceive of yourself disappearing into nothingness; it hurts, it frightens. And if you look
deep inside yourself, you will find yourself trembling with the
idea of being nothing. You want to be, you want to remain, you
want to persist. You want to persist forever. That's why people who don't know anything about their inner being go on
believing that the soul is immortal; not because they know, but
because of fear. Because of that trembling they have to believe
that the soul is immortal. That is a kind of wish fulfillment.

So any idiot who is talking about the immortality of the
soul will appeal to you. You will get hooked. Not that you have
understood what he is saying – he may not have understood
himself – but it will be very appealing. In India people believe in
the immortality of the soul, and you cannot find more cowardly
people anywhere else. For one thousand years they remained
slaves, slaves to very small countries. Anybody who came to
India conquered it with no difficulty at all. It was so simple. And
these are the people who believe in the immortality of the soul.
In fact, a country that believes in the immortality of the soul
cannot be conquered at all, because nobody will be afraid to
die. How can you conquer a person who is not afraid to die?
They would have all died, but they would not have yielded to
any kind of submission, they could not have yielded to any
conqueror. But for one thousand years, India remained a slave.
It remained a slave very easily.

England is a very small country, there are a few districts in
India which are bigger. England could rule over this big country easily; it was not difficult. Why? And these people believed
that the soul is immortal! But the belief is not their experience,
the belief is out of fear. Then everything is explained. These
are cowardly people, afraid, afraid to die; hence they cling to

the idea that the soul is immortal. Not that they know, not that they have experienced; they have never experienced anything like that, they have only experienced the death that surrounds. They are so afraid because of death. So on the one hand they go on believing in the immortality of the soul; on the other hand, anybody can torture them and they are ready to submit and touch the feet.

It is out of fear that man believes in immortality. It is out of fear that man believes in God. It is out of trembling. Søren Kierkegaard is right about the ordinary mind.

Another existentialist philosopher, Jean-Paul Sartre, says: "Man is condemned to be free." Why "condemned"? Why this ugly word *condemned*? Freedom – is it a kind of condemnation? Yes, for the ordinary mind it is, because freedom means danger. Freedom means you cannot rely on anything, you have to rely only on yourself. Freedom means all props have been taken away, all supports disappear. Freedom basically means nothingness. You are free only when you are nothing.

Listen to what Sartre says: "Man, as freedom, becomes anguish." Anguish? Out of freedom? Yes, if you are not ready for it, if you are not prepared to go into it, it is anguish. Nobody wants to be free, notwithstanding what people go on saying. Nobody wants to be free. People want to be slaves because in slavery the responsibility can be thrown on somebody else. You are never responsible, you are just a slave: what can you do? You did only that which was ordered.

But when you are free, you are afraid. Responsibility arises. Each act, and you feel responsible: if you do this, this may happen; or if you do the other thing, then something else may happen. Then choice is yours, and choice creates trembling. And Jean-Paul Sartre is right about the ordinary mind: freedom creates anguish.

He says, "Man is condemned to be free," because freedom creates dread. It is dreadful freedom. Nothing can guarantee me against myself when I am free. There is no value given to me in which I can take shelter. I have to create those values myself. I decide the meaning of myself and my universe, alone, unjustifiable, and without excuse. I am one unveiling of freedom, you are another. My freedom is a constant unveiling of my being, so is yours. Our uniqueness consists in the fact that each of us does this in his own way.

But Sartre thinks freedom creates anguish, and freedom is a kind of condemnation, a curse. And Kierkegaard says, "Man is a constant trembling." And Buddha wants you to go into this freedom, into this nothingness. Naturally, you have to be prepared for it.

Sariputra is ready now.

Therefore, O Sariputra, it is because of his non-attainmentness that a bodhisattva, through having relied on the perfection of wisdom, dwells without thought-coverings. In the absence of thought-coverings he has not been made to tremble,
he has overcome what can upset, and in the end he attains to nirvana.

...he has overcome what can upset... and he has no trembling in this nothingness.

It looks almost impossible to the ordinary mind: how can you remain without trembling when you are disappearing? When you are melting into the unknown how can you remain unscared? How can you manage not to escape? How can you manage not to start finding props and shelters and supports so that you can again create that feeling of being the ego, the self?

That's why Buddha had to wait for twenty years. And then, too, he stated this truth to Sariputra in a personal dialogue, not as a public sermon. And if people did not believe Sariputra, they are also right because Buddha had been saying something else to them.

Remember this about me! Remember this: my statements are contradictory because they are made to different people, they are made to different consciousnesses. And the more you grow, the more I will be contradictory; the more I will have to refute what I have said before because it will no longer be relevant to you. With your growing consciousness I will have to respond in a different way. Each turn in your consciousness will be a turn in my statements. And when I am gone don't create thirty-six schools – because thirty-six won't do!

Nothingness brings freedom. Freedom from the self is the ultimate freedom. There is no freedom higher than that. Nothingness is freedom. And it is not anguish, as Jean-Paul Sartre says, and it is not trembling, as Kierkegaard says. It is benediction, it is the ultimate bliss. It is not trembling because there is nobody to tremble.

Meditation prepares you for that, because as you enter into meditation you find less and less of yourself every day. And the less you find yourself, in the same proportion grow your blessings, your benediction, your blissfulness. Slowly, slowly, you learn the mathematics of the inner world – that the more you are, the more in hell; the less you are, the more in heaven. The day you are not, it is nirvana; the ultimate home has arrived. You have come full circle, you have become a child again. There is no self any more.

Remember, freedom does not mean the freedom of the self. Freedom means: freedom *from* the self. To Sartre it means "freedom of the self." That's why it feels like a condemnation; the self remains. It becomes free, but it remains and that's why there is fear.

If freedom is such that the self has disappeared in it, and there is only freedom and nobody free, then who can tremble, and who can feel the anguish, and who can feel condemned? Then there is no question of choice; that freedom acts on its own. One acts out of choicelessness, and there is no responsibility left – because there is nobody who can feel any responsibility. Nothingness acts. *Wei-wu-wei* – non-action acts. It is a response between the inner nothingness and the outer nothingness, and there is nothing obstructing.

...it is because of his non-attainmentness that a bodhisattva, through having relied on the perfection of wisdom – alone – dwells without thought-coverings. Now there is no thought-covering. And thought-covering is the barrier that divides you from the outer nothingness. That's what I was saying last night to Neelamber, the ex-Mark that I talked about yesterday.

Yesterday evening he entered into sannyas; he became

Neelamber. *Neelamber* means blue sky. What is dividing the outer sky from the inner sky? Your thought-coverings. Those are the clothes that don't allow your nudity to be in touch with the sky, your nude being to be bridged with the sky. The thought that you are a Hindu, the thought that you are a Christian, the thought that you are a Communist or a Fascist, divides. The thought that you are beautiful or ugly divides. The thought that you are intelligent or unintelligent divides. Any kind of thought – and the division. And you have millions of thoughts. You will have to peel yourself like you peel an onion, covering after covering. You peel one cover, another layer is there; peel it, another layer is there. And naturally when you peel an onion tears come to the eyes; it is painful. When you start uncovering your being, it is more painful. It is not like taking your clothes off, it is like taking your skin off.

But if you go on peeling, one day you come to when the whole onion has disappeared and only nothingness is left in your hands. That nothingness is bliss.

Buddha says a bodhisattva ...*dwells without thought-coverings*. He is here, but he is nobody; he is here, but he has no ideas; he is here, but he has no thoughts. Not that he cannot use thoughts: I go on using thoughts continuously. I am talking to you right now, I have to use the mind and thoughts – but they don't cover me. They are by the side. Whenever I need, I use them. Whenever I am not using them, they are not there – my inner sky and the outer sky are one. And even while I am using them I know that they cannot divide me. They are instrumental, you can use them, but you are not in any way covered by them.

...*dwells without thought-coverings*. Buddha says there are three kinds of thought-coverings. The first is *karma averna* – incomplete acts. Untotal acts cover your being. Each act wants to be completed. There is an intrinsic urge in everything to complete itself. Whenever you allow some act to hang around you incomplete, it covers you: *karma averna*, karma that covers you.

The second is *klesas averna*. Greed, hate, jealousy and

things like that: they are called *klesas*, impurities; they cover you.

Have you seen it? An angry person remains almost always angry – sometimes less, sometimes more, but angry all the same. He is ready to jump upon anything. He is ready, with any excuse, to go into rage. He is boiling within. And so is the jealous person: the jealous person goes on searching to find something about which he or she can be jealous. The jealous wife goes on looking in the pockets of the husband to see if she can find something, in his letters, in his files to see if she can find something.

Whenever Mulla Nasruddin comes home there is a fight, for something or the other. His wife is such a great searcher that she always finds something or other. A phone number in his diary, and she becomes suspicious. A hair on his coat, and she goes into a great investigation – where has this hair come from?

One day she could not find anything, not even a hair. Mulla had done everything that day; she still started crying and weeping.

And Mulla said, "Now what is the matter? Not even a single hair have you been able to find on my coat...?"

She said, "That's why I'm crying. So now you have started going with bald women!"

It is very difficult, really, to find a bald woman, but that is the mind of a jealous person. These are coverings. Buddha calls them *klesas*, impurities; the egoist is always in search of something to either brag about or to feel hurt about. The possessive person is always in search of finding something so that he can show his possessiveness, or in finding something negative so that he can fight for it.

People go on – and I'm not talking about others, I am talking about you. Just watch your mind, watch what you go on searching for. Watch your mind for twenty-four hours and you will come across all these coverings, *avarnas*.

There are either incomplete acts, or impurities; or, the

third is called *ghaya avarnas* – beliefs, opinions, ideologies, knowledge coverings. They don't allow you to know, they don't give you enough space to see. These three coverings have to be dropped.

When these three coverings are dropped, then one dwells in nothingness. That word *dwelling* is also to be understood.

Buddha says: "He dwells in nothingness." It is his home, nothingness is his home. He dwells in it, it is a dwelling. He loves it, he is utterly in tune with it. It is not alien, he does not feel like an outsider there. And he does not feel like he's staying in a hotel and tomorrow he will have to leave it. It is his dwelling. When thought-coverings have been dropped, nothingness is your home. You are in utter harmony with it.

Kierkegaard and Sartre have never been there. They have only speculated about it. They only think about it, about how it will be. That's why Kierkegaard feels trembling. He simply thinks, as you think...

Just think how it will be when you die, and you will be put on a funeral pyre, and you will be finished forever. And then you will not be able to see these beautiful trees, these beautiful people, and you will not laugh again, and you will not love again, and you will not see the stars. And the world will continue, and you will not be here at all. Can't you feel a shivering? Can't you feel a trembling? All will continue – the birds will sing and the sun will rise and the oceans will roar and some eagle will go on and on flying higher and higher, and the flowers will be there and their fragrance, and the fragrance of the wet earth – all that will be there. And suddenly one day you will not be, and your body will be dead. This beautiful body that you have been living with and you have been taking so much care of: it was ill and you were disturbed and one day it will be so useless that the people who had loved it, the same people, will take it to a funeral pyre and set it on fire. Just visualize it. Speculate, and trembling comes.

Kierkegaard must have speculated about it. He must have been a very fear-oriented person. A story is told about him that he was a rich man's son: the father died; he had left Kierkegaard enough money so he never worked, he continuously contemplated. He could easily afford it; there was nothing to do. He had enough money in the bank. The first day of every month he would go to the bank – that was his whole work – to take some money. And then he would live and meditate. In his sense of meditation it means contemplation, brooding, thinking. That's what the English word *meditation* means. It is not a right translation for *dhyana*.

When people come to me and I tell them to meditate they say, "On what?" The English word means meditating upon something, some object. The Indian word *dhyana* means being in it, not meditating on something. It is a state, not an activity.

So he would contemplate and think, and brood and philosophize. It is said that he fell in love with a beautiful woman, but could not decide to marry or not to marry. The very phenomenon of love became a trembling in him. For three years he brooded over it, and finally he decided not to marry. And he was in love. His whole life he could not forget the woman, his whole life he felt miserable for the woman. The woman was in love, he was in love; still he decided not to marry. Why? – because the very idea of love created trembling in him.

Love is a kind of death. If you really love a person you die in him, you disappear in him.

When you make love... I have to use this word *make* – it is not right, but no language is really right. So remember, I have to use words with all their limitations. Love cannot be made. "Making love" is a wrong expression: it happens. But when it happens, when you are in a loving space with somebody, fear comes because you are disappearing. That's why very, very many people, millions of people, never attain to orgasm, because orgasm is a death.

And Kierkegaard was so much in love that he became afraid that he may lose himself in this woman. That fear was too much. He dropped the idea. He refused, he would not marry; he suffered for his whole life – that he accepted – but because of fear... He was a fear-oriented person.

He lived perfectly well, doing nothing, just philosophizing. And there is a very strange anecdote of the day he died. He died when he was coming from the bank. It was the first day of some month; he was coming from the bank, taking his money, but this was the last money. He died on the road. It is thought that he died out of fear, because now no more money was left in the bank. He was perfectly healthy, he was not ill, there was no reason for him to die so suddenly. But coming from the bank – and the bank manager had said, "This is the last; your money is finished" – he could not reach his home. He died on the road.

He could not have experienced the nothingness Buddha is talking about. He must have only thought about it – hence, the fear. And Jean-Paul Sartre also has not been in that space called meditation. He is not a meditator; he is again a thinker, and utterly Western. He has not known the Eastern way to go in. Hence freedom looks like a condemnation, and freedom looks like anguish.

The truth is just the opposite. If you go into freedom, into nothingness, there is bliss. If you go into that utter death called love, there is satori, *samadhi*. Buddha says: "He dwells in that nothingness, it is his house." It is not anguish, it is not trembling, it is not a condemnation. He dwells there. It is his home.

...he has not been made to tremble, he has overcome what can upset, and in the end he attains to nirvana. Buddha does not say anything else. He says: "Go into this state of nothingness, then nirvana is a natural outcome. In the end it comes on its own accord." You need not worry about it; you cannot do anything about it in the first place. You just go into this nothingness, and then nothingness starts growing, growing, becomes vaster and vaster, and one day becomes your whole existence. Then there is nirvana – you have ceased to be. You have disappeared into the universe.

Somebody asked Buddha, "When you are gone and you will never be coming into the body again, what will happen to you?"

And he said, "I will disappear into existence. If you taste existence, you will taste me."

And yes, that is true: if you taste existence you will taste all the buddhas – Krishna, Christ, Buddha, Mahavira, Zarathustra,

Lao Tzu, Kabir, Nanak. You will taste all the buddhas. The day you enter into that nothingness, you will be welcomed by all the buddhas. The whole existence is throbbing with buddhahood because so many buddhas have disappeared into it. They have raised the very level of existence.

You are fortunate, because before you so many buddhas have entered into existence. When you go there, you will not be unwelcome.

All those who appear as buddhas in the three periods of time
fully awake to the utmost, right and perfect enlightenment
because they have relied on the perfection of wisdom.

The only refuge is the perfection of wisdom, the perfection of meditation. In the past it has been so, in the present it is so, in the future it will be so. Anybody who becomes a buddha becomes one through meditation. Take refuge in meditation. Take refuge in nothingness.

Enough for today.

CHAPTER 8

the path of intelligence

The first question:

Osho,
Can the intellect be a door to enlightenment, or is
enlightenment only achieved through surrender?

Enlightenment is always through surrender, but surrender is achieved through intelligence. Only idiots cannot surrender. To surrender you need great intelligence. To see the point of surrender is the climax of insight; to see the point that you are not separate from existence is the highest that intelligence can give to you.

There is no conflict between intelligence and surrender. Surrender is through intelligence, although when you surrender intelligence is also surrendered. Through surrender intellect commits a suicide. Seeing the futility of itself, seeing the absurdity of itself, seeing the anguish that it creates, it disappears. But it happens through intelligence. And especially with Buddha, the path is of intelligence. The very word *buddha* means awakened intelligence.

In the *Heart Sutra* one-fourth of the words used mean intelligence. The word *buddha* means awake, *bodhi* means awakening, *sambodhi* means perfect awakening, *abhisambuddha* means the fully awake, *bodhisattva* means ready to become fully awake. All go back to the same root, *budh*, which means intelligence. The word *buddhi*, intellect, also comes from the same root. The root *budh* has many dimensions to it. There is no single English word that can translate it; it has many implications. It is very fluid and poetic. In no other language does any word like *budh* exist, with so many meanings. There are at least five meanings to the word *budh*.

The first is to awake, to wake oneself up, and to awaken others, to be awake. As such, it is opposed to being asleep, in the slumber of delusion from which the enlightened awakens as from a dream. That is the first meaning of intelligence, *budh*: to create an awakening in you.

Ordinarily man is asleep. Even while you think you are awake, you are not. Walking on the road, you are fully awake – in your mind. But looked at from the vision of a buddha, you are fast asleep, because a thousand and one dreams and thoughts are clamoring inside you. Your inner light is very clouded. It is a kind of sleep. Yes, your eyes are open, obviously, but people can walk in a dream, in sleep, with eyes open. And Buddha says: "You are also walking in sleep, with eyes open."

But your inner eye is not open. You don't know yet who you are; you have not looked into your own reality. You are not awake. A mind full of thoughts is not awake, cannot be awake. Only a mind which has dropped thoughts and thinking, which has dispersed the clouds around it – and the sun is burning bright, and the sky is utterly empty of clouds – is the mind which has intelligence, which is awake.

Intelligence is the capacity to be in the present. The more you are in the past or are in the future, the less intelligent you are. Intelligence is the capacity to be here-now, to be in this moment and nowhere else. Then you are awake.

For example, you are sitting in a house and the house suddenly catches fire; your life is in danger. Then for a moment you will be awake. In that moment you will not think many thoughts. In that moment you forget your whole past. In that moment you will not be clamored at by your psychological memories – that you had loved a woman thirty years earlier, and boy, it was fantastic! Or, the other day you had been to the Chinese restaurant, and still the taste lingers on, and the aroma and the smell of the freshly cooked food. You will not be in those thoughts. No, when your house is on fire you cannot afford this kind of thinking. Suddenly you will rush to *this* moment: the house is on fire and your life is at stake. You will not dream about the future, about what you are going to do tomorrow. Tomorrow is no longer relevant, yesterday is no longer relevant, even today is no longer relevant! – only this moment, this split moment. That is the first meaning of *budh*: intelligence.

And then there are great insights. A man who wants to be really awake, wants to be really a buddha, has to live each moment in such intensity as you live only rarely, rarely, in some danger.

The first meaning is opposite to sleep. And naturally, you can see reality only when you are not asleep. You can face it, you can look into the eyes of truth – or call it godliness – only when you are awake. Do you understand the point of intensity, the point of being on fire? Utterly awake, there is insight; that insight brings freedom, that insight brings truth.

The second meaning of *budh* is to recognize: to become aware of, acquainted with, to notice, give heed to. And so a buddha is one who has recognized the false as the false, and has his eyes opened to the true as the true. To see the false as the false is the beginning of understanding what truth is. Only when you see the false as the false can you see what truth is. You cannot go on living in illusions, you cannot go on living in your beliefs, you cannot go on living in your prejudices if you want to know truth. The false has to be recognized as false. That is the second meaning of *budh*: recognition of the false as false, of the untrue as untrue.

For example, you have believed in God; you were born a Christian or a Hindu or a Mohammedan. You have been taught that God exists, you have been made afraid of God: that if you don't believe you will suffer, that you will be punished, that God is very ferocious, that God will never forgive you. The Jewish God says, "I am a very jealous God. Worship only me and nobody else!" The Mohammedan God also says the same thing: "There is only one God, and no other God; and there is only one prophet of God, Mohammed, and there is no other prophet."

This conditioning can go so deep in you that it can go on lingering even if you start disbelieving in God.

Just the other day Mulla Nasruddin was here, and I asked him, "Mulla Nasruddin, since you have turned into a Communist, you have become a comrade, what about God?"

He said, "There is no God! – and Mohammed is the only prophet."

A conditioning can go so deep: Mohammed remains the prophet.

You have been brought up to believe in God, and you have believed. This is a belief. Whether God exists or not has nothing to do with your belief. Truth has nothing to do with your belief. Whether you believe or not makes no difference to truth. But if you believe in God you will go on seeing – at least, thinking – that you see God. If you don't believe in God, that disbelief in God will prevent you from knowing. All beliefs prevent, because they become prejudices around you, they become thought-coverings – what Buddha calls *avarnas*.

The man of intelligence does not believe in anything, and does not disbelieve in anything. The man of intelligence is simply open to recognizing whatsoever is the case. If God is there he will recognize – but not according to his belief; he has no belief. Only in a nonbelieving, nondisbelieving intelligence can truth appear. When you already believe you don't allow truth any space to come to you. Your prejudice is enthroned, already enthroned. You cannot see something which goes against your belief; you will become afraid, you will become shaky, you will start trembling. You have put so much into your belief – so much life, so much time, so many prayers, five prayers every day. For fifty years a man has been devoted to his belief; now how can he suddenly recognize the fact that there is no God? A man has put his whole life into Communism, believing that there is no God; how can he come to see if God is there? He will go on avoiding.

I'm not saying anything about whether God is or is not. What I am saying is something concerned with you, not with God. A mind, a clear mind, is needed, an intelligence is needed which does not cling to any belief. Then you are like a mirror: you reflect that which is, you don't distort it. That is the second meaning of *budh*.

An intelligent person is neither a Communist nor a Catholic. An intelligent person does not believe, does not disbelieve. That is not his way. He looks into life, and whatsoever is there he is ready to see it. He has no barriers to his vision; his vision is transparent. Only those few people attain to truth.

The third meaning of the root *budh*, intelligence, is to know, to understand. The Buddha knows that which is; he understands that which is, and in that very understanding is free from all bondage: to know in the sense of to understand, not in the sense of knowledgeability. Buddha is not knowledgeable. An intelligent person does not care much about information and knowledge. An intelligent person cares much more for the capacity to know. His real authentic interest is in knowing, not in knowledge.

Knowing gives you understanding; knowledge only gives you a feeling of understanding without giving you real understanding. Knowledge is a pseudo-coin, it is deceptive. It only gives you a feeling that you know, and you don't know at all. You can go on accumulating knowledge as much as you want, you can go on hoarding, you can become very, very knowledgeable. You can write books, you can have degrees, you can have PhD's, DLitt's, and still you remain the same ignorant, stupid person you have always been. Those degrees don't change you; they *can't* change you. In fact your stupidity becomes stronger: it has degrees now! It can prove itself through certificates. It cannot prove through life, but it can prove through the certificates. It cannot prove in any other way, but it will carry degrees, certificates, recognitions from the society; people think you know, and you also think you know.

Have you not seen this? The people who are thought to be very knowledgeable are as ignorant as anybody, sometimes more ignorant. It is very rare to find intelligent people in the academic world, very rare. I have been in the academic world, and I say it through my experience. I have seen intelligent farmers, I have not seen intelligent professors. I have seen intelligent woodcutters, I have not seen intelligent professors. Why? What has gone wrong with these people?

One thing has gone wrong: they can depend on knowledge. They need not become knowers, they can depend on knowledge. They have found a secondhand way. The firsthand way needs courage. The firsthand way, knowing, only few people can afford – the adventurers, people who go beyond the ordinary path where crowds move, people who take small footpaths into the jungle of the unknowable. The danger is they may get lost. The risk is high.

When you can get secondhand knowledge, why bother? You can just sit in your chair. You can go to the library or to the university, you can collect information. You can make a big pile of information and sit on top of it. Through knowledge your memory becomes bigger and bigger, but your intelligence does not become bigger. Sometimes it happens when you don't know much, when you are not very knowledgeable, that you will have to be intelligent in some moments.

I have heard...

A woman bought a tin of fruit but she could not open the tin. She did not know how to. So she rushed to her study to look in the cookbook. By the time she looked in the book and found out the page and the reference, and came rushing back ready to open the tin, the servant had already opened it.

She asked, "But how did you do it?"

The servant said, "Madam, when you can't read, you have to use your mind."

Yes, that's how it happens. That's why farmers, gardeners, woodcutters, are more intelligent, have a kind of freshness around them. They can't read, so they have to use their minds. One has to live and one has to use one's mind.

The third meaning of *budh* is to know, in the sense of understanding. The Buddha has seen that which is. He understands that which is, and in that very understanding is free from all bondage. What does it mean? It means you are afraid.

For example, these *Heart Sutra* talks are making many people feel fear. Many people have sent their messages: "Osho, no more! You make us afraid of nothingness and death." Prageet is very afraid. Vidya is very afraid, and many more. Why? You don't want to get rid of fear? If you want to get rid of fear you will have to understand fear. You want to avoid the fact that the fear is there, the fear of death is there.

Now Prageet, on the surface, looks a strong man – a Rolfer – but deep down he's very afraid of death; he is one of the most afraid persons around here. Maybe that's why on the surface he has taken the stance of strength, power, a bully. That's what a Rolfer is!

I have heard that recently the Devil in hell is appointing Rolfers: they torture people for their own sakes, and they torture very technically.

If you are afraid inside, you will have to create something strong around you, like a hard shell, so nobody comes to know that you are afraid. And that is not the only point – you also will not know that you are afraid because of that hard shell. It will protect you from others, it will protect you from your own understanding.

An intelligent person does not escape from any fact. If it is fear he will go into it – because the way out is to go through. If he feels fear and trembling arising in him, he will leave everything aside: first this fear has to be gone through. He will go into it, he will try to understand. He will not try: "How *not* to be afraid?" He will not ask that question. He will simply ask one question: "What is this fear? It is there, it is part of me, it is my reality. I have to go into it, I have to understand it. If I don't understand it then a part of me will always remain unknown to me. And how am I going to know who I am if I go on avoiding parts? I will not understand fear, I will not understand death, I will not understand anger, I will not understand my hatred, I will not understand my jealousy, I will not understand this and that." Then how are you going to know yourself?

All these things are you! This is your being. You have to go into everything that is there, every nook and corner. You have to explore fear. Even if you are trembling it is nothing to be worried about: tremble, but go in. It is far better to tremble than to escape, because once you escape, that part will remain unknown to you, and you will become more and more afraid to look at it because that fear will go on accumulating. It will become bigger and bigger if you don't go into it right now, this moment. Tomorrow it will have lived twenty-four hours more. Beware! – it will have got more roots in you, it will have bigger foliage, it will become stronger; and then it will be more difficult to tackle. It is better to go right now, it is already late.

And if you go into it and you see it... Seeing means without prejudice. Seeing means that you don't condemn fear as bad from the very beginning. Who knows? – it is not bad. Who knows that it is? The explorer has to remain open to all the possibilities; he cannot afford a closed mind. A closed mind and exploration don't go together. He will go into it. If it brings suffering and pain, he will suffer the pain but he will go into it. Trembling, hesitant, but he will go into it: "It is my territory, I have to know what it is. Maybe it is carrying some treasure for me? Maybe the fear is only there to protect the treasure."

That's my experience, that's my understanding: if you go deep into your fear you will find love. That's why it happens that when you are in love, fear disappears. And when you are afraid you cannot be in love. What does this mean? A simple arithmetic – fear and love don't exist together. That means it must be the same energy that becomes fear; then there is nothing left to become love. It becomes love; then there is nothing left to become fear.

Go into fear, Prageet, Vidya, and all others who are feeling afraid. Go into it, and you will find a great treasure. Hidden behind fear is love, and hidden behind anger is compassion, and hidden behind sex is *samadhi*.

Go into each negative thing and you will find the positive. And knowing the negative and the positive, the third, the ultimate happens – the transcendental. That is the meaning of understanding, *budh*, intelligence.

The fourth meaning is to be enlightened and to enlighten. Buddha is the light, he has become the light. And since he's the light and he has become the light, he shows the light to others too, naturally, obviously. He is illumination. His darkness has disappeared, his inner flame is burning bright. Smokeless is his flame. This meaning is opposite to darkness and the corresponding blindness and ignorance. This is the fourth meaning: to become light, to become enlightened.

Ordinarily you are darkness, a continent of darkness, a dark continent, unexplored. Man is a little strange: he goes on exploring the Himalayas, he goes on exploring the Pacific, he goes on reaching for the moon and Mars; there is just one thing he never tries: exploring his inner being. Man has landed on the moon, and man has not landed yet in his own being. This is strange. Maybe landing on the moon is just an escape, going to Everest is just an escape. Maybe he does not want to go inside, because he's very afraid. He substitutes with some other explorations to feel good, otherwise you will have to feel very, very guilty. You start climbing a mountain and you feel good, and the greatest mountain is within you and is yet unclimbed. You start going, diving deep into the Pacific, and the greatest Pacific is within you, and uncharted, unmapped. And you start going to the moon – what foolishness! You are wasting your energy in going to the moon, and the real moon is within you – because the real light is within you.

The intelligent person will go inwards first. Before going anywhere else he will go into his own being; that is the first thing, and it should have the first preference. Only when you have known yourself can you go anywhere else. Then wherever you go you will carry a blissfulness around you, a peace, a silence, a celebration.

So the fourth meaning is to be enlightened.

Intelligence is the spark. Helped, cooperated with, it can become the fire, and the light, and the warmth. It can become light, it can become life, it can become love: those are all included in the word *enlightenment*. An enlightened person has no dark corners in his being. All is like the morning – the sun is on the horizon; the darkness of the night and the dismalness of the night have disappeared, and the shadows of the night have disappeared. The earth is again awake. To be a buddha is to attain to a morning, a dawn within you. That is the function of intelligence, the ultimate function.

And the fifth meaning of *budh* is to fathom. A depth is there in you, a bottomless depth, which has to be fathomed. Or, the fifth meaning can be to penetrate, to drop all that obstructs and penetrate to the very core of your being, the heart. That's why this sutra is called the *Heart Sutra*, *Prajnaparamita Hridayam Sutra* – to penetrate.

People try to penetrate many things in life. Your urge, your great desire for sex is nothing but a kind of penetration. But that is a penetration into the other. The same penetration has to happen into your own being: you have to penetrate yourself. If you penetrate somebody else it can give you a momentary glimpse, but if you penetrate yourself you can attain to the universal cosmic orgasm that remains and remains and remains.

A man meets an outer woman, and a woman meets an outer man: this is a very superficial meeting – yet meaningful, yet it brings moments of joy. When the inner woman meets the inner man... And you are carrying both inside you: a part of you is feminine, a part of you is masculine. Whether you are man or woman does not matter; everybody is bisexual.

The fifth meaning of the root *budh* means penetration. When your inner man penetrates your inner woman there is a meeting; you become whole, you become one. And then all desires for the outer disappear. In that desirelessness is freedom, is nirvana.

The path of Buddha is the path of *budh*. Remember that "buddha" is not the name of Gautama the Buddha, buddha is the state that he has attained. His name was Gautam

Siddhartha. Then one day he became a buddha, one day his *bodhi,* his intelligence bloomed.

Buddha means exactly what *Christ* means. Jesus' name is not Christ: that is the ultimate flowering that happened to him. So is it with Buddha. There have been many buddhas other than Gautam Siddartha.

Everybody has the capacity for *budh.* But *budh,* that capacity to see, is just like a seed in you – if it sprouts, becomes a big tree, blooms, starts dancing in the sky, starts whispering to the stars, you are a buddha.

The path of Buddha is the path of intelligence. It is not an emotional path, no, not at all. Not that emotional people cannot reach; there are other paths for them – the path of devotion, Bhakti yoga. Buddha's path is pure Gyan yoga, the path of knowing. Buddha's path is the path of meditation, not of love.

And just like *budh,* there is another root, *gya,* at the basis of *gyanam. Gyanam* means cognition, knowing. And the word *prajna,* which means wisdom – *prajnaparamita* – the wisdom of the beyond; or *sangya,* which means perception, sensitivity; or *vigyanam* which means consciousness, these roots come from *gya. Gya* means to know.

You will find these words repeated so many times in the sutra – not only in this sutra, but in all the sutras of the Buddha. You will find a few more words, repeated very often, and those words are *ved* – *ved* means to know; from *ved* comes the Hindu word *veda* – or *man,* which means mind; *manan* which means minding; or *chit,* which means consciousness; *chaitanya,* which again means consciousness. These words are almost like paved stones on the Buddha Way. His path is that of intelligence.

One thing more to be remembered: the sutra, it is true, points to something that lies far beyond the intellect. But the way to get to that is to follow the intellect as far as it will take you.

The intellect has to be used, not discarded; has to be transcended, not discarded. It can be transcended only when you have reached to the uppermost rung of the ladder. You have to go on growing in intelligence. Then a moment comes when intelligence has done all that it can do. In that moment say goodbye to intelligence. It has helped you a long way, it has brought you far enough, it has been a good vehicle. It has been a boat you crossed with: you have reached the other shore, then you leave the boat. Then you don't carry the boat on your head; that would be foolish.

Buddha's path goes through intelligence but goes beyond it. A moment comes when intelligence has given you all that it can give, then it is no longer needed. Then finally you drop it too, its work is finished. The disease is gone, now the medicine has to go too. And when you are free of the disease and the medicine too, only then are you free. Sometimes it happens that the disease is gone, and now you have become addicted to the medicine. This is not freedom.

A thorn is in your foot and is hurting. You take another thorn so that the thorn in your foot can be taken out with the help of the other. When you have taken the thorn out you throw both away; you don't save the one that has been helpful. It is now meaningless. The work of intelligence is to help you to become aware of your being. Once that work has happened and your being is there, now there is no need for this instrument. You can say goodbye, you can say thank you.

Buddha's path is the path of intelligence, pure intelligence, although it goes beyond it.

The second question:

Osho,
Is it true that one has to go through hell?

You need not go through hell because you are already there. Where else will you find hell? This is your ordinary state – hell. Don't think that hell is somewhere deep down below the earth. Hell is you. You, unaware, is what hell is. You, functioning unintelligently, that's what hell is. And because so many people are functioning unintelligently the world is always in anguish – so many neurotic people on the earth. Unless you are enlightened you remain neurotic, more or less. So many destructive people – because creativity is possible only when your intelligence is awakened.

Creativity is a function of intelligence. Stupid people can only be destructive. And that's what goes on: people go on preparing for more and more destruction. That's what your scientists do, that's what your politicians do.

I have heard a beautiful story:

After the Second World War, God was very puzzled. He could not believe his own eyes. Seeing Hiroshima, Nagasaki – he could not believe that he had created this kind of man. He started to think again, as if he had committed a mistake: he should have stopped with animals, he should not have created Adam and Eve because man was becoming so destructive.

To give a last chance he called three representatives from the world, one Russian, one American, one English. Those were the powerful people after the Second World War. He asked the Russian, "Why do you go on preparing for more and more destruction? If you need something, just ask me, and I will fulfill it immediately. But no more destruction."

The Russian looked very arrogantly at God and said, "Listen, first we don't believe that you are! We have our own trinity: Marx, Lenin, Stalin" – a very unholy trinity, but Communists have that trinity. "We believe in them, we don't believe in you. But if you want us to believe in you, you will have to give us proof."

"What is the proof?" God asked.

And the Russian said, "Destroy America, destroy it absolutely! Not a trace of this disease called America should be left behind. Then we will worship you, then our churches will start praying again, our temples will open. We will make new shrines for you."

God was very shocked: the very idea of destroying the whole of America!

Seeing him silent, the Russian said, "And if you cannot do it, don't be worried. We are going to do it anyway. It will take a little longer for us, but we are going to do it. You don't need to look so sad. If you cannot do it, just say you cannot do it."

God looked at the American and said, "What's your desire? What do you want?"

He said, "Nothing much, a very simple desire – that there should be no place for the Soviet Union on the map. We don't want to see the U.S.S.R. on the map. Not much, just remove... Everything is okay; it is just this U.S.S.R. that hurts. It hurts very much, it drives us crazy, and we will do anything to remove it. And if you don't do anything, with your blessings we are going to do it!"

Now God was even more puzzled and confused. It was okay from the Russian representative, because they don't believe in God. It's okay. But America? America believes in God, so there seems to be no difference between the believer and the nonbeliever, between the capitalist and the Communist, between the dictatorial and the democratic. There seems to be no essential difference, their desire is the same. He was thinking the English representative may be more human, understanding; at least he would be gentlemanly – and he was!

God asked him, "What is your desire? What do you want?"

The Englishman said, "We don't have any desire. Fulfill the desires of both of these simultaneously, and our desire is fulfilled!"

But this is how man has existed, down the ages: much more interested in destruction, destroying the other, than in living oneself, than in enjoying life. Man seems to be death-obsessed: wherever man moves he brings death, destruction.

This neurotic society exists because individuals are neurotic. This world is ugly because you are ugly! You contribute your ugliness to this world. And everybody goes on pooling ugliness, neuroses, and the world becomes more and more of a hell. You need not go anywhere else; this is the only hell there is.

But you can come out of it. By understanding how your mind is helping to create this hell, you can withdraw. And a single person withdrawing himself from creating this hell, non-cooperating, rebellious, becomes a great source of bringing heaven on the earth, becomes a gateway.

You need not go to hell, you are already there. You need to go to heaven now. And in fact when I say you need to go to heaven, what I mean exactly is that heaven needs to come to you. Be open to heaven. Let all your destructive energies be offered to creativity, let your darkness become a light, let your awareness become meditative, and you will become a door to God, and God can come through you into the world again.

That is the meaning of the Christian parable that Jesus is born to a woman, Mary, who is a virgin. This is a parable – significant, it has great meaning in it. But foolish people try to say that she was really physically a virgin. That is non-sense. But she was virgin: she was pure, utterly pure. She was heaven on the earth – only then could Jesus enter through her, only then could God extend his hand into the world.

Become a vehicle: let God play some instrument through you – a veena, a sitar. Let God play a song through you; you become his flute, a hollow bamboo. And that's what I have been telling you all these days: if you become a nothing-ness, you will be a hollow bamboo. You can become a flute, and God's song can descend unto the earth. It is needed very much. If even a little health is possible through you in this mad world... It is needed very much, it is needed urgently.

The third question:

Osho,
You said the other day that if you were a cab driver nobody
would be able to recognize you. I don't agree. At least I for
one would recognize you.

Madam, I don't believe you. You don't know enough about yourself. I appreciate your love for me, but I cannot say that you would be able to recognize me.

I will tell you a real story:

I used to stay with a family in a certain city in India for many years, a very rich family, millionaires. He was very respectful to me, he was a follower. When I used to go to his town he would touch my feet as many times as possible – at least four, five times every day.

Then after seven, eight years, he wanted to come to visit the place where I used to stay in Jabalpur. He came. Just to puzzle him, just to confuse him, I went to receive him at the station. That he had not expected, that I would come to receive him at the station.

He used to fall at my feet. That day he touched my feet, but halfheartedly – because a great ego arose in him: that I have come to receive him. He used to come to receive me for seven years and each year at least three or four times I used to visit his town. He had not expected this; he had expected that somebody would be there to take him to me. But that I myself would come to receive him? – that was not even in his dreams. He must have argued inside: "I am somebody, a millionaire…" That day he bowed down, but very halfheartedly. How can you bow down to somebody who has come to receive you at the station, with great respect?

We came out of the station, and when he saw that I was going to drive him back home, then all his respect disappeared. Then he started talking like a friend. The millionaire became very "famil-lionaire"! And after three days, when he left – I had gone to say goodbye, to give him a send-off – he did not touch my feet.

And the family that I used to live with all knew that I was playing a joke on him, and the poor fellow had got hooked in it. They all laughed when the train left. I said "Wait. Next time, let him come; he will expect me to touch his feet. And it will be no wonder if he forces me to touch his feet."

That's how things go, that's how mind functions. You recognize me, you love me, but you don't know your own mind. And in that experiment I lost one of my millionaire followers. I have been losing many followers that way, but I go on experimenting.

The fourth question:

Osho,
Why is it so hard for me to surrender to a man?

Then don't surrender. Why unnecessarily create trouble for yourself? Who is telling you to surrender to a man in the first place? Don't surrender. Why do you start taking unnecessary troubles on your head? If you don't feel like surrendering, don't surrender.

Just the other day a woman asked me, wrote a letter saying, "I have come here, but I don't feel that this place is for me. What should I do?" Go away! Get lost! Why bother?

She also has asked, "Should I listen to my heart, or should I trust you?" Listen to your heart, lady, and get lost as fast as you can. How can you trust me against your heart? Who will trust me? The heart trusts: if the heart is against, who is going to trust me? And why are you creating such a division in yourself? You will go schizophrenic, one part trying to surrender and forcing, and another part wanting to go. Either be here totally or go. If you can't surrender, don't surrender. Nobody is interested in your surrender.

Surrender cannot be done, you cannot force it. It comes when it comes. If you can't surrender to a man, that means you can't love a man. Out of love surrender comes naturally. If there is no love, surrender cannot be managed. Forget about it.

Maybe the questioner is a lesbian: perfectly good, surrender to a woman! At least surrender to somebody that you can surrender to. Maybe through that surrender you will learn to surrender to a man too. That's how one learns.

Each child is auto-sexual when born: he loves only himself, he cannot love anybody else. Then the child becomes homosexual: he loves somebody like him, he cannot love the opposite. Then, still growing, he becomes heterosexual: now he can love the opposite. That's what Jesus says: "Love your enemy" – enemy means the woman. Enemy means the opposite; that is the highest in love. Then a moment comes when sex disappears, the person becomes asexual. But that is the highest point, and it can be reached only through these stages. Maybe the questioner is hooked somewhere in homosexuality. Nothing is wrong. Wherever you are, in what-soever stage you are, be loving, be surrendering. Out of that stage the other stage will come, will grow on its own accord. Don't force it.

I am not here to make you feel guilty; I am not here to create any kind of rift in your being. I'm all for relaxation, because only through relaxation will you come to know who you are. So whatsoever is easy, go into it. Don't be a masochist and don't try to create troubles for yourself. Move happily, in a relaxed way. And whatsoever is easy for you right now, go on doing it. Through it something better will happen, but only through it. You cannot suddenly jump out of it.

The fifth question:

Osho,
What is the point of the physical universe if man's destiny is
ultimately to transcend it?

That is the point: otherwise, how will you transcend? The universe is needed to transcend. The misery is needed to transcend, the darkness is needed to transcend, the ego is needed to transcend – because only when you transcend is there joy, benediction.

I understand your question. It is a very ancient question, asked again and again and again because it puzzles the mind. If God has created the world, then why has he created misery in it? He could have given you bliss as a gift. Then why has he created ignorance? Is he not potent enough to create enlight-ened beings from the very beginning?

He is, and that's what he is doing. But even God is not potent enough to make impossibles happen. Only the possi-ble is possible. You can only know what health is when you are capable of being ill; otherwise you cannot know it. You can only know light when you know what darkness is. You can know relaxation only when you know what tension is, you can know freedom only when you know what bondage is – they go in pairs. Even God is not potent enough to simply give you freedom. With freedom, in the same package, comes bondage. And you have to go through bondage to have the taste of freedom. It is just as if you are not hungry, so you cannot enjoy food.

What you are asking is: "What is the need for hunger? Why can we not go on eating without hunger?" Hunger creates the pain, hunger creates the need, and then you eat and there is joy. Without hunger there will be no joy. You can ask the very, very rich people who have lost their hunger: they don't enjoy their food, they cannot. It is the intensity of hunger that brings joy. That's why once you have eaten, for six, seven, eight hours you have to fast to enjoy food again.

Existence is dialectical: darkness–light, life–death, summer–winter, youth–old age; they all go together.

You ask: "What is the point of the physical universe if men's destiny is ultimately to transcend it?" Precisely, that is the point. The universe is created for you to transcend. Otherwise, you will never know what transcendence is. You can remain blissful, but you will not know what bliss is. And to remain blissful without knowing what bliss is, is not worth it. And the knowing is possible only through the opposite – that's why.

The sixth question:

Osho,
Everybody is, of course, getting whatever they get, and not
getting what they don't get. And the line between getting
that you are getting it, and not getting that you are getting
it, seems to be rather thin. Is getting what you get different
from getting it? Having asked that, I realize in a sense it is, of
course, different, because the word is ambiguous. Get means
to both receive and to understand. Blah, blah, blah... Please
clarify.

You seem to be an EST-hole. Blah, blah, blah...

The seventh question:

Osho,
Why should I take sannyas?

Because tomorrow you may not be. The next moment you may not be. And sannyas is nothing but a vision of living this moment utterly, totally, absolutely.

Sannyas simply means, "I will not postpone life anymore." Sannyas simply means, "I will not live in dreams anymore, I will take hold of this moment and squeeze the whole juice out of it right now." That's what sannyas is: it is a way of intense living, of sensitive living.

And remember, life is very accidental. One never knows.

Listen to this story:

A salesman came home unexpectedly one day, and the first words he said when he came in the door were, "Where is he? I know he is here! I can feel it in my bones!"

His wife, who was cleaning the dishes at the time said, "Who are you looking for?"

Salesman: "Don't give me that. You know who I am looking for, and I will find him!"

He looked in the closet, under the bed, and in the attic. He happened to glance out of the second floor apartment window and saw a young light-haired man get into a red convertible.

"There he is!" he said, and grabbed the refrigerator and rolled it to the window and pushed it out. He crushed the fellow in the car and died of a heart attack himself.

Saint Peter: "What happened to you, young man?"

Young man: "I got crushed to death by a fridge."

Saint Peter: "And you?"

Salesman: "While pushing a fridge through a window I died of a heart attack."

Saint Peter to the third man: "What did you die of?"

Third man: "Well, I was sitting in this fridge, minding my own business, and..."

Life is very accidental! One never knows from where the fridge will come. Somebody may be sitting in it, minding his own business... That's why I say become a sannyasin: this is the only moment to live, and there is no other moment.

Enough for today.

CHAPTER 9

gone, gone, gone beyond!

*Therefore one should know the prajnaparamita as the great
spell, the spell of great knowledge, the utmost spell, the
unequalled spell, allayer of all suffering, in truth – for what
could go wrong? By the prajnaparamita has this spell been
delivered. It runs like this: Gone, gone, gone beyond, gone
altogether beyond, O what an awakening, all-hail! This
completes the heart of perfect wisdom.*

Teilhard de Chardin divides human evolution into four stages.
The first he calls *geosphere*, the second, biosphere, the third,
noosphere, and the fourth, Christosphere. These four stages
are immensely significant. They have to be understood.
Understanding them will help you to understand the climax of
the *Heart Sutra*.

The *geosphere* is the state of consciousness which is absolutely asleep, the state of matter. Matter is consciousness
asleep. Matter is not against consciousness, matter is a state
of consciousness asleep, not yet awakened. A rock is a sleeping buddha; one day or other the rock is going to become a

buddha. It may take millions of years; that doesn't matter. The difference will be only of time, and time does not matter much in this eternity. That's why in the East we have been making statues out of stone – it's very symbolic: the rock and the buddha are bridged through a stone statue. The rock is the lowest and buddha is the highest. The stone statue says that even in stone is hidden a buddha. The stone statue says that buddha is nothing but the rock come to manifestation; the rock has expressed its whole potential.

This is the first stage: *geosphere*. It is matter, it is unconsciousness, it is sleep, it is pre-life. In this state there is no freedom, because freedom enters through consciousness. In this state there is only cause and effect. The law is absolute. Not even an accident is possible. Freedom is not known. Freedom enters only as a shadow of consciousness; the more conscious you become, the more free. Hence Buddha is called a *mukta*: utterly free. The rock is utterly in bondage, fettered from everywhere, from all sides, in all dimensions. The rock is soul in imprisonment, Buddha is the soul on wings. There are no longer any chains, any bondages, any imprisonments; no walls surround Buddha. He has no borders to his being. His being is as vast as existence itself. He is one with the whole.

But in the world of the *geosphere*, cause and effect is the only *dhamma,* the only law, the only Tao. Science is still confined to the *geosphere*, because it still goes on thinking in terms of cause and effect. Modern science is a very rudimentary science, very primitive, because it cannot conceive of anything more than matter. Its conception is very limited, and hence it is creating more misery than it solves. Its vision is so finite, its vision is so tiny, small, that it cannot reconcile itself with the totality of existence. It is looking from a tiny hole and thinks that's all. Science is still confined to the *geosphere*. Science is still in bondage, it does not yet have wings. It will get wings only when it starts moving beyond cause and effect.

Yes, little sparks are there. The nuclear physicist is entering into the world which is beyond cause and effect, crossing the boundary. Hence, the principle of uncertainty is arising, arising with great force. Cause and effect is the principle of certainty: you do this, and this is bound to happen. You heat the water to a hundred degrees and the water evaporates – that's cause and effect. The water has no freedom. It cannot say, "Today I am not in the mood, and I am not going to evaporate at a hundred degrees. I simply say no!" It cannot say that; it cannot resist, it cannot fight against the law. It is very law-abiding, very obedient. Some other day, when the water is feeling very happy, it cannot say, "You need not bother too much. I am going to evaporate at fifty degrees. I am going to oblige you." No, that is not possible.

The old physics, the old science, had no glimpse about the principle of uncertainty. The principle of uncertainty means the principle of freedom. Now, little glimpses are happening. Now they are not as certain as they used to be. Now they see that at the deepest, in matter too, there is a certain quality of freedom. It is very difficult to say whether the electron is a particle or a wave: it behaves both ways, sometimes this way, sometimes that way. And there is no way to predict it. It is a quanta. And not only that, its freedom is such that sometimes it behaves simultaneously like a wave and like a particle. That is utterly impossible for the old scientist even to conceive or understand. Aristotle would not be able to understand it, Newton would not be able to understand it. That is impossible to see. That is saying that something is behaving like a line and a dot simultaneously; it is illogical. How can something behave like a dot *and* a line? Either it is a line or it is a dot.

But now the physicist is starting to have glimpses of the innermost core of matter. In a very, very roundabout way they are stumbling on one of the greatest factors of life: freedom. But in the *geosphere* it doesn't exist. It is *sushupti*.

The word *sushupti* means absolute sleep – not even a dream stirs. The rocks are not even dreaming, they cannot dream. To dream they will have to be a little more conscious. The rock is simply there. It has no personality, it has no soul – at least not in actuality. It cannot even dream; its sleep is undisturbed. Day, night, year-in, year-out, it goes on sleeping. For millennia it has slept, and for millennia it will sleep. Not even a dream disturbs it.

In Yoga we divide consciousness into four stages. They are very, very relevant to de Chardin's division. The first is *sushupti*, deep sleep. The *geosphere* corresponds to that. The *geosphere* is more like death than like life. That's why matter appears to be dead. It is not. It is waiting for its life to grow, it is like a seed. It appears dead: it is waiting for its right moment to explode into life. But right now it is dead; there is no mind.

Remember, in the last stage also there will be no mind again. A buddha is in a state of no-mind, and a rock is also in the state of no-mind. Hence the significance of a stone statue: the meeting of two polarities. The rock being in a state of no-mind means the rock is still below mind. A buddha is in a state of no-mind: that means the buddha has gone beyond mind. There is a similarity, just as there is a similarity between a child and a saint. The child is below mind, the saint is beyond mind. The rock will have to go through all the turmoil of life that the buddha has passed through. He has gone and gone and gone, and gone beyond, *utterly* beyond. But there is a similarity: he again exists in a state of no-mind. He has become so fully conscious that the mind is not needed. The rock is so unconscious that the mind cannot exist. In the rock the unconsciousness is absolute, hence the mind is not possible. In the buddha the consciousness is absolute and the mind is not needed. Let me explain it to you; it is one of the most important things to learn, to understand.

Mind is needed only because you are not really conscious. If you are really conscious, then there is insight, there is no thinking. Then you act out of insight, you don't act out of your mind. Then mind is not needed. When you see a thing as true, that very seeing becomes your action.

For example, you are in a house and the house is on fire. You *see* it – it is not a thinking. You simply see it, and you jump out of the house. You don't wait, you don't ponder, you don't brood over it. You don't inquire, you don't consult books, you don't go to ask somebody's advice about what to do.

You are coming from an evening walk, and just on the road you come across a snake. You jump! Before any thinking enters, you jump. It is not out of thinking that you jump, it is out of insight. Great danger is there; the very danger makes you alive, intense, conscious, and you take the jump out of consciousness. It is a no-mind jump.

But these moments are rare in your life because you are not yet ready to live your consciousness intensely and totally. For a buddha, that is his normal way. He lives so totally that the mind is never needed, never consulted.

The first sphere, the *geosphere*, is a no-mind sphere. There is no self, obviously, because without the mind the self cannot exist. Again, in the fourth, there will be no self – because without the mind how can the self exist? The mind needs to function out of a center, hence it creates the ego, the self. The mind has to keep itself in control, the mind has to keep itself in a certain pattern, order. It has to hold itself. To hold itself it creates a center, because only through the center can it keep control. Without a center it will not be able to keep control. So once the mind comes in, ego is on the way. Sooner or later the mind will need the ego. Without the ego the mind will not be able to function. Otherwise who will control, who will manage, who will manipulate, who will plan, who will dream, who will project? And who will be there to be referred to as a constant thing? – because the mind goes on changing. One thought after another: it is a procession of thoughts. You will be lost if you don't have any ego; you will not know who you are, and where you are going, and for what.

In the *geosphere* there is no mind, no self, and no time. It is below time. Time has not entered yet. The rock knows no past, no present, no future. And so is the case with a buddha. He also is beyond time. He knows no past, no present, no future. He lives in eternity. In fact that is the real meaning of being in the present. Being in the present does not mean that space which is between past and future. In the dictionary that is the meaning given: the space between past and future is called the present. But that is not the present. What kind of present is this? It is already becoming past; it is going out of existence. This moment, if you call it the present, the moment you have called it the present it is already gone into the past; it is no longer the present. And the moment that you were calling future – the moment you called it future it has become the present and is moving towards becoming the past. This present is not a real present. The present that is between past and future is just part of past and future, of the time procession.

The present that I talk about, the *now* that I talk about, or Buddha talks about, or Christ when he says, "Don't think of the morrow. See the lilies in the field – they toil not, they spin not, and look how beautiful they are. How incredibly beautiful! Even Solomon was not so beautiful arrayed in all his glory. Look at the lilies of the field"... Those lilies are living in a kind of nowness; they don't know the past, they don't know the future.

The buddha knows no past, no future, and no present. He knows no division. That's the state of eternity. Then the now is absolutely there. There is only now, and only here, and nothing else. But the rock is also in that state – unconscious, of course.

The second sphere is the biosphere. It means life, pre-consciousness. The first sphere was matter, the second sphere is life: trees, animals, birds. The rock cannot move, the rock has no life anywhere, no life visible anywhere. The tree has more life, the animal still more, the bird still more. The tree is rooted in the ground, cannot move much. It moves a little bit, sways, but cannot move much; it does not have that much freedom. A little freedom is certainly there, but the animal has more freedom. He can move, he can choose a little more freedom: where to go, what to do. The bird has even a little more freedom: it can fly. This is the sphere called the biosphere, the life sphere. It is pre-consciousness; just rudimentary consciousness is coming into being. The rock was absolutely unconscious. You cannot say the tree is so absolutely unconscious. Yes, it is un-conscious, but something of the consciousness is filtering in, a ray of consciousness is coming in. And the animal is a little more conscious.

The first state corresponds with Patanjali's *sushupti*: deep, deep sleep. The second state corresponds with Patanjali's *swabana*: the dream state. Consciousness is coming like a dream. Yes, dogs dream. You can see – you can watch a dog asleep and you will see he is dreaming. In a dream some-times he will try to catch flies. And sometimes you will see he is sad, and sometimes you will see he looks happy. Watch a cat, and sometimes she is jumping on a mouse in her dream, and you can see what she is doing in the dream: eating the mouse, cleaning her mustache. You can watch the cat; dream has entered, things are happening in the world of conscious-ness. Consciousness is surfacing. Cause and effect is still predominant, but not so much as in a rock. A little freedom becomes possible, and hence accidents start happening. The animal has a little bit of freedom. He can choose a few things, he can be temperamental: he can be in a good mood and be friendly towards you; he can be in a bad mood and will not be friendly towards you. A little bit of decision has come into his being, but a very little bit, just the beginning. The self is not yet integrated. It is a very loose self, hodgepodge, but it is coming up. The structure is taking shape, the form is arising.

The animal is past-oriented; it lives out of the past. The animal has no idea of the future: it cannot plan for the future, it cannot think ahead. Even if sometimes it thinks ahead, that is very, very fragmentary. For example when the animal is feeling hungry it can think ahead, a few hours ahead – that he will get food. He has to wait. But the animal cannot think about one month, two months, three months into the future. The animal cannot conceive of years; it has no calendar, no time concept. It is past-oriented. Whatsoever has been hap-pening in the past it expects to happen in the future too. Its future is more or less the same as the past; it is a repetition. It is past-dominated. Time is entering through the past, self is entering through the past.

The third sphere is the noosphere; mind, self-conscious-ness arises. The first was unconsciousness, the second was pre-consciousness, the third is self-consciousness. Conscious-ness comes, but there is a calamity with it – the self. It cannot come otherwise; the self is a necessary evil. Consciousness comes with the idea of "I." Reflection starts, thinking starts, personality comes into existence. And with mind comes future orientation: man lives in the future, animals live in the past.

Developed societies live in the future, undeveloped societies live in the past. Primitive people still live in the past. Only civilized people live in the future. To live in the future is a higher state than to live in the past. Young people live in the future, old people start living in the past. Young people are more alive than old people. New countries, new cultures, live in the future. For example, America lives in the future, India lives in the past. India goes on carrying five thousand, ten thousand years of past. It is such a burden, it is so difficult to carry it, it is crushing, but one goes on carrying it. It is the heritage, and one is very proud of the past.

To be proud of the past is simply an uncivilized state. One has to reach into the future, one has to grope into the future. The past is no longer, the future is going to be – one has to prepare for it.

You can watch it in many ways. The Indian mind is thrilled only by past events. Still, people go on playing the drama of Rama every year, and they are very thrilled. Thousands of years have passed and they have been playing the same drama again and again and again, and again they will play it. And they are very thrilled. They were not so thrilled when the first man walked on the moon; they were not so thrilled as they were and have always been thrilled by the drama of Rama. They know the story, they have seen it many times, but it is their heritage; they are very proud of it.

You will be surprised to know that there are Hindu mahatmas and Jaina mahatmas in India who have been trying to prove that man has not walked on the moon, that the Americans were deceiving. Why? – because the moon is a god. How can you walk on the moon? And there are people who listen to them and follow them.

A Jaina monk came to see me once in Gujarat and he said, "Support me – and I have got thousands of followers!" And he did have. And the whole thing, the theme of his life, was that the Americans have been deceiving, that those photographs are all photographic tricks that have been produced, that those rocks that have been brought from the moon have been brought from Siberia or from somewhere on the planet.

Nobody has ever gone and nobody can ever go to the moon, because in the Jaina *shastras,* in the Jaina scriptures, it is written that the moon is a god. How can you walk on God? This is past-orientation. This is very deadening. That's why India cannot grow, it cannot evolve, it cannot progress. It is stuck with the past.

With the noosphere, with mind, self-consciousness, reflection, thought, personality, future-orientation comes into being. And the more you start preparing for the future, of course the more anxious you become. So Americans are the tensest people, restless. Indians are very restful, so restful that they don't have any efficiency at all. Do you know that when Indians change an electric bulb, three Indians are needed? – one to hold the bulb and two to turn the ladder. Very restful people, relaxed; they don't suffer from any anxiety, they don't know what anxiety really is.

Anxiety enters with the future, because you have to plan. You cannot just go on repeating the old ways of your life. And when you do something new there is a possibility of a mistake, more possibility of a mistake. The more you try the new, the more anxious you become. That's why, psychologically, America is the most disturbed country, India the most undisturbed.

Animals don't have anxiety. To live in the past is a lower state of mind – of course more comfortable, more convenient. And the Hindu mahatmas go on saying to the world, "Look how peaceful we are. No neurosis exists. Even if we starve, we starve very, very silently. Even if we die, we die very, very acceptingly. And you are going mad!"

But remember, progress comes through anxiety. With progress there is anxiety, there is trembling – of going wrong, of doing something wrong, of missing the point. With the past there is no problem: you go on repeating it. It is a settled past, the ways of it are perfectly known. You have traveled on them, your parents have traveled on them, and so on and so forth, backwards to Adam and Eve. Everybody has done it; there is no possibility of going wrong. With something new, anxiety, fear, fear of failure enters.

This third sphere, the noosphere, is the sphere of anxiety, tension. If you have to choose between the second and the third, choose the third, don't choose the second. Although there is no need to choose between the third and the second, you can choose between the third and the fourth; then choose the fourth. Always choose the higher.

Remember, when I condemn the Indian mind, I am not condemning Buddha and I am not condemning Krishna. They have chosen the fourth: they are also at rest, they are also relaxed but their relaxation comes from dropping time itself, not by living in the past. They are utterly relaxed, they have no anxiety, no neurosis. Their mind is a calm, rippleless lake – but not by choosing the second but by choosing the fourth; not by remaining below mind but by going beyond mind. But that's how things go.

People in India have seen Buddha, and they have seen the silence, and they have seen the benediction of the man, and they have seen the grace, and they have seen that life can be lived in such relaxation. Why not live such a life? But they have not made any effort to go to the fourth stage. On the contrary, they relapsed from the third and settled in the second stage. It gives something like Buddha's silence; but it is "something like," it is not exactly that. It is always easier to settle in the past and become more convenient and comfortable. Buddha has not settled with the past; he has not even settled with the future. He has not settled with time itself: he has dropped time, he has dropped the mind that creates time. He has dropped the ego that creates anxiety.

Indians have chosen to drop the future because it seems to create anxiety: "Future creates anxiety? You can drop the future." Then you will slip back, you will relapse into the previous state. Drop the ego, and then you go beyond.

The third sphere is like what Patanjali calls wakefulness. The first is sleep, the second is dream, the third is wakefulness – your wakefulness of course, not the wakefulness of a buddha. Your so-called wakefulness: eyes are open but dreams are roaming inside you; the eyes are open but sleep is there inside you. You are full of sleep even when you are awake. This is the third state. And it is always helpful: if you become tired of the day, you fall into a dream, it gives you relaxation. Then you fall into deep sleep; it gives you even more relaxation. In the morning you are again fresh. You fall backwards to become restful because that is what you know already, and it is there in your system; you can go into it.

The fourth state has to be created; it is not in your system. It is your potential but you have never been in it before. It is arduous, it is going upstream, uphill. The fourth state is the Christosphere – you can call it the Buddha-sphere, it means the same thing; you can call it the Krishna-sphere, it means the same. With the third state there is kind of freedom, a pseudo-freedom, the freedom known as choice. This has to be understood, it is of great importance.

At the third stage you simply have a pseudo kind of freedom, and that freedom is the freedom of choice. For example, you say, "My country is religiously free." That means you can choose: you can go to a church or to a temple, and the country and its law will not create any trouble for you. You can become a Mohammedan or a Hindu or a Christian: you can choose. "The country is free" means you can choose your life, where you want to live, what you want to do, what you want to say. The choice of expression, the freedom of expression is there. This is what is thought to be freedom: that you can say whatsoever you like, that you can do whatsoever you like, that you can choose any religious or political style. You can be a Communist, you can be a fascist, you can be a liberal, you can be a democrat, and all that nonsense. You can choose. It is only a pseudo-freedom. Why do I call it pseudo freedom? – because a mind which is full of thoughts cannot be free.

If you have lived for fifty years and your mind has been conditioned by your parents and the teachers and the society, do you think you can choose? You will choose out of your conditioning. How is it going to be a choice? First, you have been conditioned.

It is like when you hypnotize somebody. You can take somebody to Santosh, our hypnotist, and he can hypnotize him and tell him, "Tomorrow morning you will go to the market and you will purchase a certain kind of a cigarette, a certain brand." He can suggest this to that person in deep hypnosis. Tomorrow morning he will get up and he will not have any idea that he is going to purchase a certain brand of cigarettes in the market, because the conditioning has entered the unconscious, has been put into the unconscious. His conscious mind is unaware. He will not even have any idea of why he is going to the market. But he will find some rationalization: he will say, "Let us go shopping today." Why today? Why not tomorrow? Why not the day after tomorrow? Why today? He will say, "This is my freedom. Whenever I want to go I will go. Who are you to prevent me? This is my freedom." And he's unaware, completely unaware that this is not freedom at all.

He will go to the market with the idea that he is free, and he may not even think for a single moment that he's going to purchase a certain brand of cigarettes. Then suddenly he comes across a shop and he says to himself, "Why not purchase a packet of cigarettes? You have not smoked for so long." He is thinking that *he* is thinking it! And he goes to the shop and he says, "Give me this brand of cigarettes, 555." And if you ask him, "Why not Panama? Why not Wills? Why not Berkeley?" he will say, "This is my choice. I am free to choose!" And he will purchase 555, and he remains free – at least according his idea. He's not free, he has been conditioned.

You have been conditioned as a Hindu, a Christian, as a Mohammedan, as an Indian, as a Chinese, as a German. How can you be free? You have been conditioned by your parents, by your society, by your neighborhood, by your school, college, university. How can you be free? Your freedom is pseudo. It is bogus: it only gives you the feeling of freedom and makes you happy; otherwise there is no freedom in it. When you go to church are you going out of your freedom? When you go to the Hindu temple are you going out of your freedom? Look into it and you will find it is not out of freedom; you were born in a Hindu family.

Sometimes it can happen – you were born in a Christian family and still you want to go to a Hindu temple. That too is a conditioning – a different kind. Maybe your parents were too Christian, *too* much, and you could not absorb that much non-sense. There is a limit. You became antagonistic, you started rebelling against it; you became a reactionary. They used to pull you to the church. And they were powerful, and you were a small child, and you could not do anything; you were help-less. But you were always thinking, "I will show you." The day you became powerful you stopped going to church.

Now this idea, "I will show you," has been implanted by their obsession with the church. It is again hypnosis – in the reverse order, but it is still hypnosis. You are reacting, you are not free. If you want to go to church you will not be able to go, you will find yourself pulling away. You will not go because this is the church your parents used to take you to. You *cannot* go to this church; you will become a Hindu. You will start doing things which your parents had never wanted you to do just to show them. This is reaction. The first is obe-dience, the second is disobedience, but there is no freedom in either.

One thing more: it is not only a question of condition-ing that you are not free. When you choose between two things, maybe nobody has conditioned you about those two things; there are millions of things for which you have not been conditioned at all. When you choose between two things your choice is out of confusion, and out of confusion there can be no freedom. You want to marry this girl or that; how are you going to choose? You are confused.

Every day I receive letters from people: "I am torn apart between two women. What should I do? This woman is beau-tiful bodily, in proportion, has very, very beautiful eyes, a kind of charm; the body is vibrant, radiant, alive but psycholog-ically she is very ugly. The other woman is psychologically beautiful, but physically ugly. Now, what to do?" And you are torn apart.

I have heard about a man who was thinking to marry. He was in love with a woman, but she was very poor. She was beautiful, but she was very poor. And another woman was in love with him who was very rich but very ugly. But one thing was beautiful in her too – her sound, her voice. She was a great singer.

Now he was torn apart. The beautiful woman had not that voice, that singing voice; and he was a lover of music. She had a beautiful face, but form was not so important to him as voice. And then he was poor, and he wanted a woman who would bring much money with her so there would be security; he could go into his music totally, wholeheartedly, so he need not worry about money and things like that. He wanted to devote his whole life to music. That woman had two things: the money and a beautiful voice but she was utterly ugly. It was very difficult to look at her, her face was repulsive. The poor woman was beautiful, but her voice was ordinary and she had no money. So if he chose that woman he would have to drop his love affair with music. He would have to become a clerk in some stupid office, or a teacher or something. And then he would not be able to devote himself to music. Music needs total devotion, music is a very jealous mistress – it does not allow you to go anywhere, it wants to absorb you utterly, totally. So he was torn part. And finally his love for music won, and he married the ugly woman.

He came home, they went to sleep. The dark nights were okay because he was not looking at the woman, so there was no problem. But in the morning, when the sunrays filtered in and he was awake, and he looked at the face of the woman, it was so repulsive. He shook the woman hard and said, "Sing! Sing immediately! Sing immediately!" – just to protect himself from that ugliness.

People write to me: "We are torn apart between two women, or between two men. What should we do?" This confusion arises because you are motivated. There is a motivation: money, music, security. There is no love; that's why you are torn apart. If love is there, intense love is there, passionate love is there, then there would be no choice. That passion itself would decide. You would not be choosing, you would not be torn apart. But people are not that intelligent and not that intense. They live very lukewarm, so-so; they don't live intensely; their lives have no fire.

Real freedom happens only when your life becomes so total in each moment that there is no need to decide; that totality decides. Do you follow me? – the totality itself decides. You are not facing two alternatives: whether to marry this woman or that. Your heart is *totally* with one. There is no motive so you are not divided, and there is no confusion. If you decide out of confusion you will create conflict. Confusion will take you into deeper confusion. Never decide out of confusion.

That's why Krishnamurti goes on talking about choicelessness. Choicelessness is freedom. You don't choose, you simply become totally intense. You just become absolutely alert, aware, attentive.

For example, you are listening to me: you can listen in a lukewarm way – half asleep, half awake, yawning, thinking a thousand and one things, planning, last night still hanging around you, hangovers of a thousand and one types – and you are listening too. Then there is a question of whether I am telling the truth or not. If you are passionately listening, if you are utterly herenow, that very passion will decide. In that intensity you will know what truth is. If I say something which is true, it will immediately strike in your heart because you will be so intelligent, how can you miss it? Your intelligence will be so alert, how can you miss it? And if there is something which is not true, you will see it immediately. The vision will come, immediate. There will be no decision on your part: "Should I follow this man or not?" That is out of confusion. You have not listened, you have not seen me.

See the point of it. With truth you need not agree or disagree. The truth has to be heard totally, with sensitivity, that's all. And that very sensitivity decides. You see, you immediately feel the truth of it. In that very feeling you have moved into truth – not that you agreed or disagreed; not that you were convinced by me, converted by me. I'm not converting anybody; truth converts. Truth is not a belief, and truth is not an argument; truth is a presence. If you are present you will feel it. If you are not present you will not feel it.

So on the third stage, the noosphere, there is pseudo-freedom. Out of confusion, you decide; hence confusion goes on growing. Confusion brings conflict, because there are always two sides in you: to do this or to do that, to be or not to be. And whatsoever you decide, the other side will remain there and wait for its time to take revenge. Freedom happens only at the fourth stage.

The Christosphere is the fourth. With the Christosphere, no-mind comes into existence – the no-mind of a Buddha, of a Christ, not of a rock. With the fourth comes consciousness, without a center, with no self in it; just pure consciousness with no border to it, infinite consciousness. Then you can't say "I am conscious." There is no "I" to it, it is just consciousness. It has no name and no form. It is nothingness, it is emptiness. With this consciousness, thinking is not needed; insight starts functioning, intuition starts functioning.

Intellect lives on tuition; others have to teach you, that's what tuition is. Nobody has to teach you intuition: it comes from within, it grows out of you, it is a flowering of your being. This is the quality of consciousness called meditation, intuition, insight, consciousness without a center, timelessness; or you can call it the now, the present. But remember, it is not the present between past and future; it is the present in which past and future have both dissolved.

De Chardin calls it "the omega point," Buddha calls it nirvana, Jainas call it *moksha*, Christ calls it "God the Father." These are different names. This whole sutra is concerned with from the third to the fourth, from the noosphere to the Christosphere, from intellect to intelligence, from self-consciousness to no self-consciousness. The third is like waking, ordinary waking, and the fourth is what Patanjali calls *turiya*, "the fourth." He has not given it any name, and that seems to be very beautiful. Call it "Christosphere," and it looks Christian; call it "Krishnasphere," and it looks Hindu; call it Buddhasphere, and it looks Buddhist. Patanjali is very, very pure; he simply calls it "the fourth." That contains everything. He has not given it a particular name. He gives names to three because they have forms, and wherever form is, names are relevant. The formless cannot have any name – *turiya*, "the fourth."

This whole *Prajnaparamita Sutra* is from the third to the fourth. Sariputra is at the peak of the third: the noosphere – reflection, thinking, self-consciousness. He has traveled to the uttermost into the third, he has reached the maximum of it. There is no more to it. He's standing on the boundary line.

Therefore, O Sariputra... Buddha is standing beyond the boundary and calling Sari-putra forth: "Come, come, and yet come." The whole sutra is condensed today in this last sutra. All of the sutras, up to now, were just preparation for this last peak.

Tasmaj jnatavyam: prajnaparamita maha-mantro maha-vidyamantro "nuttara-mantro" samasama-mantrah...

Therefore one should know...

Tasmaj jnatavyam... Therefore the only thing worth knowing is this. This is the conclusion of this whole beautiful dialogue. The dialogue is between two energies, Buddha and Sariputra, because Sariputra has not said a single word. This is a far superior dialogue than exists between Arjuna and Krishna in the Gita, because Arjuna says something. It is verbal. Arjuna is more like a student than like a disciple. He becomes a disciple only at the very end. When he becomes the disciple, Krishna becomes the master. If the disciple is not a disciple, how can the master be a master? If the disciple is just a student, then the master is just a teacher.

Where the Gita ends, that is the point where this *Prajna-paramita Sutra* starts. Sariputra is a disciple: utterly silent, has not uttered a single word, has not even asked a question – not verbally. He's a guest, not a questioner. His whole being is asking, not his mind. He's not verbalizing; his existence is a question mark. He's standing before Buddha, his whole being thirsty, on fire, afire. Seeing his state Buddha goes on saying things on his own. Not that the disciple has to ask; the master knows when the disciple needs. The master knows far better than the disciple himself what his need is. The disciple has to wait. Maybe Sariputra *has* waited for many years, for almost twenty years, for this moment: when the master would see the need, when the master would feel his hunger and thirst, when he would be worthy of receiving a gift from the master. That day has come, that fortunate moment has arrived.

Tasmaj jnatavyam... Buddha says, "Therefore, O Sariputra, this is the only thing that is worth knowing." And now he condenses his whole message into a few small words, into a small sentence, into a mantra, into a maxim, into a formula. This is the greatest mantra, because Buddha has contained in it all that is needed for the whole journey. He has put everything into this small, this very small formula.

> *Therefore – the only thing worth knowing is – the*
> *prajnaparamita as the great spell, the spell of great knowledge,*
> *the utmost spell, the unequalled spell...*

Buddha praises it like anything; he goes through all the superlatives possible. He says, "This is the great spell!" Spell, mantra, means a magic formula. What a mantra is has to be understood. A mantra is a very, very special thing to be understood. It is a spell, a magic formula. It implies the phenomenon that whatsoever you have is not really there, and whatsoever you think you do not have, is there! A magic formula is needed. Your problem is not real – that's why a magic formula is needed.

For example, a parable:

It happened...

A man was very afraid of ghosts. Unfortunately he had to pass the cemetery every day, coming and going. And sometimes he was late, and he had to pass the cemetery in the night. His house was behind the cemetery, and very close to it. And he was so afraid of ghosts that his life was a constant torture. He could not sleep: the whole night he was disturbed by the ghosts. Sometimes they were knocking on the doors, and sometimes moving inside the house, and he could hear their footsteps and their whisperings. Sometimes they would come very close to him and he could even feel their breath. He was in a constant hell.

He went to a master, and the master said, "This is nothing. You have come to the right person" – just like I say to you – "Take this mantra. It is enough, and you need not be worried. Just put this mantra in a small golden box and carry the box always. You can hang it around your neck."

It is just like the locket: it is a mantra; or it is like the magic box that I give to sannyasins who are going far away from me. It is a magic box, it is a mantra.

The master said, "Keep this mantra. You need not even repeat it; it is so potent that it need not be repeated. You just keep it in the box. Keep the box with you and no ghost will ever trouble you." And it really happened: that day he passed through the cemetery almost as if he was going for a morning walk. Never before had it been so easy. He used to run; he used to scream and shout, and he had to sing songs while passing. That day he walked very slowly with the box in his hand, and it really worked! No ghosts. He was even standing in the middle of the cemetery, waiting for somebody to come, and no ghost turned up. It was utter silence.

Then he went home. He put the box underneath his pillow. That night nobody knocked on the door, nobody whispered, nobody came close to him. That was the first time in his whole life that he slept well. It was a great mantra. But then he became too attached to the box. He could not leave it anywhere, he had to carry it everywhere the whole day.

People started asking, "Why do you go on carrying this box?"

And he said, "This is my safety, my security."

He became so afraid that now if some day this box was lost, "I will be in great trouble, and those ghosts will take great revenge!" Eating – and he had his box. And in the toilet – he had his box. Making love to his woman – and he had his box. He was going crazy! And now the fear was too much: if it is stolen, if somebody plays a trick or if he loses it somewhere, or if something happens to the box, then what? "Then for months those ghosts are hankering to create trouble for me! They will jump upon me from everywhere, and they will kill me!"

The master inquired one day about how things were going.

He said, "Everything is good. Everything is perfectly good, but now I am being tortured by my own fears. Again I cannot sleep. The whole night I have to see whether the box is still there. Again and again I have to wake myself up and search for the box. And if sometimes it slips here and there in the bed and I cannot find it, it is so frightening! I get so scared!"

The master said, "Now I will give you another mantra. Throw away the box."

The man asked, "Then how am I going to protect myself from the ghosts?"

The master said, "They are not there. This box is just nonsense. Those ghosts are not there; that's why this box has worked. Those ghosts are only in your imagination. If they were really there they would not be afraid of the box. It is just your idea, those ghosts were your idea. Now you have got a better idea, because you have got a master. And the master has given you a box, a magic spell. Now be more understanding: the ghosts are not there, that's why this box has helped. Now there is no need to get so obsessed with the box. Throw it away!"

A mantra is a spell to take away things which are not really there. For example, a mantra will help you to drop the ego. The ego is a ghost, just an idea. That's why I say to you that I am here to take away things which are not really with you, and to give you things which are really there. I am here to give you that which you already have, and I have to take away that which you never had but which you think that you have. Your miseries, your hurts, your ambitions, your jealousies, your fears, greeds, hatreds, attachments – those are all ghosts.

A mantra is just a trick, a strategy to help you drop your ghosts. Once you have dropped those ghosts then the mantra has to be dropped too. One need not carry the mantra anymore the moment he feels the ghosts have disappeared. And then you will laugh at the whole absurdity: the ghosts were false and the mantra was false – but it helped.

It happened...

A man got the idea in a dream that a snake had entered his mouth, and that it was there in his stomach. And he would feel the movement of the snake. You know such snakes; everybody knows. And he became very disturbed. He went to the doctors and was X-rayed, but... He would say, "It is there, even if the X-ray is not showing it. It doesn't matter. I am suffering, my suffering is real."

Then he went to a Sufi master. Somebody had said, "Go to a Sufi master. Only a master can help with this. Doctors won't be of much help. They treat real diseases; masters treat unreal diseases. Go to a master."

So he went, and the master said, "Right, I will do something. Tomorrow morning it will come out."

The next morning the master arranged it: he found a snake, gave it to the man's wife and said, "Make arrangements so when the man wakes up in the morning he finds the snake crawling out of the bed."

And the man shrieked, and he screamed and jumped. And he said, "Here! Here it is! That snake! And those foolish doctors: they were saying that there is no snake, nothing. And here it is!" But since that day the problem disappeared.

This was a mantra. The problem was not really actual.

All your problems are your creations. A mantra is a strategy to take away your illusions, and when the illusions are taken away, that which remains behind is the truth. The mantra only takes the false. It cannot give you the real, it can only take the false. But that's enough. Once the false is taken, once the false is understood as false, the truth arises. And truth liberates. Truth is liberation.

Buddha says:

> ...the prajnaparamita, as the great spell, the spell of great knowledge, the utmost spell, the unequalled spell – sarva-duhkha prasamanah – allayer of all suffering.

Buddha says this small mantra is so potential, it is enough for all your suffering. Just this mantra will do, will take you to the farther shore.

...satyam amithyatvat.

...in truth – for what could go wrong?

Buddha says it will only show you the false as the false. And when you know the truth, then what can go wrong? Then nothing can go wrong – *satyam amithyatvat.*

This word *amithya* comes from a root *mithya*. *Mithya* means false, *amithya* means not false. The word *mithya* exists in the English word *myth*. *Myth* means the false. *Myth* comes from the same root, *mithya*. A myth is that which appears but is not real.

The same root, *mithya* also exists in another English word, *miss*, as in "to miss." *Misunderstanding* – that "mis" comes from *mithya*. Or when we say, "He missed," that "to miss" also comes from *mithya*.

Truth is that which we go on missing. We go on missing because we go on clinging to the false. We miss the truth because we cling to the false. If we drop the false there is no missing at all. And that is the root meaning of the word *sin* too. *Sin* means to miss, to miss the target. Whenever you cling to the false you commit a sin, because clinging to it, you miss the truth.

You cling to the idea of God and that is false. All ideas are false. You cling to a certain idea of God and that is your barrier. Buddha says this mantra will take all your barriers; it will give you only nothingness. In nothingness, truth arises, because there is nothing to obstruct. *Nothingness* means nothing to obstruct anymore, all false ideas have been dropped on the way. You are just empty, you are just receptive, open; you come nude, naked, empty, to truth – that is the only way to come to it. Then nothing can go wrong.

...prajnaparamitayam ukto mantrah –

By the prajnaparamita has this spell been delivered.

And Buddha says, "I have given the last, the ultimate in it. There is no more to it, and there is no more possibility to improve upon it."

And I also say to you that there is no more possibility to improve upon it. "Nothing" is the greatest mantra. If you can enter into nothingness, then nothing else is needed. And that is the whole message of the *Prajnaparamita Sutra*.

...tadyatha...

It runs like this...

Now Buddha condenses the whole scripture, the whole dialogue, the whole message into a few words.

...tadyatha...

It runs like this...

...gate gate paragate parasamgate bodhi svaha.

...Gone, gone, gone beyond, gone altogether beyond. O, what an awakening, all hail!

Buddha uses *gone* four times. These are the four things that he uses *gone* for: the *geosphere*, the biosphere, the noosphere, the Christosphere. Gone from matter: gone from the body, gone from the visible, the tangible. He again uses *gone* a second time: gone from life, the so-called wheel of life and death. The third time he uses *gone*: now gone beyond mind, thought, thinking, self, ego. Gone altogether beyond – now he uses it a fourth time – even gone beyond the beyond, the Christosphere. Now he has entered into the uncreated.

Life has moved a full circle. This is the omega point, and this is the alpha too. This is the symbol you must have seen in many books, in many temples, in old monasteries: the symbol of the snake holding its own tail in its mouth.

...*Gone, gone, gone beyond, gone altogether...* You have come back home. *O, what an awakening...* What satori! What *samadhi!* This is awakening, the buddhahood.

All-hail! ...Alleluia! You can ask Aneeta: she goes on singing "Alleluia." This is the alleluia. This is the state of alleluia: when all is gone, when all has disappeared and only pure nothingness is left behind. This is the benediction – alleluia! This is the ecstasy everybody is searching for. Rightly or wrongly, but everybody is searching for this ecstasy.

You are a buddha, and you are not yet a buddha: that's the dilemma, that's the paradox. You are meant to be a buddha but you are missing. This sutra bridges you, this sutra helps you to become that which you are destined to become. This sutra helps you to fulfill your being. Remember, this sutra is not just to be repeated as it has been done down the centuries in China, Korea, Thailand, Japan, Ceylon. They go on repeating: "*Gate gate paragate parasamgate bodhi svaha.*" That repetition is not going to help.

This mantra is not just to be repeated. It has to be understood, it has to become your being. Go on moving beyond every name and form, go on moving beyond every identity, go on moving away from every limitation. Go on becoming bigger and bigger, huge, enormous. Even the sky is not your limit. Go on...

Gate gate paragate parasamgate bodhi svaha. Svaha is the expression of the ultimate ecstasy. It does not mean anything; it is just exactly like alleluia. It is a great exclamation of joy. The benediction has happened; you are fulfilled, utterly fulfilled. But this sutra is not just to be repeated, remember. Buddha has condensed it into few words so that you can remember it. In these few words he has put the whole message, his whole life's message.

You are a buddha, and unless you recognize it as that, you will suffer. This sutra declares you to be a buddha. That's why I started these discourses by saluting the buddha in you. I declare you to be buddhas! Recognize it!

The word *recognition* is beautiful. It means: just turn back and look. Respect yourself. The word *respect* is also good: it means respect, look again. That's what Jesus means when he says "Repent!" The original Aramaic word means return; it has nothing to do with Christian repentance. *Repent* means return: a hundred-and-eighty-degree turn. Patanjali calls it *pratiyahar*: go in, withdraw inwards. And Mahavira calls it *pratikrama*: don't go out, come in, come home.

The gap between the unreal you and the real you is obviously a false gap, because you are the real you all the time – just dreaming, thinking that you are somebody else. Drop that. Just look at who you are. And don't be deceived by beliefs and ideologies and scriptures and knowledge. Drop all! Drop it unconditionally! Unload all the furniture that you are carrying in your being. Just make an empty room there, and that empty room will reveal the truth to you. In that recognition, *svaha*, alleluia! Great ecstasy bursts forth in song, in dance, in silence, in creativity.

One never knows what is going to happen. How that ecstasy will be expressed by you, one never knows; everybody is going to express it in his own way – Jesus in his way, Buddha in his, Meera in hers. Everybody expresses it in his own way. Somebody becomes utterly silent: silence is his song. Somebody starts singing: a Meera, a Chaitanya, singing is their silence. Somebody dances: not knowing how to say it, goes into a crazy dance; that's his way. Somebody may paint, somebody may compose music, somebody may sculpt, or somebody will do something else. There are going to be as many expressions as there are people. So never imitate; just watch for your own expression to take possession of you. Let your *svaha*, your alleluia, be yours, authentically yours. And that happens when you are a nothingness.

Nothingness is the taste of this whole sutra. Become nothing and you will be all. Only the losers can be the winners in this game. Lose all and you will have all. Cling, possess, and you will lose all.

Buddha is known as Mantra Adipatti, bestower of spells; master of spells, Mahaguru – but not in the sense that the word has fallen to and become a dirty thing. In modern times *guru* has become a four letter dirty word – not in that sense. Krishnamurti says that he's allergic to gurus. It is true.

Buddha is really a *mahaguru*. The word *guru* means heavy with heaven, heavy with joy, heavy with ecstasy, heavy with *svaha*; heavy like a cloud full of rain, ready to shower on anybody who is thirsty, ready to share. *Guru* means heavy, heavy with heaven.

Guru also means one who destroys the darkness of others. I'm not talking about so-called gurus who go on roaming around the world. They don't destroy your darkness; they impose their darkness upon you, they impose their ignorance upon you. And these gurus are mushrooming like anything. You can find them everywhere: one Muktananda mushrooming here, another Maharishi Mahesh Yogi mushrooming there; they are mushrooming everywhere.

A guru is one who makes you free. A guru is one who delivers you freedom. A guru is one who liberates you. Buddha is one of the *mahagurus*. His message is the greatest that has ever been delivered to man. And this sutra is one of the greatest expressions of Buddha. He has talked for forty-two years, and he has said many things, but nothing compared to this. This is unique. You are fortunate that you have been here to listen to it and to meditate upon it. Now be even more fortunate – become it.

Enough for today.

CHAPTER 10

truth is a presence

The first question:

Osho,
What are the qualities of a sannyasin?

It is very difficult to define a sannyasin, and more so if you are going to define my sannyasins.

Sannyas is basically a rebellion about all structures, hence the difficulty of defining. Sannyas is a way of living life unstructuredly. Sannyas is to have a character which is characterless. By "characterless" I mean you no longer depend on the past. Character means the past, the way you have lived in the past, the way you have become habituated to living: your character is all your habits and conditionings and beliefs and your experiences. A sannyasin is one who no longer lives in the past or through the past; who lives in the moment, hence, is unpredictable.

A man of character is predictable; a sannyasin is unpredictable because a sannyasin is freedom. A sannyasin is not only free, he *is* freedom. It is living rebellion. But still, I will try; a few hints can be given, not exact definitions, a few indications, fingers pointing to the moon. Don't get caught with the fingers. The fingers don't define the moon, they only indicate. The fingers have nothing to do with the moon. They may be long, they may be short, they may be artistic, they may be ugly, they may be white, they may be black, they may be healthy, they may be ill – that doesn't matter. They simply indicate. Forget the finger and look at the moon.

What I am going to give is not a definition; that is not possible in this case. And, in fact, a definition is never possible about anything that is alive. A definition is possible only about something which is dead, which no longer grows, which no longer blooms, which has no more possibility, potentiality, which is exhausted and spent. Then a definition is possible. You can define a dead man, you cannot define an alive man.

Life basically means that the new is still possible.

So these are not definitions. The old sannyasin has a definition, very clear-cut; that's why he is dead. I call my sannyas "neosannyas" for this particular reason: my sannyas is an opening, a journey, a dance, a love affair with the unknown, a romance with existence itself, in search of an orgasmic relationship with the whole. Everything else has failed in the world. Everything that was defined, that was clear-cut, that was logical, has failed. Religions have failed, politics have failed, ideologies have failed – and they were very clear-cut. They were blueprints for the future of man. They have all failed. All programs have failed.

Sannyas is not a program anymore. It is exploration, not a program. When you become a sannyasin I initiate you into freedom, and into nothing else. It is great responsibility to be free, because then you have nothing to lean upon. Except your own inner being, your own consciousness, you have nothing as a prop, as a support. I take all your props and supports away; I leave you alone, I leave you utterly alone. In that aloneness: the flower of sannyas. That aloneness blooms on its own accord into the flower of sannyas.

Sannyas is characterlessness. It has no morality; it is not immoral, it is amoral. Or, it has a higher morality that never comes from the outside but comes from within. It does not allow any imposition from the outside, because all impositions from the outside convert you into serfs, into slaves. And my effort is to give you dignity, glory. My effort here is to give you splendor.

All other efforts have failed. It was inevitable, because the failure was built-in. They were all structure-oriented, and every kind of structure becomes heavy on the heart of man, sooner or later. Every structure becomes a prison, and one day or other you have to rebel against it. Have you not observed it down through history? – each revolution in its own turn becomes repressive. In Russia it happened, in China it happened. After every revolution, the revolutionary becomes antirevolutionary. Once he comes into power he has his own structure to impose upon society. And once he starts imposing his structure, slavery changes into a new kind of slavery, but never into freedom. All revolutions have failed.

This is not revolution, this is rebellion. Revolution is social, collective; rebellion is individual. We are not interested in giving any structure to society. Enough of structures! Let all structures go. We want individuals in the world – moving freely, moving consciously, of course. And their responsibility comes through their own consciousness. They behave rightly not because they are trying to follow certain commandments; they behave rightly, they behave *accurately,* because they care.

Do you know, this word *accurate* comes from *care?* The word *accurate* in its root means "to care about." When you care about something you are accurate. If you care about somebody, you are accurate in your relationship.

A sannyasin is one who cares about himself, and naturally cares about everybody else – because you cannot be happy alone. You can only be happy in a happy world, in a happy climate. If everybody is crying and weeping and is in misery, it is very, very difficult for you to be happy. So, one who cares about happiness, about his own happiness, becomes careful about everybody else's happiness – because happiness happens only in a happy climate. But this care is not because of any dogma. It is there because you love, and the first love, naturally, is the love for yourself. Then other loves follow.

Other efforts have failed because they were mind-oriented. They were based in the thinking process, they were conclusions of the mind. Sannyas is not a conclusion of the mind. Sannyas is not thought-oriented; it has no roots in thinking. Sannyas is insightfulness; it is meditation, not mind. It is rooted in joy, not in thought. It is rooted in celebration, not in thinking. It is rooted in that awareness where thoughts are not found. It is not a choice: it is not a choice between two thoughts, it is the dropping of all thoughts. It is living out of nothingness.

Therefore, O Sariputra, form is nothingness, nothingness is form. Sannyas is what we were talking about the other day – *svaha,* alleluia! It is joy in being.

Now how can you define joy in being? It cannot be defined, because each one's joy in being is going to be different. My joy in being is going to be different from your joy in being. The joy will be the same, the taste of it will be the same, but the flowering is going to be different. A lotus flowers, a rose flowers, a marigold flowers – they all flower, and the process of flowering is the same but the marigold flowers in his own way, and the rose in his, and the lotus in his. Their colors are different, their expressions are different, although the spirit is the same. And when they bloom, and when they can whisper to the winds, and when they can share their fragrance to the sky, they are all joyous.

Each sannyasin will be a totally unique person. I am not interested in the society. I am not interested in the collectivity. My interest is absolutely in individuals – in you!

Meditation can succeed where mind has failed, because meditation is a radical revolution in your being – not the revolution that changes the government, not the revolution that changes the economy, but the revolution that changes your consciousness, that transforms you from the noosphere to the Christosphere, that changes you from a sleepy person into an awakened soul. And when you are awakened, all that you do is good.

That's my definition of "good" and "virtue": the action of an awakened person is virtue, and the action of an unawakened person is sin. There is no other definition of sin and virtue. It depends on the person – his consciousness, the quality that he brings to the act. So sometimes it can happen that an act may be virtuous and the same act may be sinful: the acts may apparently be the same, but the people behind the acts can be different.

For example, Jesus entered the temple of Jerusalem with a whip in his hand to throw out the moneychangers. He upset their money-changing boards. Alone, single-handedly, he threw all the moneychangers out of the temple. It looks very violent – Jesus with a whip, throwing people out of the temple. But he was not violent. Lenin doing the same thing will be violent, and the act will be sinful. Jesus doing the same act is virtuous. He is acting out of love; he cares. He cares about these moneychangers too! It is out of his care, concern, love, awareness, that he is acting. He is acting drastically because only that will give them a shock and will create a situation in which some change is possible.

The act can be the same, but if a person is awake the quality of the act changes.

A sannyasin is a person who lives more and more in alertness. And the more there are people who exist through awareness, the better the world that will be created. Civilization has not yet happened.

It is said that somebody asked the Prince of Wales, "What do you think about civilization?" And the Prince of Wales is reported to have said, "It is a good idea. Somebody needs to try it. It has not happened yet."

Sannyas is just a beginning, a seed of a totally different kind of world where people are free to be themselves, where people are not constrained, crippled, paralyzed, where people are not repressed, made to feel guilty, where joy is accepted, where cheerfulness is the rule, where seriousness has disappeared, where a nonserious sincerity, a playfulness has entered. These can be the indications, the fingers pointing to the moon.

First: an openness to experience. People are ordinarily closed; they are not open to experience. Before they experience anything they already have prejudices about it. They don't want to experiment, they don't want to explore. This is sheer stupidity!

A man comes and wants to meditate, and if I tell him to go and dance, he asks, "What will be the outcome of dancing? How can meditation come out of dancing?" I ask him, "Have you ever danced?" He says, "No, never." Now this is a closed mind. An open mind will say, "Okay. I will go into it and see. Maybe through dancing it can happen." He will have an open mind to go into it, with no prejudice. This man who asks, "How can meditation happen out of dance?" even if he is persuaded to go into meditation, he will carry this idea in his head: "How can meditation happen out of dance?" It is not going to happen to him. And when it does not happen, his whole prejudice will be strengthened. And it has not happened *because* of the prejudice.

This is the vicious circle of the closed mind. He comes full of ideas, he comes readymade. He is not available to new facts, and the world is continuously bombarded with new facts. The world goes on changing and the closed mind remains stuck in the past. And the world goes on changing, and every moment something new descends into the world. Existence goes on painting the world anew again and again and again, and you go on carrying your old, dead ideologies in your heads.

So the first quality of a sannyasin is an openness to experience. He will not decide before he has experienced. He will *never* decide before he has experienced. He will not have any belief systems. He will not say, "This is so because the Bible says it." He will not say, "This is so because Buddha says it." He will not say, "This is so because it is written in the Vedas." He will say, "I am ready to go into it and see whether it is so or not."

Buddha's departing message to his disciples was this: "Remember" – and he was repeating this for his whole life, again and again, the last message also was this – "Remember, don't believe in anything because I have said it. Never believe anything unless you have experienced it."

A sannyasin will not carry many beliefs; in fact, none. He will carry only his own experiences. And the beauty of experience is that the experience is always open, because further exploration is possible. Belief is always closed; it comes to a full point. Belief is always finished. Experience is never finished, it remains unfinished. While you are living, how can your experience be finished? Your experience is growing, it is changing, it is moving. It is continuously moving from the known into the unknown and from the unknown into the unknowable. And remember, experience has a beauty because it is unfinished. Some of the greatest songs are those which are unfinished. Some of the greatest books are those which are unfinished. Some of the greatest music is that which unfinished. The unfinished has a beauty.

I have heard a Zen parable:

A king went to a Zen master to learn gardening. The master taught him for three years, and the king had a beautiful, big garden – thousands of gardeners were employed there – and whatsoever the master would say, the king would go and experiment in his garden. After three years the garden was absolutely ready, and the king invited the master to come and see the garden. The king was very nervous because the master was strict: "Will he appreciate?" This was going to be a kind of examination: "Will he say, 'Yes, you have understood me'?"

Every care was taken. The garden was so beautifully complete; nothing was missing. Only then did the king bring the master to see it. But the master was sad from the very beginning. He looked around, he moved in the garden from this side to that, he became more and more serious. The king became very frightened. He had never seen him so serious: "Why does he look so sad? Is there something so wrong?"

Again and again the master was shaking his head, and saying inside "No."

The king asked, "What is the matter, sir? What is wrong?

Why don't you say? You are becoming so serious and sad, and you shake your head in negation. Why? What is wrong? I don't see anything wrong? This is what you have been telling me, and I have practiced it in this garden."

The master said, "It is so finished that it is dead. It is so complete; that's why I am nodding my head and I am saying no. It has to remain unfinished. Where are the dead leaves? Where are the dry leaves? I don't see a single dry leaf!" All the dry leaves were removed – on the paths there were no dry leaves; in the trees there were no dry leaves, no old leaves which had become yellow. "Where are those leaves?"

The king said, "I have told my gardeners to remove everything. Make it as absolute as possible."

And the master said, "That's why it looks so dull, so manmade. God's things are never finished." And the master rushed out, outside the garden. All the dry leaves were heaped: he brought a few dry leaves in a bucket, threw them to the winds, and the wind took them and started playing with the dry leaves, and they started moving on the paths. He was delighted, and he said, "Look, how alive it looks!" Sound had entered with the dry leaves – the music of the dry leaves, the wind playing with the dry leaves. Now the garden had a whisper; otherwise it was dull and dead like a cemetery. That silence was not alive.

I love this story.

The master said, "It is so complete, that's why it is wrong."

Just the other night Savita was here. She was telling me that she is writing a novel, and she is very puzzled about what to do. It has come to a point where it can be finished, but the possibility is that it can be lengthened; it is not yet complete. I told her, "Finish it. Finish it while it is unfinished, then it has something mysterious around it: that unfinishedness. And I told her, "If your main character still wants to do something, let him become a sannyasin. And then things are beyond your capacity. Then what can you do? Then it comes to a finish, and yet things go on growing."

No story can be beautiful if it is utterly finished. It will be utterly dead. Experience always remains open – that means unfinished. Belief is always complete and finished. The first quality is an openness to experience.

Mind is all your beliefs collected together. Openness means no-mind; openness means you put your mind aside and you are ready to look into life again and again in a new way, not with the old eyes. The mind gives you the old eyes, it gives you again ideas: "Look through this." But then the thing becomes colored; then you don't look at it, then you project an idea upon it. Then the truth becomes a screen on which you go on projecting. Look through no-mind, look through nothingness: *shunyata.* When you look through no-mind your perception is efficient, because then you see that which is. And truth liberates. Everything else creates a bondage, only truth liberates.

In those moments of no-mind, truth starts filtering into you like light. The more you enjoy this light, this truth, the more you become capable and courageous to drop your mind. Sooner or later a day comes when you look and you don't have any mind. You are not looking for anything, you are simply looking. Your look is pure. In that moment you become *avalokita,* one who looks with pure eyes. That is one of the names of Buddha – Avalokita: he looks with no ideas, he simply looks.

Once it happened that a man spat on Buddha's face. He wiped his face and asked the man, "Have you anything more to say?"

His disciples were very shocked and angry. His chief disciple, Ananda, said to him, "This is too much! We cannot do anything because you are here; otherwise we would have killed this man. This man has spat on you, and you are asking, 'Have you anything more to say?'"

Buddha said, "Yes, because this spitting is a way of saying something. Maybe the man is so angry that words are not adequate; that's why he has spat." When words are not adequate, what do you do? You smile, you cry, tears come, you hug, you slap; you *do* something. If there is too much anger what will you do? You cannot find a strong enough, violent enough word. What will you do? – you spit.

Now this is Buddha's vision – without mind. He looks into the man: "What is the matter? Why is he spitting on me?" He's not involved in it at all. He does not bring his past experiences or ideas that spitting is bad, that this is insulting and humiliating. No idea interferes. He simply looks into the reality of this man who is spitting on him. He's utterly concerned: "Why? This man must be in trouble, a linguistic trouble. He wants to say something but he does not have the right words to do it. Hence, awkwardly, he is spitting."

Buddha said, "That's why I'm asking if you have anything more to say." The man himself was shocked because this was not his expectation. He had come to humiliate Buddha, but Buddha was not humiliated. Buddha's compassion was showering on the man. He could not sleep that night. Again and again he thought about it. It was so difficult for him to absorb it: "What kind of man is this? What manner of man is this? I spit, and he simply asks – and with tremendous love – 'Have you anything more to say?'"

In the early morning he went back, fell at Buddha's feet and said, "Sir, excuse me, forgive me. I could not sleep the whole night."

Buddha laughed, and he said, "You fool! Why? I slept perfectly well. Why should you get so disturbed about such a small thing? It has not hurt me. You see my face is as it was before. Why did you get so worried?"

The man said, "I have come to become your disciple. Initiate me. I want to be with you. I have seen something unique, superhuman. But first, forgive me."

Buddha said, "This is nonsense. How can I forgive you? – because I have not even taken any note of it. I was not angry, so how can I forgive you?" Twenty-four hours had passed, and they were sitting on the bank of the Ganges. And Buddha said, "Look at how much water has passed down the Ganges in twenty-four hours: that much life has passed in you, that much life has passed in me. It is no longer the same Ganges. I am not the same man. In fact, you had never spat on me, it was somebody else; twenty-four hours have passed. And you are not the same man who had spat, so who can forgive whom? Let the gone be gone."

This is the vision of no-mind. It can work miracles. The sannyasin lives an openness to everything.

The second quality is existential living. He does not live out of ideas: that one should be like this, one should be like that, one should behave in this way, one should not behave in this way. He does not live out of ideas, he is responsive to existence. He responds with his total heart, whatsoever is the case. His being is here-now. Spontaneity, simplicity, natural-ness – these are his qualities.

He does not live a readymade life. He does not carry maps – how to live, how not to live. He allows life; wherever it leads he goes with it. A sannyasin is not a swimmer, and he does not try to go upstream. He goes with the whole, he flows with the stream. He flows so totally with the stream that by and by he is no longer separate from the stream, he becomes the stream. That's what Buddha calls *srotapanna*: one who has entered the stream. That is the beginning of Buddha's sannyas too – one who has entered the stream, one who has come to relax in existence. He does not carry valuations, he's not judgmental.

Existential living means each moment has to decide on its own. Life is atomic; you don't decide beforehand, you don't rehearse, you don't prepare how to live. Each moment comes, brings a situation; you are there to respond to it, you respond. Ordinarily people live a very strange kind of life. If you are going to give an interview, you prepare, you think what is going to be asked and how you are going to answer it, how you are going to sit and how you are going to stand. Every-thing becomes phony because it is rehearsed. And then what happens? When you go with such a rehearsal, you are *never* totally there. Something is being asked and you are searching in your memory, because you are carrying a prepared answer – whether that will suit with it or not, whether this will do or not. You go on missing the point. You are not totally there; you cannot be totally there, you are involved in the memory.

And then the next thing happens: when you are coming out then you start thinking, "I should have answered this way." This is called "the staircase wit": when you are coming down the staircase, and you start thinking, "I should have answered this, I should have said this." You become very wise again. Before you are wise, after you are wise; in the middle you are otherwise! And in the middle is life. Existence is there.

The third quality of a sannyasin is a trust in one's own organism. People trust others, the sannyasin trusts his own organism. Body, mind, soul, all are included. If he feels like loving he flows in love. If he does not feel like loving he says "Sorry," but he never pretends.

A non-sannyasin goes on pretending. His life is a life lived through masks. He comes home, he hugs the wife, and he does not want to hug her. He says, "I love you," and those words sound so phony because they are not coming from the heart. They are coming from Dale Carnegie. He has been reading *How to Win Friends and Influence People* and that kind of nonsense. And he is full of that nonsense, and he carries it and he practices it. His whole life becomes a false, pseudo life, a parody. And he is never satisfied, naturally; he cannot be, because satisfaction comes only out of authentic living. If you are not feeling loving you have to say so; there is no need to pretend. If you are feeling angry you have to say so. You have to be true to your organism, you have to trust your organism. And you will be surprised: the more you trust, the more the organism's wisdom becomes very, very clear to you.

Your body has its own wisdom; it carries the wisdom of the centuries in its cells. Your body is feeling hungry and you are on a fast because your religion says that this day you have to fast – and your body is feeling hungry. You don't trust your organism, you trust a dead scripture, because in some book somebody has written that this day you have to go on a fast, so you go on a fast. Listen to your body. Yes, there are days when the body says, "Go on a fast!" – then go. But there is no need to listen to the scriptures. The man who wrote that scripture has not written it with you in his mind at all. He could not have conceived of you. You were not present to him, he was not writing about you. It is as if you fall ill and you go to a dead doctor's house and look into his prescriptions, and find a prescription and start following the prescription. That prescription was made for somebody else, for some other disease, in some other situation.

Remember to trust your own organism. When you feel that the body is saying don't eat, stop immediately. When the body is saying eat, then don't bother whether the scriptures say to fast or not. If your body says eat three times a day, perfectly good. If it says eat one time a day, perfectly good. Start learning to listen to your body, because it is *your* body. You are in it; you have to respect it, and you have to trust it. It is your temple; it is sacrilegious to impose things on your body. For no other motive should anything be imposed. And this will not only teach you trust in your body, this will teach you, by and by, a trust in existence too – because your body is part of existence. Then your trust will grow, and you will trust the trees and the stars and the moon and the sun and the oceans: you will trust people. But the beginning of the trust has to be trust in your own organism. Trust your heart.

Now somebody has asked a question: he has decided to live with his wife because he thinks that to live with one's wife and never leave her, never separate, and never make love to another woman, is a great spiritual quality. For some it may be, maybe not so for others. It depends.

Now the questioner says, "I have decided this, and there are problems. I feel attracted to other women: I feel guilty. And I don't feel attracted towards my wife – then too I feel guilty. I don't want to make love to my wife because the desire does not arise. But I have to make love to my wife to satisfy her. If I make love to her, then I feel guilty about myself, that I am being untrue to myself. And it looks like a dragging affair."

When you don't want to make love, then love is the ugliest thing in the world. Only the most beautiful can be the most ugly. Love is one of the most beautiful experiences, but only when you are flowing in it, when it is spontaneous, when it is passionate, when you are full of it, overpowered by it, possessed by it, drunk with it, absorbed in it – only then. Then it takes you to the highest peak of joy. But if you are not possessed in it, and you are not even feeling any love for your wife or your husband, and you are *making* it... Then the English expression is right: making love. Then you are making it, it is not happening. It is ugly, it is prostitution. To whom you are doing it is not the point; it is prostitution. It is criminal. And this is not going to make you spiritual in any way. You will only become sexually repressed, that's all. If you make love you will feel guilty, if you don't make love you will feel guilty.

Now this man has an idea of how a husband and wife should be. Now the wife must be suffering also. Both are hooked, both are bored with each other, both want to get rid of each other but cannot because they don't trust their organism. If your organisms are saying, "Be together, grow together, flow together"; if your organism is feeling happy and thrilled and excited and there is ecstasy, go with the woman one life, two lives, three lives, as many lives as you want be together, and you will be coming closer and closer to godliness. And your intimacy will have a quality of spirituality.

But not this kind of intimacy. A forced intimacy will make you more and more unspiritual, and your mind will start, naturally, seeking some ways: your mind will become more and more obsessed with sex. And when there is too much obsession, how can you grow in spirituality?

Listen to the organism, and be courageous enough to do that which your organism says. I'm not saying to separate from your wife. But if that has to come, that has to come. And it will be good for you both. At least that much you owe to your wife. If you care at all about the wife, and you don't love her anymore, then you have to say so. In deep sadness: the parting will be sad, but what can be done? You are helpless. You will not part in anger, you will not part with a grudge and complaint. You will part with immense helplessness in your heart. You wanted to be with her, but your organism is saying no. What can you do? You can force your organism, and the organism can go there, and go on continuing in the relationship, but there will be no joy. And without joy how can you be in a relationship? Then the marriage is false; legal, but otherwise false.

A sannyasin is one who trusts in his own organism, and that trust helps him to relax into his being, and helps him to relax into the totality of existence. It brings a general acceptance of oneself and others. It gives a kind of rootedness, centering. And then there is great strength and power, because you are centered in your own body, in your own being. You have roots in the soil. Otherwise you see people uprooted, like trees that have been pulled up from the soil. They are simply dying, they are not living. That's why there is not much joy in life. You don't see the quality of laughter; the celebration is missing. And even if people celebrate, that too is false.

For example, it is the birthday of Krishna and people celebrate. How can you celebrate Krishna's birthday? You have not even celebrated your own birthday. And how are you concerned with somebody who was born five thousand years ago; how can you celebrate it? It is all phony. How can you celebrate Jesus Christ's birthday? It is impossible. You have not celebrated the God that has come to you, that is inside you. How can you celebrate some other God who was born in a stable two thousand years ago?

In your very body, in your very being, this very moment, godliness is there and you have not celebrated it. You cannot celebrate. Celebration has to happen first in your own home, at close quarters. Then it becomes a great tidal wave and spreads all over existence.

The fourth is a sense of freedom. The sannyasin is not only free, he is freedom. He always lives in a free way. Freedom does not mean licentiousness. Licentiousness is not freedom, licentiousness is just a reaction against slavery; so you move to the other extreme. Freedom is not the other extreme, it is not reaction. Freedom is an insight: "I have to be free, if I have to be at all. There is no other way to be. If I am too possessed by the church, by Hinduism, by Christianity by Mohammedanism, then I cannot be. Then they will go on creating boundaries around me. They go on forcing me into myself like a crippled

being. I have to be free. I have to take this risk of being free.
I have to take this danger."

Freedom is not very convenient, is not very comfortable.
It is risky. A sannyasin takes that risk. It does not mean that
he goes on fighting with each and everybody. It does not mean
that when the law says to keep to the right or keep to the left,
he goes against it, no. He does not bother about trivia. If the
law says keep to the left, he keeps to the left because it is not
a slavery. But about important, essential things… If the father
says, "Get married to this woman because she is rich and
much money will come," he will say, "No. How can I marry a
woman when I am not in love with her? That would be disre-
spectful to the woman." If the father says, "Go to church every
Sunday because you are born in a Christian home," he will
say, "I will go to church if I feel, I will not go because you say
so." Birth is accidental; it does not matter much. The church
is very essential: "If I feel like it, I will go."

I'm not saying don't go to church, but go only when your
feeling has arisen for it. Then there will be a communion.
Otherwise, no need to go.

About essential things the sannyasin will always keep
his freedom intact. And because he respects freedom, he
will respect others' freedom too. He will never interfere with
anybody's freedom, whosoever that other is. If your wife has
fallen in love with somebody you feel hurt, you will cry tears of
sadness, but that is your problem. You will not interfere with
her. You will not say, "Stop it because I am suffering!" You will
say, "This is your freedom. If I suffer, that is my problem. I
have to tackle it, I have to face it. If I feel jealous, I have to get
rid of my jealousy. But you go on your own. Although it hurts
me, although I would have liked that you had not gone with
anybody, that is my problem. I cannot trespass your freedom."

Love respects so much that it gives freedom. And if love is
not giving freedom it is not love, it is something else.

A sannyasin is immensely respectful about his own
freedom, very careful about his own freedom, and so is he
about other's freedom too. This sense of freedom gives him
an individuality; he is not just a part of the mass mind. He

has a certain uniqueness – his way of life, his style, his climate, his individuality. He exists in his own way, he loves his own song. He has a sense of identity: he knows who he is, he goes on deepening his feeling for who he is, and he never compromises.

Independence, rebellion – remember, not revolution but rebellion – is the quality of a sannyasin. And there is a great difference. Revolution is not very revolutionary. Revolution also goes on functioning in the same structure.

For example, in India, for centuries the untouchables, the lowest caste has not been allowed into temples. The brahmins have never allowed them to enter the temple: "The temple will become dirty if they come in." For centuries in India the untouchables have not gone into the temple. This is ugly. Then came Mahatma Gandhi: he tried hard, he struggled hard. He wanted the untouchables to be allowed into the temples; his whole life was a struggle for it. It is revolutionary but not rebellious. Why revolutionary? Then what is rebellion?

Somebody asked J. Krishnamurti about Gandhi's struggle for the untouchables to be permitted into the temples. And do you know what J. Krishnamurti said? He said, "But God is not in the temples." This is rebellion.

Gandhi's approach is revolutionary, but he also believes that God is in the temples as much as the brahmins do. The structure is the same. He believes it is very, very important for people to go into temples; if they don't go into the temples they will miss God. That is the idea of the brahmin, that is the idea of the society that has repressed the untouchables from entering, prohibited them from entering. The idea is the same: that God lives in the temples, and those who are going to get into the temples will come close to God, of course. And those who are not allowed will miss. Gandhi is revolutionary, but revolution believes in the same structure. It is a reaction.

J. Krishnamurti is rebellious. He says, "But God is not in the temples, so why bother? Neither brahmins are getting it there, nor will the untouchables get it. Why bother? It is stupid." All revolutions are reactionary, reactions to a certain pattern. Whenever you react it is not much of a revolution because you believe in the same pattern. Of course you go against it, but you believe. The deep down substratum is the same.

Gandhi is thinking that brahmins are enjoying very much; they are getting God so much. And the untouchables? – they are deprived. But he has not looked at the brahmins: down the centuries they have been worshipping in the temples and they have got nothing. Now this is foolish! Those who are inside the temple have got nothing, so why bother? And why bring people in who are not inside? It makes no sense.

A sannyasin is rebellious. By rebellion I mean his vision is utterly different. He does not function in the same logic, in the same structure, in the same pattern. He is not against the pattern – because if you are against a certain pattern you will have to create another pattern to fight with it. And patterns are all alike. A sannyasin is one who has simply slipped out. He's not against the pattern, he has understood the stupidity of all patterns. He has looked into the foolishness of all patterns and he has slipped out. He is rebellious.

The fifth is creativity. The old sannyas was very uncreative. It was thought that somebody becomes a sannyasin and goes to a Himalayan cave and sits there, and that was perfectly all right. Nothing more was needed. You can go and see the Jaina monks: they are sitting in their temples, doing nothing – absolutely uncreative, dull and stupid looking, with no flame of intelligence at all. And people are worshipping and touching their feet. Ask, "Why are you touching his feet?" and they say, "This man has renounced the world" as if renouncing the world is in itself a value. "What has he done?" and they will say, "He has fasted. He fasts for months together," as if not eating is a value in itself.

But don't ask what he has painted, what beauty he has created in the world, what poem he has composed, what song he has brought into existence, what music, what dance, what invention – what is his creation? They will say, "What are you talking about? He is a sannyasin!" He simply sits in the temple and allows people to touch his feet, that's all. And there are so many people sitting like this in India.

My conception of a sannyasin is that his energy will be

creative, that he will bring a little more beauty into the world, that he will bring a little more joy into the world, that he will find new ways to get into dance, singing, music, that he will bring some beautiful poems. He will create something, he will not be uncreative. The days of uncreative sannyas are over. The new sannyasin can exist only if he is creative.

He should contribute something. Remaining uncreative is almost a sin, because you exist and you don't contribute. You eat, you occupy space, and you don't contribute anything. My sannyasins have to be creators. When you are in deep creativity you are close to godliness. That's what prayer really is, that's what meditation is. God is the creator, and if you are not creators you will be far away from godliness. God knows only one language, the language of creativity. That's why when you compose music, when you are utterly lost in it, something of the divine starts filtering out of your being. That is the joy of creativity, that's the ecstasy – *svaha!*

The sixth is a sense of humor, laughter, playfulness, non-serious sincerity. The old sannyas was unlaughing, dead, dull. The new sannyasin has to bring more and more laughter to his being. He has to be a laughing sannyasin, because your laughter is your relaxation, and your laughter can create situations for others also to relax. The temple should be full of joy and laughter and dance. It should not be like a Christian church. The church looks so cemetery-like. And with the cross there it seems to be almost a worship of death, a little morbid. You cannot laugh in a church. A belly-laugh would not be allowed; people would think you are crazy or something. When people enter a church they become serious, stiff, long faces.

To me, laughter is a religious quality, very essential. It has to be part of the inner world of a sannyasin: a sense of humor.

The seventh is meditativeness, aloneness, the mystical peak experiences that happen when you are alone, when you are absolutely alone inside yourself. Sannyas makes you alone; not lonely, but alone; not solitary, but it gives you a solitude. You can be happy alone, you are no longer dependent on others. You can sit alone in your room and you can be utterly happy. There is no need to go to a club, there is no need to always have friends around you, there is no need to go to a movie. You can close your eyes and you can fall into inner blissfulness: that's what meditativeness is all about.

The eighth is love, relatedness, relationship. Remember, you can relate only when you have learned how to be alone, never before it. Only two individuals can relate. Only two freedoms can come close and embrace each other. Only two nothingnesses can penetrate into each other and melt into each other. If you are not capable of being alone, your relationship is false. It is just a trick to avoid your loneliness, nothing else.

That's what millions of people are doing. Their love is nothing but their incapacity to be alone. So they move with somebody, they hold hands, they pretend that they love, but deep down the only problem is that they cannot be alone. So they need somebody to hang around, they need somebody to hold onto, they need somebody to lean upon. And the other is also using them in the same way, because the other can also not be alone, is incapable. He or she also finds you instrumental as a help to escape from himself.

So two persons that you say are in love are more or less in hate with themselves. And because of that hate, they are escaping. The other helps them to escape, so they become dependent on the other, they become addicted to the other. You cannot live without your wife, you cannot live without your husband because you are addicted. But a sannyasin is one...

That's why I say the seventh quality is aloneness, and the eighth quality is love-relationship. These are the two possibilities: you can be happy alone and you can be happy together too. These are two kinds of ecstasies possible for humanity. You can move into *samadhi* when alone and you can move into *samadhi* when together with somebody, in deep love. And there are two kinds of people: the extroverts will find it easier to have their peak through the other, and the introverts will find it easier to have their greatest peak while alone. But the other is not antagonistic; they can both move together. One will be bigger, and that will be the decisive factor whether you are an introvert or an extrovert. The path of Buddha is the path of the introvert; it talks only about meditation. The path of Christ is extrovert; it talks about love.

My sannyasin has to be a synthesis of both. An emphasis will be there: somebody will be emphatically more in tune with himself than with others, and somebody will be just the opposite – more in tune with somebody else. But there is no need to get hooked into one kind of experience. Both experiences can remain available.

The ninth is transcendence, Tao, no ego, no-mind, nobodiness, nothingness, in tune with the whole.

That is the whole message of *Prajnaparamita Sutra*, the *Heart Sutra*: *gate gate paragate: gone, gone, gone beyond. Parasamgate bodhi svaha: gone altogether beyond.* What ecstasy! Alleluia!

Transcendence is the last and the highest quality of a sannyasin.

But these are only indications, these are not definitions. Take them in a very liquid way. Don't start taking what I have said in a rigid way. Very liquid, in a vague kind of vision, in a twilight vision – not like when there is a full sun in the sky. Then things are very defined. In a twilight, when the sun has gone down and the night has not yet descended, it is both, just in the middle, the interval. Take whatsoever I have said to you in that kind of way. Remain liquid, flowing. Never create any rigidity around you. Never become definable.

The second question:

Osho,
If you were a cab driver, would I really not recognize you? Firstly, instead of taking me straight down to MG Road, you would drive me nuts for one and a half hours. Secondly, you would refuse to accept the fare and instead demand my life. Thirdly, while leaving me in total distress, you would drive off with a heavenly smile and light your sign: "Enough for today." Could I still miss this cab-driver? Then I had better go by foot.

The question is from Adi. Adi is so crazy that I cannot be very certain whether he would be able to recognize me or not. He may! Crazy people are crazy people. About crazy people you cannot be so certain. Yes Adi, it is possible: you may recognize me even as a cab driver.

And you say, "Firstly, instead of taking me straight down to MG Road, you would drive me nuts for one and a half hours." That's true. Help me to drive you nuts because your sanity is of no worth. Your sanity is just like a rock on your heart. Let me remove it from you. It is a kind of surgery: it hurts, it pains. You would like to cling to the rock. You would like to go straight to MG Road. But my whole approach is that there is nowhere to go, no MG Road. There is no goal in life; life is a journey without destination. So I have to take you zigzag, on and on and on, till you are really tired and you say, "Enough! Enough for today!"

"Secondly, you would refuse to accept the fare and instead demand my life." That too is right, Adi. Less than that won't do. Less than that is worthless. That's my whole teaching: that you have nothing to lose except everything!

"Thirdly, while leaving me in total distress, you would drive off with a heavenly smile, and light your sign: 'Enough for today'!" That depends on you. You can participate with me in my "heavenly smile." Courage is needed. You have invested so much in your distress that you go on keeping it. But remember, the more you keep it, the more the investment goes on becoming bigger and bigger every day. Drop it! Today it is easier: tomorrow it will be more difficult, because you will have invested twenty-four hours more into it. Drop it as quickly as possible. Don't postpone, because all postponement is dangerous. While you go on postponing, your distress goes on becoming stronger and goes on spreading its roots into your being.

I know why you are clinging to your distress – because your idea is that, "Something is better than nothing." And my whole approach is: nothing is godliness. You go on holding your distress because it gives you a feeling that you have something, at *least* something – maybe it is distress, anxiety, misery, but something, at least something: "I am not empty."

You are so afraid of emptiness, and it is only emptiness that godliness comes through.

Let me help you to become nothingnesses. And then there comes that heavenly smile; it comes out of nothingness. When inside you is nothingness, you will have a smile all over you. It is not only on the lips, it is all over you. It is the smile of nothingness.

See that you are carrying a great load of distress, and see that *you* are carrying it. And see that you are responsible for carrying or for not carrying: you can drop it this very moment. Dropping it is what sannyas is all about.

I will have to say about Adi: I'm afraid he would recognize me even if I were a cab driver. Maybe he would recognize me far better than he recognizes me now. He is just crazy.

There are many more people who will recognize me anyway, anywhere. Only those are the people who are with me – who will recognize me anywhere.

Jesus died. His body was kept in a cave after crucifixion. Mary Magdalene went to see him on the third day, and the body was not there. So she looked around to inquire, and she saw a gardener working outside. So she went to the gardener and asked, "Have you seen where Jesus' body has been removed to?"

The gardener started laughing, and he said, "Can't you recognize me?" He was Jesus himself, resurrected. When Jesus spoke, then, only then, did Magdalene recognize him. But she was a woman. She did well – not perfectly well, because first she thought that he was a gardener. But still, immediately, the moment he uttered a single word and she looked into his eyes, she recognized him.

But then Jesus went in search of his other disciples. He met two disciples on the way – they were going to another town, and they were talking continuously of what had happened to their master: he had been crucified, and what the repercussions of it were going to be, and no miracle had happened, and they were waiting for the miracle... And Jesus walked with them, and they were talking to Jesus also, thinking that he was a stranger. For four miles they walked together and they could not recognize Jesus, and he talked and they could not recognize him. They never looked at him. Then they sat in a restaurant to eat, and the moment Jesus broke his bread, then they recognized him because the way he used to break his bread was simply his, unique. That gesture was his; nobody could have imitated it: with such respect, reverence, with such prayer, as if bread was God. Then they recognized him, but it took a long time. For four miles they walked, for four miles they talked, and they could not recognize him.

Many are here who will recognize me in any form. But many are here also who have not even recognized me in this form. It depends on you. If you are carrying certain conceptions then it is very difficult.

Somebody has written to me that he is a follower of Sri Aurobindo; he is puzzled, and he wants to choose. And he cannot choose whether he should remain with Aurobindo or with me. And he tells me, "You decide."

How can *I* decide this? And if I decide it will be wrong. You will have to look into it. I'm not saying to choose, I'm saying *look* into it. If you have really loved Sri Aurobindo, then what is the point of coming here? If it has happened through him, it has happened; there is no need to come here. If it has not happened and you have come to me, then say goodbye to him. But people are very clever: they want to ride both horses. You will be in trouble.

This is happening every day. People come to me and they are hooked somewhere else. If they are hooked somewhere, then their eyes are not ready to see me. Now this man says, "If you can say that Sri Aurobindo himself has sent me to you, it will be very easy for me to accept you" – through Aurobindo. Now, I have to tell this lie. Why should Aurobindo send you to me? And why do I have to tell you this? – so that somehow you can make a compromise, so you can say, "Good, so it is Aurobindo's will. So I am not going against Aurobindo." How cowardly you are! How afraid to lose hold of anything! If something has happened, I'm not saying lose hold of it: go,